CAMBRIDGE TEXTS

HISTORY OF PHIL

NOVALIS

Fichte Studies

CAMBRIDGE TEXTS IN THE HISTORY OF PHILOSOPHY

Series editors

KARL AMERIKS
Professor of Philosophy, University of Notre Dame

DESMOND M. CLARKE
Professor of Philosophy, University College Cork

The main objective of Cambridge Texts in the History of Philosophy is to expand the range, variety and quality of texts in the history of philosophy which are available in English. The series includes texts by familiar names (such as Descartes and Kant) and also by less well-known authors. Wherever possible, texts are published in complete and unabridged form, and translations are specially commissioned for the series. Each volume contains a critical introduction together with a guide to further reading and any necessary glossaries and textual apparatus. The volumes are designed for student use at undergraduate and postgraduate level and will be of interest not only to students of philosophy but also to a wider audience of readers in the history of science, the history of theology and the history of ideas.

For a list of titles published in the series, please see end of book.

NOVALIS

Fichte Studies

EDITED BY

JANE KNELLER

Colorado State University

CAMBRIDGE
UNIVERSITY PRESS

PUBLISHED BY THE PRESS SYNDICATE OF THE UNIVERSITY OF CAMBRIDGE
The Pitt Building, Trumpington Street, Cambridge CB2 1RP, United Kingdom

CAMBRIDGE UNIVERSITY PRESS
The Edinburgh Building, Cambridge, CB2 2RU, UK
40 West 20th Street, New York, NY 10011–4211, USA
477 Williamstown Road, Port Melbourne, VIC 3207, Australia
Ruiz de Alarcón 13, 28014 Madrid, Spain
Dock House, The Waterfront, Cape Town 8001, South Africa

http://www.cambridge.org

First published 2003

Printed in the United Kingdom at the University Press, Cambridge

Typeface Ehrhardt 11/13 pt. *System* LaTeX 2ε [TB]

A catalogue record for this book is available from the British Library

ISBN 0 521 64353 8 hardback
ISBN 0 521 64392 9 paperback

Contents

Preface

The preparation of this translation and introduction of Novalis' manuscript has been a lengthy and somewhat daunting enterprise, during the course of which I have become indebted to many generous and helpful folk. I would especially like to thank the series editor, Karl Ameriks, and editor Hilary Gaskin at Cambridge University Press for advice, encouragement, and patience that bordered on the saintly. Pauline Marsh did an extraordinary job with the painstaking work of copy-editing the typescript and was a joy to work with at all times. I am extremely grateful to Mathias Thierbach for his diligent work on a final reading of the translation, and also to Noell Birondo for compiling the index. Violetta Waibel gave extremely helpful last-minute advice on Novalis' reference to "players" in #445, as well as other useful suggestions and moral support.

Finally I want to thank my colleagues in the Department of Philosophy at Colorado State University, who never doubted the worthiness of this time-consuming and somewhat unorthodox philosophical enterprise. I owe special thanks to James Maffie for encouraging me to take on the project, and to Michael Losonsky for insisting that I finish.

Introduction

Georg Friedrich Phillip von Hardenberg is primarily known to Anglo-American philosophers, if at all, as a German Romantic poet, not as a philosopher. Indeed, until rather recently, the idea that early German Romanticism might comprise a philosophical as opposed to a purely literary phenomenon has hardly been taken seriously in anglophone philosophical circles at all.[1] Hence the name "Novalis," as Hardenberg chose to call himself, typically conjures up images of a somewhat effete young man with large, moony eyes who fell in love with a child destined to die before she was old enough to marry him, and who himself died, romantically, as it were, of tuberculosis at the early age of twenty-nine. Even his literary efforts tend to be dismissed by analytically minded contemporary philosophers as paradigms of a stereotyped Romanticism: dreamy and mystical, valorizing medieval times, idealizing nature and human individuals, and worst of all, tending toward irrationalism. But just as the engraving of Novalis adorning the jackets and covers of books about him for the last hundred and fifty years is arguably a distortion,[2] so is this dismissive view of his work. The aim of this translation is to make accessible to an English-speaking audience the early, formative, and provocative

[1] A recent exception is Richard Rorty, who quotes Novalis in comparing pragmatism to Romanticism in "Truth without Correspondence to Reality," in *Philosophy and Social Hope* (New York: Penguin, 1999), p. 27; an interesting nineteenth-century exception is John Stuart Mill, who was fond of Novalis' work. He quotes Novalis (from Carlyle's translation) in his Berkeley essay, "Berkeley's Life and Writings," in *Collected Works*, Vol. XI, ed. J. M. Robson (London: Routledge, 1996), p. 466; and also in his *System of Logic*, Book VI, Ch. II, "Of Liberty and Necessity" (*Collected Works*, Vol. VIII), p. 843.

[2] William Arctander O'Brien discusses the mythologizing of Novalis, including the retouching of his portrait, in *Novalis: Signs of Revolution* (Durham & London: Duke University Press, 1995), pp. 25–26.

philosophical struggles of a remarkable young thinker living in a remarkable time and place.

Friedrich von Hardenberg was born May 2, 1772 in Oberwiederstedt in Thuringia. His father, Heinrich von Hardenberg, traced his family origins to nobility in lower Saxony as far back as the twelfth-century. The father was what we would now call a "born again" pietist of the Herrnhuter or Moravian brethren sect. His involvement with the children, when he was not traveling, centered around their religious upbringing, and he remained a rather distant and cold figure in Novalis' life. His mother, Auguste von Bolzig, with whom he always remained close, was the daughter of impoverished nobility and happy to be married to Heinrich. Friedrich was the first of her eleven children, all but one of whom died before her own death in 1818. Novalis was a sickly child and perhaps for that reason received her special attention, but whatever the cause, his attachment to her was strong, and eventually was reflected in the glorified mother-figures of his writings.

In 1784, the family moved to Weißenfels near Leipzig when the father was appointed director of the Saxon salt mines. Novalis was educated at home by private tutors and in 1790 enrolled in gymnasium and soon tested into the university at Jena in the fall. There he studied philosophy with the Kantian Reinhold and history under none other than Friedrich Schiller, with whom he developed a personal acquaintance and a love for poetry, much to the chagrin of his stern father. To satisfy his father's concern that he study law, Novalis shifted his study in the fall of 1791 to the University of Leipzig and law. Although he failed to finish the degree there he became friends with Friedrich Schlegel and had an ill-starred love affair that foundered on the rocks of his father's disapproval. The law degree was finally obtained in June, 1794 at the University of Wittenberg.

That fall, Novalis' father apprenticed him to a director in the Prussian civil service in Tennstedt, where on a visit to a landowner in nearby Grüningen he met Sophie von Kühn, one of his daughters. She was at the time twelve years old. For Novalis, it was the proverbial love at first sight ("A quarter-hour determined it for me," he wrote to his brother); for the adolescent girl it was perhaps a mildly entertaining visit. Novalis' persistence prevailed and they were engaged the following March, two days before her thirteenth birthday. Novalis hid their engagement for fear once again of his father's disapproval, but the older Hardenberg liked Sophie, and consented to the marriage.

The affair with Sophie has since become the stuff of myth (or Gothic romance), although recent biographers, both historical and fictional, have helped to recover the human dimension of this pair. Sophie developed what was probably a liver inflammation and fell ill in November of that same year, 1795. In the meantime Novalis had met Fichte in the home of the philosopher Niethammer, and had vowed to himself to make a serious study of the philosopher's work, a pledge which he kept that fall. The result was the so-called *Fichte Studies*, notes written in fits and starts over the course of an eventful year, until the fall of 1796. Sophie's illness recurred at the beginning 1796 and by the following summer she was taken to Jena for what turned out to be a series of excruciatingly painful operations. She returned worse than ever to her home in December of that year and died, two days after her fifteenth birthday, in March of 1797.

Sophie's death followed the completion of the *Fichte Studies* by only a few months, and traces of the impending tragedy are evident in the later sections. The study of philosophy during this period of his life is inseparable from his personal development: "The study dearest to me is basically named the same as my bride: it is called philosophy – philosophy is the soul of my life and the key to my real self."[3] Novalis' "love of sophia" was through and through determined by his love of Sophie – by his admiration for her courage in suffering combined with childish playfulness and ordinary common sense: an odd, compelling combination of resignation and fantastical hope (what F. Schlegel somewhat peevishly called "Herrnhuterei" and "absolute Schwärmerei" – pietism and absolute fanaticism[4]) that also characterizes the search for the true nature of the "I" in the *Fichte Studies*.

Professionally, Novalis' life took an important turn when he was appointed assistant to the directorate of the Saxonian saltworks in Weißenfels (under the direction of his father). He moved from Tennstedt to Weißenfels to take up the job in February of 1796. His interest in mining was not incidental to his philosophical explorations and it is no coincidence that a year later, after enrolling in the Mining Academy in Freiburg, he immediately took up again his studies of the philosophies of Fichte, Kant, and Hemsterhuis. That same year (1797) Novalis met August Wilhelm

3 Letter to Friedrich Schlegel, July 8, 1796.

4 Quoted in Gerhard Schulz, *Novalis in Selbstzeugnissen und Bilddokumenten* (Reinbek bei Hamburg: Rowolht, 1969), p. 57.

Schlegel, brother of Friedrich and Caroline von Schlegel, as well as Friedrich Schelling. The Schlegel brothers, as co-editors of the journal *Athenäum* (1798–1800), were the leading figures of the so-called Jena Romantics, the early German Romantics whose circle included Caroline Schlegel (later Caroline Schelling), Schelling, Friedrich Schleiermacher, Dorothea Mendelssohn Schleiermacher, and Ludwig Tieck. Novalis became a key figure in this short-lived but enormously influential group. It was also during this year that Novalis undertook a serious study of mathematics, chemistry, physics, and geology.

By the end of 1798 Novalis was engaged to Julie von Charpentier, for whom he had developed a more tempered but deep love over the past year. The marriage never occurred. He was diagnosed with tuberculosis and spent a month at the spa in Teplitz "taking the cure," but was plagued by progessively poor health from that time forward. Just as his poetic program was coming to fruition, his physical health began to decline. Nevertheless, this year saw the publication of Novalis' first major works, including *Blütenstaub* (*Pollen*), for the first time under the pen-name "Novalis," and *Glaube und Liebe* (*Faith and Love*). He wrote *Die Lehrlinge zu Sais* (*The Apprentices of Sais*) and the "Teplitz Fragment" and began notes for the *Allgemeine Brouillon* as well.

In spite of increasing ill-health, 1799 was another active year for him. He met Tieck and Goethe, studied Schleiermacher's work, wrote *Die Christenheit oder Europa* (*Christianity or Europe*) and *Geistliche Lieder* (*Spiritual Songs*), and began *Heinrich von Ofterdingen* and the *Hymnen an die Nacht* (*Hymns to the Night*). It was during this year, from November 11–14, that he took part in the historic meeting that might be called the only "real" Jena Circle, at the home of August Schlegel in Jena. There he read his *Geistliche Lieder* and *Die Christenheit oder Europa* to Friedrich Schlegel, Schelling, Tieck, and Jean Paul Ritter. His work life, meanwhile, continued to flourish: at the end of the year he was appointed associate director of the saltworks of Saxony.

Novalis continued to write during the following year, made plans to improve his financial and career status, and even began a geological survey tour of several regions in Saxony. But his weakened condition declined even further, and by October he was seriously ill. In December he was appointed circuit director of the Thuringian saltworks administration, but by January of 1801 his condition was so serious that he was forced to return to the family home in Weißenfels. On March 25 of that year he died, in the company of his closest friend Friedrich Schlegel and to the strains of the piano that his brother Karl was playing for him.

Novalis' Fichte critique

Novalis undertook his serious study of Fichte's *Wissenschaftslehre* just months after having met Fichte, along with Hölderlin, in the home of a mutual friend, the philosopher Niethammer, in Jena. Little is known about that encounter except for an entry in Niethammer's diary stating that they "spoke much of religion and revelation, and that in this area many questions still remained for philosophy," but Mähl speculates that the meeting may have spurred Novalis' determination to engage with Fichte's philosophy more seriously and as soon as possible.[5] In the set of notes beginning with reflections on Fichte's *Wissenschaftslehre*, which comprises the bulk of the manuscript (about 400 pages) and which has been called "the most significant philosophical work of early Romanticism," Novalis comes to grips with the early philosophy of this thinker who had claimed, and nearly won, ascendency to Kant's throne in German philosophy.[6]

Fichte's work was exciting to the young Romantics, since among other things it aimed to resolve the "crisis" of metaphysics in Kant caused by his relativization of knowledge to human modes of cognititon. Insofar as it intended to say something definite and positive about the nature of the self as it is in itself, Fichte hoped to ground human freedom on a firm foundation and to rescue this fundament of ethics from the precarious status of an unknowable postulate. Novalis, like everyone in Jena, was fascinated by this bold attempt, and the *way* Fichte philosophized was an inspiration to Novalis, but after submerging himself in his work, Novalis moved away from and ultimately rejected much of the *Wissenschaftslehre*. In particular, he criticized Fichte's account of self-consciousness, especially his view that the I of self-consciousness is to be understood as beginning with an act of "self-positing," and is not a representation, but a kind of intellectual intuition that, in Fichte's words, is "that act which does not and

5 *Novalis: Schriften*, Vol. II, *Das philosophische Werk I*, ed. Richard Samuel in collaboration with Hans-Joachim Mähl and Gerhard Schulz, revised by Richard Samuel and Hans-Joachim Mähl (Stuttgart, Berlin, Cologne, Mainz: Kohlhammer, 1981), p. 31. All further page references in the text to Mähl's Introduction to the *Fichte Studies* will be to this volume. References to the *Fichte Studies* themselves will be by paragraph number following this edition.

6 Manfred Frank, in *Einführung in die Frühromantische Ästhetik* (Frankfurt-on-Main: Suhrkamp, 1989), p. 248. Hereafter, references to Frank in the text will be to this work.

cannot appear among the empirical states of our consciousness, but rather lies at the basis of all consciousness and alone makes it possible."[7] For Fichte

> The self is to be equated with, and yet opposed to, itself. It is all one consciousness, but a consciousness that involves an absolute self, on the one hand, and a divisible, limited self on the other. (p. 109)

Novalis' problem with Fichte's account of self-consciousness has to do with the latter's view that it is possible to postulate an absolute self outside of presenting it to ourselves in reflection. As Novalis saw it, self-consciousness *must* be representational. Insofar as self-consciousness involves thought of oneself, it must be about some thing, an object one represents to oneself. But Fichte's "I" is supposed to be *non*-represented, an original fact-act (*Tathandlung*) that can only be described as immediate consciousness, or a kind of "intellectual intuition." The self-posited "I" is supposed to unite in an intellectual intuition the subject of consciousness with the self as object of consciousness. As Manfred Frank argues in his lecture on Novalis' *Fichte Studies*, "Immediacy and self-reference are incompatible with each other" (p. 253). That is, self-reference requires a vehicle, something that points to the self, a means, or medium for referring. For Novalis, intellectual intuition can only be a reflection, an act of representing that is directed toward the only thing we can experience immediately, namely a feeling. (At #11 Novalis identifies sensible intuition with feeling.) Because self-consciousness is a reflective act, an attempt to reach an intuition (feeling) in thought, the best it can accomplish is still only a reflection of this feeling. It is the feeling grasped in thought – the thought of the feeling – but this grasping is not identical to the feeling itself (as the thought that something is funny is not itself funny). In other words, and in essence, Novalis refuses to grant Fichte's very un-Kantian starting point – he refuses, as Kant certainly refused, to allow the conflation of intuition and thought, even in the guise of a pre-reflective "thought-act."

Of course, there is more to Fichte's story. The "conflation" or *Tathandlung* is an original act that brings consciousness into existence, but self-consciousness contains further moments that involve the positing of

[7] *Fichte: The Science of Knowledge (Wissenschaftslehre)*, ed. and trans. Peter Heath and John Lachs (Cambridge: Cambridge University Press, 1982), p. 93. Page references in the text hereafter will be to this edition.

opposition in general, that is, the positing of a not-self in opposition to and limited by the self. Novalis' reading of Fichte was based on lecture notes that were published in haste by Fichte and later revised, and it may be objected that Fichte's most sophisticated account was not open to Novalis' objections.[8] Be that as it may, Novalis categorically rejects any account of consciousness that depends on a single principle ("All searching for a single principle would be like the attempt to square the circle" [#566]). Referring to Fichte's account of a unitary self-consciousness that contains a divided self, Novalis speaks of "the famous struggle within the I" (#5). But Novalis argues that the struggle begins already in the (allegedly) "absolute *Urhandlung*" of self-positing, which is, Novalis argues, nothing more than a necessary deception of a mediated I that is attempting to be absolute – unmediated – and thus comes into conflict with itself. Hence, what Fichte takes to be an immediate act of self-positing is in fact a mediated act of representation. We see self-intuition (*Selbstgefühl*) reflected in the mirror of thought and conclude that we have reached it. But in fact we are fooled: we have only the "mirror image" of self-intuition, not that intuition itself.

Self-reflection presents us with an illusion of ourselves that, Novalis says, requires a second act of reflection if we are not to be misled into thinking that we have attained objective knowledge of what is essentially non-objective. This second reflective act "corrects" the illusion of the first thought that we had of ourselves, and leads us, not to the self, but to knowledge of our ignorance of it. That is, it shows us that we are incapable of grasping the absolute ground of the self, and hence of all our knowledge. Since Novalis holds that "striving after the thought of a ground is the ground of philosophy" and "all philosophizing must end in an absolute ground"(#566), this would seem to spell the end of all philosophizing, and for Novalis, in one sense this is true: "The borders of feeling are the borders of philosophy" (#15).

But in another sense, he argues, philosophy may recognize its own absolute when it recognizes that no absolute ground is given. Even in the face of giving up the search for the absolute, or rather, precisely *because* of giving it up, the "drive to philosophize" can never be satisfied, and when

[8] For a thorough English-language account of the history of the *Wissenschaftslehre*, and a translation of the student transcripts of the later lectures, see *Fichte: Foundations of Transcendental Philosophy (Wissenschaftslehre), Novo Methodo (1796/99)* (Ithaca: Cornell University Press, 1992), Editor's Introduction.

we "freely renounce the absolute" there arises in us an "unending free activity" that is "the only possible absolute that can be given us"(#566). Thus philosophy can only ever provide a negative account of the self. But since this negative characteristic *is* indeed *one* aspect of our nature, it is at least not a falsified account of the human self (which in essence he accuses Fichte of giving). Manfred Frank nicely captures this tension-laden conception of the self propounded by Novalis as "a non-knowing that knows itself as such" (p. 255).

Novalis' philosophical theory of self-consciousness commits him to the view that no *theory* of the self will reveal us to ourselves as we are "in ourselves" or as we are "absolutely." This view marks a significant departure from Fichte's idealism, and in many respects it marks a decisive break within early German Romanticism from German idealism overall. Arguably, Novalis' repudiation of a philosophy of the absolute marks him out as far more in the spirit of Kantian Enlightenment than those in his idealist cohort.[9] Indeed, as von Molnár (pp. 41–42) points out,[10] Novalis makes frequent reference to a Kantian notion of regulative ideas, especially in regard to the nature of the "I." The absolute ego is for Novalis a regulative absolute:

> I – has, perhaps, like all ideas of reason merely regulative, classificatory use – Nothing at all in relation to reality. (#502)

Or,

> Every state, every fact-act [*Tathandlung*] presupposes an other... all quest for a First [genus] is nonsense – it is a *regulative idea*. (#472)

Given Novalis' explicit criticism of Fichtean "seeking the unconditioned," it is at least not surprising that Novalis returned, if only briefly, to the study of Kant immediately after his "Auseinandersetzung" with Fichtean philosophy.

[9] In this regard he shares company with Hölderlin. See Frank, *Einführung*, pp. 248–249, and also my "Romantic Conceptions of the Self in Hölderlin and Novalis," in *Figuring the Self: Subject, Absolute, and Others in Classical German Philosophy*, ed. D. E. Klemm and G. Zöller (Albany: State University of New York Press, 1997), pp. 134–148.

[10] Géza von Molnár, *Novalis' "Fichte Studies": The Foundations of his Aesthetics* (The Hague: Mouton, 1970). Page references in the text are to this work.

Overview of the *Fichte Studies*

The editors reorganized Novalis' notes into six distinct groups based on painstakingly careful handwriting analyses. The first (Group I) dates from fall to early winter of 1795; Group II from winter, 1795 to February, 1796; Group III from February to March, 1796; Group IV from March and April to early summer, 1796; Group V from summer of 1796, and Group VI from summer to fall, 1796.

Group I (1–210)

Novalis begins his Fichtean thought experiment by reflecting, as Fichte did in his published lectures from 1794/1795, on the form of the proposition "A = A" (p. 93). To understand what Novalis is responding to in this first crucial section it is important to keep in mind which of Fichte's works he most likely had before him. Texts that Novalis was certainly responding to when he undertook his serious study of Fichte include these lectures and also Fichte's essay "Concerning the Concept of the *Wissenschaftslehre*," published in May of 1795, as well as the first part of the *Foundations of Natural Right*, published in 1796.

In the lectures of 1794, Fichte uses the necessarily true statement "A = A" simply as a starting point, an occasion for uncovering the claim of the self's identity, "I am I," which he argues is presupposed in all other identity claims. Novalis obligingly starts here too, but immediately finds a problem in the nature of the identity claim itself, which he calls a *Scheinsatz*, an "illusory proposition" that makes an identity claim but is itself incapable of revealing the essence of identity. In this regard he gestures already to aesthetic judgment – "taste and genius" – and so his path diverges from Fichte's at the outset. Nevertheless, he continues his reading, jotting notes on the text, but almost always diverging from Fichte's line of thought, taking long detours through his own reveries on a number of philosophical issues.

Some oft-quoted highlights from this section, by no means meant to interpret the text but simply provided as signposts for the reader, include the following:

> #2, the nature of the knowledge and consciousness: "a being outside of being that is within being . . . an image of being within being"

#3, on the attempt to verbalize being in-itself through opposition, by saying "not-being": "It just grasps a handful of darkness."
#5, on Fichte's conception of the I: "Has not Fichte too arbitrarily packed everything into the I?"
#11, the "semiotic fragment,"[11] on the "theory of the sign": deals with the "miracle" of signification and communication between two "signifying agents"; first reference to the "mirror" of reflection
#15, on the nature of philosophy: "cannot be self-observation" – "eavesdropping on the self"
#17–26, the nature of the self-reflective act, intellectual intuition, Fichte's original act (*Tathandlung*)
#27–31, categories of thought
#31–50, nature and relation of the empirical and the pure I: #32, "the famous conflict within the I"; #33, subject and object in the I; #36, the rule of reverse order: "What holds of the absolute I holds also for the mediated I, only inversely [*ordine inverso*]"
#38–50, categories of the absolute and relative act of self-positing, their matter and form, feeling, unity and division; the real and ideal
#51, the "particular subject" and morality, natural rights and politics
#86–112, theoretical and practical I.

Group II (211–287)

This group begins with thoughts on the nature of the imagination and its relation to the other faculties of "feeling, understanding and reason" (#212) or "of representation and of feeling" (213). Novalis chiefly differentiates the imagination as an active power: *Einbildungskraft*. He argues for the need to ground the sciences in a "theory of intuition" (217) which would include theories of feeling and imagination (211). He goes on to speak more of the faculty of representation as well, and distinguishes in the process material and matter (*Stoff* and *Materie*) – "the latter is the substrate of intuition, the former is the substrate of representation" (226), and space and time as "conditions of material" (224). There follows (226–233) a set of thoughts on the relative, interchangeable nature of form and material (see especially #233), followed by a set of fragments on the illusory nature of truth and the truth of illusion: "Truth is the form of

[11] O'Brien's designation for this passage in *Novalis: Signs of Revolution*, pp. 97ff. Hereafter references to O'Brien in the text will be to this work.

illusion – illusion the form of truth." "Illusion is necessary everywhere" (234).

More sketches follow on the nature of other concept pairs: being/appearance, whole/part, determination/determinability, activity/passivity, reality/ideality, affirmation/negation (246), and rule/game, and the power of the imagination to mediate (or "oscillate" – Fichte's notion of *Schweben*) between the two sides of each pair. He returns to consider once more the nature of positing or affirming in the "original act" (282), introducing the importance of words as "the passage [*transitus*] upon which everything rests" (282). He ponders the implications of the subject's freedom as the substrate of reflection: "Freedom is the substrate, the sphere of the opposite, the idea," says that it must be "a non-word, a non-concept," and in a memorable aside asks: "How can that which is only a voice produce an echo?" (284).

Group III *(288–372)*

Under the heading "Principal rule" (*Hauptregel*), Novalis takes up his third set of reflections on self-consciousness: "Everything, irrespective of whether we reflect upon or sense it, is an object and so stands under the *laws* of the object." He ponders the consequences of this for reflection itself: "Presentation is also object – but what kind of object?" (290). He introduces the term "state" (*Zustand*) to express the "real essence" of that which he has referred to up to this point as the "opposite" of the object and the relation of state and object to the activity of the subject: "Activity is change. Change is unthinkable without state and object" (292–306). He then continues to explore the active as well as the suffering ("taking") nature of subject (311–324), as "drive" and "passion" (325–327). This is followed by a more fragmented set of entries on related concepts, words, and occasional musings, the scattered nature of which Mähl suggests may indicate the restlessness and frequent travel during this period of Novalis' life (p. 65). The section ends with the enigmatic question, apparently inserted later: "Where do I exit, where do I go, and how do I proceed?"

Group IV *(373–552)*

The tone of this group changes dramatically and is no doubt a reflection of troubles in Novalis' life tied to the illnesses of his brother Erasmus and his fiancée, Sophie. The first entry reiterates a Fichtean "egocentricity" that may well also portray Novalis' own distracted state as he attempts to continue his studies: "When I ask what a thing is I am asking about its representation and intuition – *I* am wondering only about *myself*." There is far less discursive continuity in this section than the preceding ones, so that it may prove frustrating for the scholar pursuing an interpretive or philosophical agenda. On the other hand it is full of provocative thoughts ("Scientist – rhapsodist, or free spirit" [394], "Is language indispensable to thought" [495]), interesting bits of self-help ("Practice slowness" [407], "Now I can do nothing better than to finish the studies and work leisurely on French...") and revealing personal asides ("Equanimity – even in the most hopeless cases, for instance, as with Sophie" [388], "Why must everything I do now be so *painful* – nothing peaceful – at leisure – calm" [504]). Passing reference is made to Schiller, Wieland, and other writers, and traces of his religiosity, or need for it, are noticeable here. Paragraphs following #437 pick up threads from the earlier notes dealing with activity, state, and object, and the relative nature of being ("Only the whole is real... The whole rests more or less – like a game in which people sit on each other's knees in a circular fashion without a chair" [445, also 454–456]). Novalis also makes several references to the merely regulative nature of philosophy in this section, as if he were learning to appreciate the wisdom of people (like his beloved brother and Sophie) who lacked scholarly wisdom ("One can also fulfill one's vocation without philosophy, if one lives in accordance with what the wisest and best did and taught, and makes experience and common sense his guide" [505]).

Group V (553–568)

This group is headed "Remarks on the *Wissenschaftslehre*" and marks a return to the original topic of his study. The page references are to Novalis' copy of Fichte's lectures, section 1 of the *Fundamental Principles of the Entire Science of Knowledge*, 1794. Novalis' gloss on the identity "a = a" explains how what seems to be a mere tautology can be understood as a kind of predication – it is a "sharpened distinction" of terms that might otherwise not have been recognized as identical. He then moves in a new and important direction by taking the basic first principle of explanation, which Fichte had assumed as a postulate given in an intellectual intuition, to be a regulative ideal which serves to give a kind of unity to the "unending body of the known" (554). He also parts company with Fichte by emphasizing the freedom of the I as a tendency grounded in *harmonious* interaction, of imaginative "oscillation" between the relata, or "opposites" (555). At #556 he expands this, adding an element of mystical sensibility into his account that is compatible with a Spinozistic naturalism. The most important, and certainly the most frequently cited, passage in this section, however, is #566, where Novalis redefines philosophy as reflecting upon a ground, that is, "an ending free activity," claiming that "All searching for *a single principle* would be like the attempt to square the circle..." This passage contains one of the clearest statements of what Novalis takes philosophy to be, and it is a cornerstone of his later thought and art.

Group VI *(569–667)*

The final group, like the fourth, is marked by a lack of continuity in tone and content, and probably for similar reasons. Sophie's illness continued, the operations proved both excruciatingly painful and useless, and Novalis was certainly distracted. He continues threads from earlier themes, including fragments on the differences between the sexes, references to faith and Christianity, and references to Fichte's views in the *Foundations of Natural Right*. In this section Novalis returns to his interest in language in a few passages on words and their use and meaning (590, 612, 622), as well as literary critical comments. There are comments on God and the "one true religion" that undermine traditional caricatures of Novalis' religiosity ("Every *fixation* on an object is as *correct*, but also as *unjust*, as a 'one true religion' – human beings draw more from it than their humanity permits..." [647]), and gesture in the direction of Feuerbach ("Up to now concepts of God were quite correct concepts of human beings" [649]). Paragraph 633 is interesting for its application of the theory of representation developed earlier to art, ending with the claim "We stand now only at the beginning of the art of the writer." In general in this last section, where Novalis returns to the original Fichtean themes it is with an eye to their relevance to art and life, and, one cannot help but surmise, to *his* art and life.

The *Studies* finish with a perplexing passage ending in a question:

> On humanity. Its pure complete development must first be in the art of the individual – and only then pass over to the great masses of people and then the species. To what extent is the species an individual? (667)

In his detailed account of the dating and ordering of the six groups, Mähl notes that since the last extant page of the *Fichte Studies* is filled to the very bottom, the question of whether there were further notes or whether this is indeed the conclusion of Novalis' project must remain open (p. 86) – an appropriate ending to this extraordinary work.

Recent interpretations of the *Fichte Studies*

The substantial contributions to literature that Novalis made in his short life have received, justifiably, much recognition beyond the German-speaking lands. It may be that the very success of his creative and artistic endeavors has obstructed perception of him as a thinker worthy of a place in the distinguished pantheon of German philosophy. It is therefore not surprising that the first major English-language study of Novalis as philosopher was published in a language series, Stanford Studies in Germanics and Slavics. This was Géza von Molnár's *Novalis' "Fichte Studies"*, published in 1970 and subtitled "*The Foundations of his Aesthetics*."

Philosophical influences on Novalis included Kant, of course, as well as Hemsterhuis, Spinoza, Plotinus, Böhme, and Plato, to name a few, but there is no question that it was the philosophy of Fichte that had the strongest impact on his thought. Novalis' family was indirectly associated with Fichte through his benefactor, Ernst Haubold Freiherr von Miltitz, Novalis' uncle. Novalis had certainly had access to Fichte's writings as soon as they were published, and as early as 1794. It is worth considering some of the leading interpreters' views on the issue of Fichte's influence, however, if only to illustrate the surprising extent to which what may at first glance appear to be a rather tangled set of notes can indeed be unraveled into fascinating and original lines of philosophical argument.

Theodor Haering, in *Novalis als Philosoph*,[12] argues that Fichte's influence was direct with respect to four points in particular: the view of philosophy

[12] Theodor Haering, *Novalis als Philosoph* (Stuttgart: Kohlhammer, 1954). References to Haering in the text will be to this work.

as a basic human drive to seek the original ground of experience in a systematic way; the view that this seeking must lead to a "creative (active)" principle that would allow human beings somehow to grasp the absolute; a dialectical account of phenomena; and finally, the view that the empirical I is a "not-I," that is, an object among other objects. Haering's fundamental assumption, one that has come to be shared by most students of Novalis' thought, is that in the course of his studies Novalis develops his own philosophy in opposition to important aspects of Fichte's philosophy. In particular, the Fichtean notion of the "I" as an original fact-act is thoroughly criticized and ultimately rejected by Novalis, according to Haering, in favor of a less idealist, more dialectical account of phenomena.[13] This opposing account, while certainly adapted from Fichte's own in the *Wissenschaftslehre*, then becomes absolutely central for Novalis' own philosophical views. According to Haering, the greater part of the *Fichte Studies* is "dedicated to the proof and development of just this dialectical character of the whole of actuality as well as of true knowing" (pp. 620–621). He argues that Novalis effectively separates Fichte's dialectical account of the self (the self can only come to be through positing an "other" or "not-self" and vice versa) from Fichtean idealism, which limits this understanding to subjectivity and the ego, or the "I." Independently of Schelling, who developed a similar approach later, and in anticipation of Hegel, Haering argues, Novalis extended Fichte's dialectical understanding of subjectivity to all natural phenomena. Nature and our knowledge of it are to be understood in terms of completion (*Ergänzung*) in a higher unity that contains both inner and outer "spheres." Haering calls this process a "sublation," using Hegel's language, and claims that it is the very notion of romanticizing for which Novalis is famous.[14]

Moreover, according to Haering, Novalis elevates the dialectical process, which Fichte only *applied*, to an object of philosophical investigation in its own right. In so doing, he calls into question the very possibility of a

[13] See *ibid.*, p. 620. Haering argues that Novalis was "quite critical" of the idealist aspect of Fichte's theory of the self, not only pointing to his famous comment that Fichte "packed too much into the I," but reminding the reader as well that Novalis' "magical idealism" was also for him a "realist idealism" (*Real-Idealismus*).

[14] See Haering, *ibid.*, pp. 45–46 and also 638. Although Haering sees Novalis as a precursor to Hegel, it is interesting to note that in the *Fichte Studies* the term *Aufheben* and its cognates occur very few times, and even in the passages quoted by Haering in support of his account of romanticizing as a kind of "(hin)aufheben" (p. 638), Novalis actually uses the term *erheben* – "to raise" or "to raise to a higher power."

successful philosophy of consciousness, answering it with what Haering calls his "philosophy of representation" – the view that the necessarily non-identical relation between representing thing and thing represented (the sign is always other than the signified and so cannot "be" the sign) holds in every area of philosophy and serves as an explanatory prototype for all relations, including that of the empirical self to the absolute. It is, in Haering's words, a metaphysics of representation, far removed from Fichte's idealism (p. 622, and pp. 152–156, 641). All in all, Haering's view is that although Novalis is deeply indebted to Fichte, especially as a stylistic and terminological source, Novalis went far beyond Fichte, forging in essence a new metaphysics whose innovativeness renders irrelevant the issue of whether he truly understood Fichte. In light of this, says Haering, the question of influence "loses interest" (p. 622).

Géza von Molnár's *Novalis' "Fichte Studies"* takes issue with Haering's "Hegelian" reading, arguing for the centrality of the Fichtean concept of the ego (or as I have preferred to translate it, the "I") in Novalis' work.[15] He makes the important point that Fichte's *Wissenschaftslehre* first and foremost involves his enjoining his students to perform an introspective exercise: "It is reasonable to assume," he argues, "that Novalis' fragments constitute subjective exercises in accordance with this Fichtean exhortation" to repeat Fichte's own introspective processes, and "the only possible object of such scrutiny is the ego itself" (p. 33). Thus von Molnár argues that what distinguishes Novalis from Fichte is not that Novalis rejects the latter's conception of the I, but rather that Novalis' view of the underlying ground of subjectivity is a "negative principle" or regulative idea (pp. 35ff.). The paradoxical fact of human existence, that we are both subject and object to ourselves, is to be understood in Novalis as a matter of perspective or aspect, of whether we are looking inward or looking outward. If the absolute is sought inwardly it gives rise to the (regulative) thought of the I as the source of all subjectivity; if outwardly, it gives rise to the regulative notion of God as the source all objectivity, i.e., of nature. The "unifying function" of the I is "the only manifestation of the absolute unity which is the absolute ego" (p. 54).

[15] Géza von Molnár, *Novalis' "Fichte Studies": The Foundations of his Aesthetics* (The Hague: Mouton, 1970). Page references in the text are to this work.

Molnár, like Haering, takes the activity of representating to be a central aspect of Novalis' philosophy, but again, he argues for a direct appropriation of Fichtean ideas. The importance of representation is tied to the Fichtean "fusion" of subject and object, agency and thought, practical and theoretical in the original activity of the I. For Novalis, von Molnár argues, the I is regulative in the sense that it represents the relation between the two:

> The schema of interrelation, where the ego is the image of nature, nature the image of the ego, and the relation between the two the image of the nameless Absolute, is obviously not a static condition but constitutes rather a dynamic relationship which we came to know as representative action (*Darstellung*). (p. 97)

The difference is not that Novalis rejects the Fichtean conception of the ego as a union of the subjective and objective self, or even that Novalis rejects Fichte's acceptance of an absolute self. He argues rather that Novalis simply gives equal emphasis to what Fichte himself, were he not such a moralist, could have emphasized, namely the equally absolute nature of world. Even here von Molnár claims that Novalis remains within Fichte's philosophy inasmuch as he maintains this emphasis by appeal to "Fichtean concepts of 'feeling' (*Gefühl*) and 'faith' (*Glaube*)":

> Novalis, to be sure, stays within the Fichtean framework, only his accentuation is more evenly distributed between self and world, since he never loses sight of the Absolute's "form-contentual" aspect, or, in Fichte's terms, he never forgets that *Tathandlung* comprises *Tat* as well as *handeln*, content as well as form . . . Fichte's absolute is the Ego . . . but Novalis can call the Absolute both God and Ego in one and the same breath, since his state of the empirical is the simultaneity of action and passion, spirit and "being", form and content, where both paths reach out to the same Infinity and where a change in name is merely indicative of the direction from which the Absolute is approached.

The conclusion of his analysis of the *Fichte Studies*, then, is that they represent a "reinterpretation" of Fichte's philosophy that by emphasizing nature as well as self allows him to replace Fichtean "absolute action" of self-positing with the absolute activity of artistic representation. Thus Novalis does not so much break with Fichte as rather recognize what is already inherent in the latter's own account of the imagination, thus placing aesthetics center stage in his philosophy.

In German scholarship, no one has argued more forcefully for the independent contributions and unique place of early German Romanticism in German philosophy than Manfred Frank. The 1989 publication of his lectures on Romantic aesthetics has been instrumental in reviving interest in the *Fichte Studies*. Novalis' debt to Fichte, in Frank's estimation, is primarily as a catalyst to his own systematic working through of the paradoxes of explaining self-consciousness in terms of reflection, a problem that he shared not only with Fichte, but, in Frank's view, with his generation.[16] Novalis uses Fichte's language at first (and confuses matters somewhat by occasionally couching Fichte's arguments in his own poetic language), but gradually comes to speak in his own voice, and, from the very start, is critical of the Fichtean (and according to Frank, also Kantian) account of self-consciousness.[17]

Frank points out that if there is a position that resembles Novalis' during this period, it can only be that of Hölderlin's in "Judgment and Being," which was written at roughly the same time. But even so, he argues, the basis for Novalis' position is far more carefully formulated than Hölderlin's view, and is the result of a philosophical struggle the depth of which makes the *Fichte Studies* one of the "most difficult [texts] in German philosophy" (p. 248). The position that Frank is referring to involves the "aesthetic consequences" Novalis draws from the failure of reflection, i.e., of judgment, to produce knowledge of the fact of self-consciousness:

> Poetics [*Poesie*] must jump into the breach where the air becomes too thin for philosophy to breathe. But this conclusion must be drawn in a completely immanent way through purely philosophical means. The thesis that the Absolute is inaccessible to reflection indeed opens the gates to poetics and invites it to achieve what philosophy was incapable of achieving; but the thesis itself is not a piece of poetic thought, but rather a work of genuine and rigorous philosophical speculation. (Frank, p. 248)

16 "One can practically explain it as a generational experience." Frank, *Einführung*, p. 249.

17 *Das Problem "Zeit" in der deutschen Romantik: Zeitbewußtsein und Bewußtsein von Zeitlichkeit in der frühromantischen Philosophie und in Tiecks Dichtung* (Paderborn: Ferdinand Schöningh, 1990), p. 130.

Frank's account of Novalis' path to his aesthetic conclusions places strong emphasis on the latter's examination of the judgment of self-identity: "I am I," or the more abstract "a is a" with which Novalis begins. Novalis is concerned that "We abandon the identical in order to present it" (#1) or, in Frank's paraphrase, "In order to present identity as it is expressed in judgment we have to step outside judgment" (p. 251). Frank takes the key to his interpretation from the Novalis claim in the same passage that "The essence of identity can only be presented in an *illusory* proposition [*Scheinsatz*]." He explains Novalis' theory of reflection as literally a kind of representational mirroring and remirroring that is "the structure of reflective inversion" (or, following Novalis, the *ordo inversus*) (p. 257).

This account of the structure of judgment is the "invariable schema" that governs the entire study, according to Frank, and the failure to recognize this basic theme in all Novalis' varied expressions of it explains why, according to Frank, Novalis' real contribution to philosophy and the theory of consciousness has been ignored or misunderstood. Judgment necessarily misrepresents, or reverses, the self at first, but upon recognition of this reversal can re-reverse itself in a second reflective act that amounts to a reversal of the error, the damage to knowledge, of the first act. What is investigated is not the absolute self, but the "unity and being" of "the incapacity of reflection" (p. 261). When we understand the self as, as it were, *absolutely* finite, and the absolute as merely a regulative idea of infinite being, we first truly grasp the nature of the self. The result, according to Frank, is that Novalis radically distances his account of consciousness from any kind of metaphysical absolutes. If Frank's reading is correct, Novalis' account of subjectivity is of interest not only for contemporary theories of self-consciousness, but also as an important and hitherto neglected precursor of postmodern theories of the subject.

In *Novalis: Signs of Revolution*, William Arctander O'Brien carries the postmodernist implications of Novalis' theorizing even further. He argues that the latter's problematizing of the nature of the self and its relation to being led him not only to reject absolutizing metaphysics, but to move beyond philosophy altogether. Novalis' revolutionary move, O'Brien claims, was to subsume it, together with the central problem of the nature of the I, under linguistic and semiotic theory:

> Hardenberg's notebooks do not so much investigate language as a philosophical problem as they approach the problematics of Fichte's philosophy understood *as* language . . . Language, which Hardenberg explicitly subsumes under the larger rubric of semiotics, is not just one philosophical problem among others in the *Fichte Studies*, and to examine it as such misses its special role in the text. To approach Hardenberg's discussions of language and semiotics as philosophical issues within the *Fichte Studies* overlooks or underestimates their most radical gesture, for they insist on just the opposite: they approach philosophy as a linguistic and semiotic problem. (p. 78)

O'Brien's reading carefully pulls together those strands in the *Fichte Studies* that deal with the nature of the image or the sign and its implications for self-knowledge. While acknowledging that Hardenberg was not only familiar with but also still in part committed to eighteenth-century linguistic theory, O'Brien is concerned to expose those aspects of the *Fichte Studies* that extend and finally break with Enlightenment linguistic traditions.

O'Brien's reading thus focuses on the explicit problematizing of representation that is a recurrent and, he believes, the most fundamental theme in the *Fichte Studies*. It is easy to underestimate the extent of late-eighteenth-century philosophy's faith in its own ability to achieve its goals. Even the post-Kantian philosophers like Fichte, who recognized difficulties for transcendental philosophy, never doubted that philosophical method was the appropriate tool for discovering the nature of consciousness. Novalis is far more critical, however, recognizing from the outset the need for a distinction between being or identity and its presentation. O'Brien points out that Novalis approaches Fichte's first principle not as a proposition, but as a *sentence*, a linguistic entity. This is the sense in which the "essence" of the principle can only be an illusory proposition or *Scheinsatz*: as a sentence it signals identity, but does not literally re-present it for transparent inspection: "By introducing the term 'sign' (*Zeichen*) for what stands in the place of what is lost, Hardenberg divorces presentation (*Darstellung*) from representation, and grounds it in semiosis" (p. 84).

Central to O'Brien's reading is what he calls the "semiotic fragment" (#11), which he sees as providing a sort of proto-structuralist account of meaning, eschewing causal accounts of the relation between sign and signified, and introducing the notion of a signifier as an "agent of semiotic invention." He glosses the entry in terms of four stages: (1) an examination of the sign/signified relation as in general an arbitrary relation between dissimilar relata; (2) an examination in light of this fact of how signifying agents manage to communicate with each other; (3) an account of communication between agents as the result of self-determination; and (4) a discussion of the role of a universal "schema" (adapted from Kant and Fichte) shared by signifying agents in guaranteeing the success of communication between them. This final move, according to O'Brien, is "epoch-making" in its implications:

> Although Hardenberg's solution here recalls Fichte's similar use of the schema, it has one radically different consequence. For whether it is used by the first or the second signifier, the schema's inherent and universal mediation between sign and signified undercuts any possibility of a stable priority of one to the other: the sign and signified are given "simultaneously" in the priority of the schema itself.

Whereas O'Brien clearly rejects the view that Novalis is still operating entirely within the framework of Fichtean metaphysics, he suggests that Novalis' semiotic theory is strongly influenced by Fichte's views on language, and thus in a way

> merely extends Fichte's thought more consequently than Fichte himself... When Hardenberg extends the function of the schema to *all* signs, he merely continues a line of reasoning already introduced, but neglected by Fichte.

O'Brien argues that Novalis even prefigures post-structuralist accounts like Derrida's in his recognition of "the signifier's lack of motivation and its differential constitution with the signified" (p. 80).

Significance for contemporary philosophy

The very fact that this unusual collection of notes can generate such vastly different interpretive enterprises over the past half-century is a tribute to its potential to continue to engage philosophers well into the future. This is not surprising if we view Novalis' study of Fichte and subsequent reworking, revolutionizing, or repudiating (depending on one's interpretation) of the philosophy of human subjectivity as a unique chapter in modern western philosophy's attempt to understand the relationship of human knowledge to its object. In Novalis' own time, Kant had pulled the rug out from under foundationalist accounts, so to speak, by arguing that building metaphysical systems from universal principles of reason was methodologically unsound and substantively unwarranted, since all human knowledge depends on human ways of knowing. The Copernican Revolution in philosophy, as it has since come to be called, was intended by Kant to circumscribe once and for all the area within which human beings can lay claim to knowledge of themselves and their world. But what for Kant seemed an enlightened and reasonable proposal was for many of his era an oppressive command to cease all efforts to find the "core" of their being and the absolute nature of the world. For all Fichte's claim to be carrying on the Kantian tradition, his effort to define the human subject in terms of an originary act of which we have an intellectual intuition was clearly a return in many respects to a Cartesian model of consciousness.

But just as the Cartesian cogito gives rise to problems in identifying the "I" that is supposed to be the conclusion of his argument (What do I know everytime I think/doubt? An idea? Or the self itself, in an intuition?), so too does Fichte's account of our grasp of the original act of positing the I (*Tathandlung*). Novalis asks, how do I grasp the true (absolute) self (as it is-in-itself, to use Kant's language) in anything *other* than representation? I might indeed "have a feeling" of myself that somehow precedes my recognition of it, but the moment that feeling is stated or asserted, it belongs to the realm of representation. Introspection won't work because consciousness is not transparent to itself. So, "the borders of feeling are the borders of philosophy":

> Philosophy cannot be self-observation, because it would not then be what we are after. Perhaps it is self-feeling?" ... "What then is a feeling? It can only be observed in reflection – the spirit of feeling is then gone. (#15)

What is the solution? Whatever interpretive approach one prefers, I believe that it is safe to say that basically, Novalis has a two-pronged answer. The first prong of the answer, which may be taken as the leading or at least most general conclusion of the *Fichte Studies*, is to accept that philosophy is fundamentally a product of an endless activity, *philosophizing*, that is a "striving after the thought of a ground" that is not given to us. We must look for but never expect to attain the "absolutes" we seek:

> Unending free activity in us arises through the free renunciation of the absolute – the only possible absolute that can be given us and that we only find through our inability to attain and know an absolute. This absolute that is given to us can only be known negatively, insofar as we act and find that what we seek cannot be attained through action. (#566)

So Novalis parts company with Fichtean idealism, but also with Cartesian foundationalism. Moreover, he argues, in a way very much prefiguring the later Wittgenstein, that the product of philosophizing – philosophy – is really a breach in the unending activity of philosophizing:

> Philosophy, the result of philosophizing, arises accordingly through *interruption* of the drive towards knowledge of the ground – through standing still at the point where one is. (#566)

The philosophy of the subject, then, cannot provide a positive solution to the nature of the I:

> The I signifies that negatively known absolute – what is left over after all abstraction – what can only be known through action and what only realizes itself through eternal lack. (#566)

Given this regulative notion of philosophy as an unending, and endless, activity, Novalis may certainly be seen as a precursor of the so-called postmodern philosophers who, in various ways, have declared the end of philosophy.

At the same time, however, Novalis moves further in the direction of transforming the modern conception of philosophy by suggesting that the activity of philosophizing may move seamlessly over into the creation of art. And this is the second prong of his solution to modern philosophy's question of the relation of thought to reality. In the very next sentence following the dramatic announcement that the self is only realized "through eternal lack," Novalis strikes a more optimistic note:

> /Thus [through the realization of the self as an eternal lack] eternity is realized temporally in spite of the fact that time contradicts eternity. The I becomes effective and determinate in itself only in its *opposite*. /Insofar as I ask "What is that?" I demand the *externalizing* of the thing in itself – I want to know – *what is* it? Of course I already

> know that it *is* this or that thing, but what sort of a thing? This is what I want to know – and here I step into the sphere of the subjective. (#566)

In other words, Novalis says, what I demand is an exhibition or external presentation of the thing as it really is, absolutely, or in itself. That, whether it be the I or any other object, can never be given to me in reflection ("I never find intuition because I must seek it through reflection and vice versa" is how Novalis ends this paragraph). A paragraph later Novalis gestures toward the second half of his solution to the problem of reflection:

> /To ground is to philosophize. To *think up [something]* [*erdenken*] is to poeticize. (#567)

Then, a few lines later, he adds an interesting parenthetical remark about Fichte's style of philosophizing:

> (Fichtean philosophy is a call to self-activity – I cannot thoroughly explain something to someone unless I refer him to himself, unless I bid him to perform the same action that clarified it for me. I can teach someone to philosophize when I teach him to do it as *I* do it – when he does what I do, he is what I am, is there, where I am.)

This is followed by the apparent non sequitur, "/All art begins with invention or imitation/." But for Novalis the connection is clear. What is most important about Fichte for Novalis, in the end, is his invitational approach to philosophy – what Cavell has called the "reseduction" of poetry and philosophy[18] – and it is precisely this invitation to imitate and reinvent another's experience that leads Novalis to the connection between philosophizing (the activity, not philosophy the product) and art. Where philosophizing ends, poeticizing may begin, and if one is doing philosophy inventively, *with feeling*, so to speak, the transition should be seamless.

In another fragmentary set of notes on Kant, Novalis suggests that the practice of philosophy itself, and practical reason, must move into a new, aesthetic dimension:

[18] Stanley Cavell, *In Quest of the Ordinary: Lines of Scepticism and Romanticism* (Chicago: University of Chicago Press, 1988), p. 75.

> Philosophizing is just scientizing [*wissenschaften*], thinking through thought, knowing knowledge – treating the *sciences* scientifically and *poetically*. Should the *practical* and the poetic be one – and the latter simply signifies absolute practice made specific? (II:390, #45)

Philosophy cannot grasp the absolute – a "handful of darkness"(#3) – but it could involve an imaginative transformation of the world – poeticizing the world, or, as he would soon come to say, romanticizing it. By "romanticizing" the world Novalis means something quite specific: to romanticize is to make what is ordinary and mundane extraordinary and mysterious, and conversely, to make what is unknown and mysterious ordinary (II: 545, #105).

> The world must be romanticized. In this way one rediscovers the original meaning. Romanticizing is nothing but a qualitative raising to a higher power [*Potenzirung*]. The lower self becomes identified with a better self. Just as we ourselves are such a qualitative exponential series. This operation is still quite unknown. Insofar as I give the commonplace a higher meaning, the ordinary a mysterious countenance, the known the dignity of the unknown, the finite an appearance of infinity, I romanticize it. The operation is precisely the opposite for the higher, unknown, mystical and infinite – these are logarithmized by this connection – they become common expressions. Romantic philosophy. Lingua romana. Alternating elevation and lowering.

There is no reason, from Novalis' perspective, to choose between philosophy and poetry. When done properly, i.e., when understood as activities, both are part of the same process. To philosophize and to poetize are to romanticize. Whatever Fichte's influence on Novalis might have been, in the final analysis it was this aspect of his philosophy that was taken over by Novalis whole-heartedly. It is worth quoting Fichte's own description of what he is actually doing in the *Wissenschaftslehre*:

> The *Wissenschaftslehre* begins with an I. But the point is not to analyze this I, for this would produce a purely empty philosophy. Instead, the *Wissenschaftslehre* allows this I to act in accordance with its own laws and thereby to construct a world. This is no analysis, but instead a continually progressing synthesis.[19]

[19] *Fichte: Foundations of Transcendental Philosophy*, ed. and trans. Breazeale, pp. 109–110.

On Fichte's own terms, Novalis never stopped "Fichtesizing."[20] Philosophy, as he himself claims in the *Fichte Studies*, is an "unending free activity." That in the course of pursuing its own end it must at some points blend into and become artistic activity is not a Fichtean conclusion, but it is the result of applying the Fichtean method to philosophy, of making philosophy itself "self-conscious." This is surely one of the most significant conclusions of Novalis' *Fichte Studies*, and no matter how one interprets them, they embody a beguiling reinvitation to philosophize about the very nature of human consciousness and creativity.

[20] This is the term he and Friedrich Schlegel used to refer to their metaphysical discussions. See letter from Schlegel, May, 1797 (*Novalis: Schriften*, Vol. IV, p. 482).

Chronology

1772	May 2: Georg Friedrich Phillip von Hardenberg (Novalis) born in Oberwiederstedt, in Thuringia.
1780 (1781)	The nine-year old Friedrich falls seriously ill.
1781	Friedrich tutored privately by Karl Christian Erhard Schmid, who later became professor of philosophy at Jena.
1784	Family moves to the town of Weißenfels, near Leipzig. Father appointed director of the Saxon salt mines.
1786	Death of Friedrich II (Frederick the Great); ascendence to throne of Friedrich Wilhelm II.
1786/1787	Friedrich sent to live for a year with his uncle, Fr. Wilhelm von Hardenberg. Meeting with Georg August Bürger, poet and author of "Lenore"; Hardenberg's first serious attempts at poetry.
1789	Storming of the Bastille; outbreak of the French Revolution.
1790	Hardenberg sent to Eisleben to the Luthergymnasium; matriculation in October at the University of Jena; acquaintance with Friedrich Schiller, Karl Reinhold and Sophie Wieland Reinhold, Johann Benjamin Erhard, among others; along with some other students, Hardenberg undertakes care of Schiller during the latter's illness.
1791	Leaves the University of Jena to return to Weißenfels in October; shortly thereafter matriculates at the

University of Leipzig; returns to Jena at Christmas to visit the ailing Schiller.

1792 Meets Friedrich Schlegel in Leipzig. Affair with Julie Eisenstuck. Revolutionary army takes Mainz.

1793 Hardenberg decides to become a soldier; changes his mind because of father's disapproval of the affair with Eisenstuck and the family's difficult financial situation. Hardenberg enrolls at Wittenberg, once more to study law.

Prussia at war with France; outbreak of the Terror in France; Mainz reclaimed by allied forces. Execution of Louis XVI.

1794 Receives law degree from Wittenberg. Moves to Tennstedt to take position as assistant to the county bailiff, Just; becomes close friends with his niece Caroline. Meets Sophie von Kühn (b. March 17, 1782) at Grüningen. Execution of Robespierre. Peace treaty between Prussia and French Republic.

1795 Secretly engaged to Sophie in March. In May, meets Fichte and Hölderlin in the home of Niethammer in Jena. Serious study of Fichte begins in the fall. In November, Sophie's illness appears. In December, appointment to Saxon salt mines directorate as assistant.

1796 Chemistry course with Johann Wiegleb in Langensalz. Moves to Weißenfels to begin new job. Sophie's operations in Jena begin over the course of the summer and fall. Several visits with Fr. Schlegel. Sophie's further deterioration and return to her home in Grüningen in December. Study of Spinoza and Zinzendorf.

1797 March: Visits Sophie, who dies nine days after this last visit. A month later the sibling to whom he was closest, Erasmus, dies. Writes the famous diary on "Mourning" and has mystical vision while visiting Sophie's grave. Meeting with August and Caroline Schlegel. Matriculation at the Mining Academy in Freiberg.

Study of Kant, Hemsterhuis, and Fichte again. Study in Freiberg under the geologist Abraham Werner: chemistry, physics, mathematics, and geology. Death of Friedrich Wilhelm II, succeeded by Friedrich Wilhelm III and Queen Luise.

1798 Meets Julie von Charpentier. Meets Goethe in Weimar. Continued contact with Schiller. Publication in *Athenäum* of *Blütenstaub*, under the pen-name "Novalis." Also publishes *Blumen* and *Glaube und Liebe*. Goes to Teplitz spa for his failing health. Meets author Jean Paul (Ritter). Engaged to Julie von Charpentier.

1799 Returns to Weißenfels and inspects Saxon salt mines. Meets and befriends Ludwig Tieck in Jena and together they visit Herder. Studies Schleiermacher's work; reads mystic philosopher Jacob Boehme. November 11–14: famous meeting of the "Jena Circle" Romantics at the home of August and Caroline Schlegel, with Friedrich Schlegel, Tieck, and Jean Paul in attendance. Appointed associate director of Saxon salt mines. During the course of this year writes *Die Christenheit oder Europa* and *Geistliche Lieder*, and begins *Heinrich von Ofterdingen* and *Hymnen an die Nacht*.

1800 Finishes *Hymnen* and the first part of *Ofterdingen*; continues his study of Boehme. Conducts a geological survey tour of several areas in Saxony. Visited by Tieck in Weißenfels. *Hymnen an die Nacht* published in *Athenäum*. September: becomes seriously ill with tuberculosis. Journeys to Siebeneichen in Meißen and to Dresden for medical help in October. Appointed circuit director of the salt mines administration for Thuringia.

1801 Taken from Dresden to Weißenfels. Friedrich Schlegel visits him on March 23, remaining by Novalis' side until his death on March 25.

Further reading

Although most of Novalis' literary works are available in English translation, his philosophical writings have gone largely untranslated. The most significant English-language translation to date is Margaret Mahony Stoljar's translated edition, *Novalis: Philosophical Writings* (Albany: State University of New York Press, 1997). Stoljar's volume does not contain selections from the *Fichte Studies*, but is fairly extensive in its translations of other important theoretical essays and fragments, and is therefore a useful companion to the *Fichte Studies*. Although prior to this volume there has been no translation of the entire *Fichte Studies*, portions have been translated in *Theory as Practice: A Critical Anthology of Early German Romantic Writings*, under the general editorship of Jochen Schulte-Sasse (Minneapolis: University of Minnesota Press, 1997). The translation of selections from the *Fichte Studies* in that volume is by Elizabeth Mittman and Mary R. Strand, and focuses on sections dealing with identity, consciousness, and signification. Their introductory essay ("Self and Other in Early German Romanticism") contains a useful section of commentary on these aspects of the *Fichte Studies*, relating them to his politics in the later work "Faith and Love." In addition to some of the readings translated in Stoljar's book, Kathleen Wheeler's *German Aesthetic and Literary Criticism: The Romantic Ironists and Goethe* (Cambridge: Cambridge University Press, 1984) contains Joyce Crick's translations of "Dialogues" and "Studies in the Visual Arts." A small selection of Novalis' fragments is also contained in translation in *German Romantic Criticism*, edited by A. Leslie Willson (New York: Continuum 1982).

In *The Early Political Writings of the German Romantics*, edited and translated by Frederick C. Beiser (Cambridge: Cambridge University

Press, 1999), the reader can find translations of "Faith and Love" as well as other essays and fragments dealing directly with political issues, including a few paragraphs from the last sections of the *Fichte Studies*. This volume also contains a translation of *The Oldest Systemic Programme of German Idealism*, a very brief but influential document attributed variously to Hölderlin, Schelling, and/or Hegel, which, although independently conceived, strikingly resembles a short précis-version of Novalis' carefully worked-out program in the *Fichte Studies*. Readers interested in Novalis' political theory might also consult Beiser's *Enlightenment, Revolution, and Romanticism* (Cambridge, Mass.: Harvard University Press, 1992), Chapter 11.

To date, there are relatively few English-language studies of Novalis' philosophical writings. The only one of these devoted exclusively to the *Fichte Studies* is Géza von Molnár's *Novalis' "Fichte Studies": The Foundations of his Aesthetics* (The Hague: Mouton, 1970). William Arctander O'Brien's more recent book, *Novalis: Signs of Revolution* (Durham & London: Duke University Press, 1995), contains a long chapter on "Language and Semiotics in the *Fichte Studies*" that is also a good source of commentary and interpretation, with an interesting discussion of paragraph 11, the so-called "semiotic fragment." Manfred Frank's *Introduction to Early Romantic Aesthetics*, soon to be available in translation, contains a ground-breaking essay on the *Fichte Studies* as well (*Einführung in die Frühromantische Ästhetik* [Frankfurt-on-Main: Suhrkamp, 1989]). Frank's Chapter 15 of this book, on Novalis' theory of temporality, represents a thorough-going integration of the *Fichte Studies* into Novalis' philosophy. A very brief but helpful discussion of the studies is also contained in John Neubauer's biography, *Novalis* (Boston: Twayne Publishers, 1980).

Ernst Behler's *German Romantic Literary Theory* (Cambridge: Cambridge University Press, 1993) also contains a chapter on Novalis that deals in part with the relationship of his philosophy to that of Fichte, with a general discussion of the role of the *Fichte Studies* in his poetic development and in comparison to Friedrich Schlegel's views on Fichte. Although little attention is given to the *Fichte Studies* in Kristen Pfefferkorn's *Novalis: A Romantic's Theory of Language and Poetry* (New Haven: Yale University Press, 1988), her overall approach views Novalis as a philosopher as well as a poet, and the book contains interesting discussions of themes first raised in the *Studies*, as well as appendices on

Fichte's and Herder's theories of language that readers might find useful for purposes of comparison.

Using Novalis' 1798 "Monologue" as catalyst, Andrew Bowie discusses the early Romantics' views on language and truth in the context of Fichtean and Kantian philosophy, and also relates the issues raised to Critical Theory and to contemporary analytic philosophical concerns (*From Romanticism to Critical Theory* [London: Routledge, 1997]). Readers interested in further developments in Novalis' theoretical program after the *Fichte Studies*, especially its elements of mysticism, may find useful Chapter 5 of Paola Mayer's *Jena Romanticism and its Appropriation of Jakob Böhme* (Montreal & Kingston: McGill-Queens University Press, 1999). Relatively recent English-language monographs dealing with Fichte's influence on Novalis' aesthetics include von Molnár's *Romantic Vision, Ethical Context* (Minneapolis: University of Minnesota Press, 1987) and Richard W. Hannah's *The Fichtean Dynamic of Novalis' Poetics* (Bern: Lang, 1981). Martha B. Helfer's Chapter 3 of *The Retreat of Representation: The Concept of "Darstellung" in German Critical Discourse* (Albany: State University of New York Press, 1996) discusses the *Fichte Studies* as part of Novalis' development of a theory of artistic presentation. In *Representation and its Discontents: The Critical Legacy of German Romanticism* (Berkeley: University of California Press, 1992), Azade Seyhan examines the role of Fichte's philosopy of self-activity in Novalis' theory of poetic creativity.

Readers interested in a biography of Novalis should consult John Neubauer's *Novalis*, and O'Brien's *Signs of Revolution* also contains significant amounts of biographical information. The recent fictionalized biography *The Blue Flower* by Penelope Fitzgerald (Boston: Houghton Mifflin, 1996) should not, of course, be taken in its details as historical fact, but is entertaining and plausible while remaining close to the actual circumstances of Novalis' life.

Note on the text

In his Introduction to the third and definitive edition of Novalis' writings, Hans-Joachim Mähl describes the recent fortunes of the work now labeled the *Fichte Studies*:

> In the archives of the Hardenberg family in Oberwiederstedt a number of manuscripts, about 500 pages in various formats, were found among Novalis' posthumous papers. These contained a critical dialogue with the philosophy of his time, especially with Fichte, Kant and Hemsterhuis, in which the author at the same time attempted to advance his own worldview. These manuscripts turned up in the possession of the Schocken family of New York at an auction in Hamburg in 1960, after having passed, like many others, into foreign lands after the Berlin auction of 1930 and were lost to scholarship for almost 30 years. They were then acquired by the Freie Deutschen Hochstift in Frankfurt. (Mähl, p. 29)

The writings were originally compiled somewhat randomly by Hardenberg's niece Sophie; an extensive selection was published by Ernst Heilborn in 1901, involving what turned out to be a rather unsuccessful attempt at a chronological ordering of the notes (see von Molnár, p. 20). This edition was improved upon dramatically by Eduard Havenstein's edition in 1909, which employed careful handwriting analyses to determine the proper ordering of the manuscript pages. Paul Kluckhohn in 1929 published a significantly expanded edition based on Havenstein's, adding new material especially to the beginning section of the manuscripts and further refining the chronology. The 1965 second edition of Kluckhohn's work, co-edited by Richard Samuel and Hans-Joachim Mähl, involved further chronological revisions but no new additional material to the *Studies*, and still stands as the definitive edition of the *Fichte Studies*.

As noted in the introduction, this translation has followed as faithfully as possible the format used by the editors of the *Novalis: Schriften*. This includes the use of numbers for each paragraph, angle brackets (< >) for material that Novalis had crossed out but that is important for making sense of the immediately following lines, and reproduction as faithfully as possible in print form of the diagrams and lists Novalis employed (see Hans-Joachim Mähl's introduction to that edition, p. 90). I have followed the German edition text in using slash marks (/) for parentheses.

In translating this unusual work, I have tried to preserve the freshness – in both senses of the word – of Novalis' style. It is important to bear in mind that these are the jottings and free speculations of a brilliant but somewhat distracted young man in his early twenties. Novalis was inspired and agitated not only by the events in his personal life, but by the new philosophies of his time. The *Studies* are generally deeply philosophical and clearly steeped in the technical language of Fichte and Kant. Yet they are also at times rather wild – rashly speculative, unrestrained in their enthusiasm, teasing and playful. One never senses disrespect for his philosophical mentors, but, as is often the best student's wont, Novalis has no problem poking a little fun now and then as he explicates their views and opposes them with his own. It is hard to avoid the conclusion that Novalis' high-spirited style is integral to the substance of this work, and I have tried as much as possible to preserve the sense of sport as well as the seriousness of these notes.

Fichte Studies

Group 1: 1–210 (fall to early winter, 1795)

Remarks

1. The proposition a is a contains nothing but a positing, differentiating and combining. It is a philosophical parallelism. In order to make *a* more distinct, *A* is divided (analyzed).[1] "Is" is presented as universal content, "a" as determinate form. The essence of identity can only be presented in an *illusory* proposition [*Scheinsatz*]. We abandon the *identical* in order to present it.[2] Either this occurs only illusorily – and we are brought by the imagination to believe it – what *occurs*, already is – naturally through imaginary separation and unification – Or we represent it through its "not-being" [what it is not], through a "not-identical" [what is not identical to it] – a sign – [using] a determined thing for an isomorphic determining thing.[3] This isomorphic determining thing must actually

[1] I have added the italics for clarity. Novalis does not use them, nor in general does he have any print conventions for distinguishing mention from use, except by context, throughout the *Studies*. I have followed suit except in cases such as this where it would be unnecessarily confusing.

[2] The translation of *Vorstellung* and *Darstellung* and their cognates is a vexed issue in German philosophy that appears to have its roots in Kant and his immediate successors. For simplicity's sake I will translate occurrences of *Darstellung* and its cognates as "presentation," "to present," etc. Similarly for *Vorstellung* I will use "representation," although "representation" is often a perfectly reasonable translation of *Darstellung* as well. Cf. Martha B. Helfer, *The Retreat of Representation: The Concept of Darstellung in German Critical Discourse* (Albany: State University of New York Press, 1996). *Darstellung* in its technical, Kantian sense connotes an element of sensation or sensibility in presentation tied to the notion of schematism. Hence Lacoue-Labarthe and Nancy refer to it problematically as a "staging" or "figuration" (see Philippe Lacoue-Labarthe and Jean-Luc Nancy, *The Literary Absolute* [Albany: State University of New York Press, 1988], p. 31).

[3] The discussion of an isomorphic, i.e., similarly formed, "sign" harks back to Kant's discussion of the schematism of the pure concepts of the understanding, in which he poses the problem of the application of the pure concepts. He argues that what is required to make such application possible

determine the communicated sign in a completely unmediated way, through just the same movements as the I, freely and yet still like the I. Taste and genius. The former [taste], if it is determined through a medium, a representation, of my act of producing the sign or simply of my *intention*, my *meaning*. The latter [genius], if it is produced immediately, without this medium, the representation of *my* causality – like the I. The former is mere taste, the latter is the taste of genius.
The proposition: If A then A, contains this [same thing]. The rest is explained by the category of relation.
Application of the above to the proposition:

I am I.

Grammatically it contains the same thing three times.
The proposition I am I contains nothing more than what lies in the mere concept of the I.
What is the I? /An absolute thetic faculty/ The sphere of the I must encompass everything for us. As itself content, it can recognize content. The recognition points to its being an I. As the ground of all determining for the I, or of all *form*, it is thus also the ground of its own determination, or form. In short: it is an independent determination of content – thus it gives *it*self *all* determination.
The spontaneity of its determination – It assumes, e.g., A, because it assumes a.
Why the original act must be a free act – because it presupposes no other – It is, because it is, not because another is. Consequently the determination of the I as I is free. /A not-free act can only be not-free through another act, and so forth. Identity/
Because the I is a thoroughly determined thing, it can only cognize the universal content in itself. Insofar as it transposes universal content outside itself, it must believe in it. The I cannot know [content outside itself] as a determination, because [to do so] it would have to be *in it*. What I don't know but feel (the I feels itself, as content) I believe. The act of positing something outside us must be free – but only mediate – it depends upon the first act – we are unaware of the latter and consequently we feel the former as unfree. Why we are not aware of the first act: because it first makes the awareness possible and consequently this lies *within* the

is a "mediating representation" that can act as an interface between the intellectual concept and the sensible intuition (*Critique of Pure Reason*, A 137/B 176ff., trans. Paul Guyer and Alan W. Wood [Cambridge: Cambridge University Press, 1998], pp. 271ff.).

sphere of the first act – the act of coming to awareness can therefore not go outside its sphere and hope to grasp the mothersphere.
Dividing and *uniting*.

Pure and empirical I.

Concerning Consciousness

[2.] Knowledge comes from something. It always refers to a something – It is a reference to Being, in the determined being in general, namely in the I.
In *knowledge* of the determined being, the *accent*, the stress is on the being; the determined [thing] is only baggage [literally: "brought along"], it is an accident. With *feeling* it is the opposite. The accent lies on the form, on the determination. The being is only baggage, is an accident.
Consciousness is the sphere of knowledge. In feeling it [consciousness] can only occur mediately.

/Knowledge is here taken exclusively in the strict sense./

What kind of a relation is knowledge? It is a being outside of being that is nevertheless within being.

/Dividing – uniting/

Consciousness is a being outside of being that is within being.
But what is that?
What is outside being must not be a proper being.
An improper being outside being is an image – So what is outside being must be an image of being within being. Consciousness is consequently an image of being within being.
A better explanation of the image. /Sign/ Theory of signs. /Theory of presentation, i.e., of not-being, within being, in order to let being be there for itself in a certain respect.
Theory of space and time in terms of the image.

3. Now if the universal content were only in the I, could one not then place determined-being in opposition to mere-being? *Belief* also forces us to take up just this illusory opposition, which we are in any case capable

of through our thetic faculty. /Thus thinking and feeling switch the roles of subjective and objective./

No modification – no concept – clings to mere-being – One cannot posit anything in opposition to it – except to say not-being. But this [word] is just a little connecting hook used for hanging things on pro forma – it only appears thus [to connect things]. It just grasps a handful of darkness.

In order *to determine* the I we must refer it to something. Reference occurs through differentiation – Both [occur] through the thesis of an absolute sphere of existence. This is mere-being – or chaos.

Should there be a still higher sphere, it would be the sphere between being and not-being. – The oscillating between the two. – Something inexpressible, and here we have the *concept* of *life*.

Life can be nothing else – a human being dies – the substance remains – the *middle-joint*, if I may call it that, between substance and annihilation is gone. – The substance becomes indeterminate – Each appropriates what it can.

Here philosophy is at a standstill and must remain so – because life consists precisely in this, that it cannot be grasped. Philosophy can aim only at *being*. Human beings feel the boundary that circumscribes everything for them, for themselves, *the first act*; they must believe it, as certainly as they know everything else. Consequently we are here not yet transcendent, but rather in the I and for the I.

In order to conceive itself the I must represent to itself another like itself, anatomize, as it were. This other being that is like the I is none other than the I itself. The I similarly becomes aware of this act of alienation and respective production only through this same conceptual exercise. – It finds that it is the same in its own case, that the act that precedes this reflection can occur in no other way.

> /Clarification of "being," "life," "thinking," "representing" etc./
> Natural path of reflection to result and from result to reflection, as to the result of the result.

Life is something composed of synthesis, thesis, and antithesis and yet none of the three.

All subsequent theses, syntheses and antitheses must have the content of the thesis and the form of the first synthesis and antithesis. Consequently Being must be the character of all theses, dividing and relating must be the character of all antitheses and syntheses.

[4.] Is not philosophy possible only for the use or purpose of reflection? Therefore it must be dogmatic and *appear* transcendent.

[5.] What do we mean by "I"?

Has not Fichte too arbitrarily packed everything into the I? With what warrant?

Can an I posit itself as *I*, without another I or Not-I -/How are I and Not-I opposable/

6. The I has a hieroglyphic power.

7. There has to be a Not-I, in order that I can posit the I as I. Thesis, antithesis, synthesis.

8. The act by which the I posits itself as I must be connected with the antithesis of an independent Not-I and of the relationship to a sphere that encompasses them – this sphere can be called God, and I.

9. The requirement of a universally valid philosophy.

10. Concept of the nothing and the something.

11.1. Theory of the sign or
what can be *true* through the medium of language?
2. of philosophy in general – the possibility of a system, etc.
3. System itself.

What is thought?

Free successive isolation outside of space.

Speech and writing?

<the same, only in a determinate way in space.>
determinate presentation of thought in space – Consequently, because space and time reciprocally *signify*, determine, and restrain each other – determinate signs of thought.

The relationship of the sign to the signified.
Both are in different spheres that can mutually determine each other.
The signified is a free effect[,] likewise the sign.
They are thus the same in the one who is doing the signifying – otherwise completely different – but this also only for the one signifying – both are related to each other only in the one who is signifying.
Insofar as the signifying [agent] is *completely free* either in the effect of the signified or in the choice of the sign, and not dependent even on its own determinate nature, then to that extent both [signified and signifier] are there in mutual relationship only for the signifying [agent], and neither of them is necessarily related to the other for a second signifying [agent].[4]
For a second signifying agent they are completely separate.
Thought, however, can be communicated to a second signifying [agent], as with all things *from outside*, only in space, via an intuition or a feeling.

> /Space is the *outer* condition, time the *inner* condition, of sensible intuition, or feeling/

Consequently only through a sign. But if, as just stated, sign and signified are completely separated, if they are related only in the first signifying [agent], then it can only be an accident or a miracle if the signified is received by the second signifying [agent] through such a sign.
Objectively and subjectively necessary signs, /which at bottom is the same/ are therefore the only things through which something that is thought can be communicated.
In order to communicate, the first signifying [agent] need only choose such signs as have a well-grounded necessary relationship to the signified in the homogeneous being of the second signifying agent. The homogeneity of the alien being with that of its own [being] in this relationship will have to be studied by it in this communication.
The necessity of the relationship of a sign to the thing signified should lie in the signifying agent. In *this* agent, however, both are freely posited. Therefore a free necessity of the relationship of both must exist in the signifying agent. It [the relationship of sign/signified] should be free with

[4] Here I am following Schulte-Sasse et al. in translating *der Bezeichnende* as a reference to an individual subject in its activity of signifying, as opposed to the sign (*das Bezeichnende*) itself. I have for that reason preferred "signifying agent" to their "signifying person." (Cf. Jochen Schulte-Sasse et al., *Theory as Practice: A Critical Anthology of Early German Romantic Writings* [Minneapolis: University of Minnesota Press, 1997], pp. 63, 93ff.)

respect to this signifying agent – it can be necessary therefore only with respect to *the signifying agent in general* or to other signifying agents. – Free necessity could be called self-determination. Consequently self-determination would be characteristic of the *signifying agent in general* or of other signifying agents – thus the essence of self-determination is synthesis – absolute positing of a sphere – thesis [is the] determinate positing of a sphere – antithesis [is the] indeterminate positing of a sphere. Every one of these three is all three and this is proof of their belonging together. The synthesis is, or can be, thesis and antithesis. The same with the thesis, and the antithesis. Original schema.[5] /One in all./ All in one./ Every *comprehensible* sign must therefore stand in a *schematic* relationship to the signified.

In order to make this clearer we must investigate the original schema more closely.

The schema stands in reciprocal action with itself. Each in its place is only what it is through the other. The first signifier [*das Bezeichnende*] finds an original schema in the second signifier – and it chooses the signs to be communicated accordingly.[6] The second signifier is only free insofar as it is necessary, and conversely, is only necessary inasmuch as it is free – in short – it is *necessarily free*. ["]Free["] must stand last, because freedom either reached the second signifier first or occurs to it last in its process of thought. It is free in the thesis – the opposite and the sphere only comprise the predicate – and must be so, so that in the schema the thesis just is the thesis – as it must be.

> /The antithesis [*Gegensatz*] is to be distinguished from the non-thesis [*Nichtsatz*]. Antipodes and antivectors./
> Here the all-uniting character of the schema is also shown in the application. The free can only be determined, that is, necessary, and the necessary can only be undetermined, that is, free. Without sphere, thesis and antithesis could become interchangeable, could be one, or nothing – which here comes to the same. Thus [an] I and [a]

[5] Fichte in "On the Faculty of Speech and the Origin of Language" (1795) borrows Kant's notion of a schematism used to map sensible intuitions to concepts of the understanding. Fichte, however, uses the notion of a mediating function as that between the sensible and the supersensible in the development of language – sense concepts are mapped imaginatively onto abstract, "supersensible" concepts so that philosophical language arises.

[6] Here Novalis uses the neuter *das* presumably to refer to the sign itself as signifying thing, as opposed to the agent's act of signification. (See Elizabeth Mittman and Mary R. Strand, "Self and Other in Early German Romanticism," in Schulte-Sasse et al., *Theory as Practice*.)

not-I, without an absolute I! Which is just sphere, only under the presupposition (co-supposition) of thesis and antithesis/

We have come this far in understanding the second signifier, and we continue to explore it further.

Question? How first to recognize this schema and then to be able orient ourselves by it

The first signifier without noticing it will have painted its own picture in the mirror of reflection, not forgetting to paint the feature, that the picture is painted in the arrangement that it [the first signifier] itself paints./

It is free according to the original schema. If I then give the signifying agent a sign that stands in schematic relation to the signified then it will find, or rather itself signify, the signified in its [the signifying agent's] necessarily free way. The first signifying agent interacts with the second. The first agent orients himself to the second in the sign, the second to the first in the signified – a *quasi*-free contract. They must both freely want it in order for the effect to succeed. The signified precedes the sign, so it is as if the first signifying agent wants [the interaction] before the second wants it. But it is only an "as if" – (because as soon as the agent thinks the sign and signified in relation, it anticipates the *will* of the other in the representation and [. . .][7] itself first of all). The will of the other must enter at exactly the same time into the actual activity that takes place *in* the first signifying agent – even if this determination is not clearly thought.

/The representation is the medium of the outer world/ more about this later/

But how will a schematic relationship between sign and signified be determined? And which?

/If the first wants to communicate something to a third signifying agent through the second, what must be presupposed in the second by way of capacities and powers, etc.? All powers and capacities must

[7] Yellowed to the point of illegibility in the original manuscript. (Cf. Richard Samuel's text revisions, *Novalis: Schriften*, Vol. II, p. 695.)

stand under the absolute synthetic or whatever one wants to call it. The *kind* of activity developed in the schema must ground everything. It must be *generic.*/

Deduction of the C[ategories?]

[12.] tangibleness – Property of the Something. Intuitability.

Life – Law of association.

The highest *presentation* of the incomprehensible is synthesis – unity of the un-unifiable.
Positing of contradiction as not-contradiction.
The *simplest thing* is Something.
What is not even 1, is 0.
Every thing can be viewed in relation to itself, and to its not self.
The simplest thing is the simplest thing. It can stand in relation to a composite[8] and to that which is not even 1. But since *relation* itself is a composite, there can be absolutely no relation between 1 and 0. /Negation is first division./

/We are speaking here only of the grounding of the possibility of reflection/or of systematic thought/
/We must make the virtually objective into the virtually subjective, bring being into a form of thinking, in order to be able to investigate it. It is easy to discern how carefully one must then abstract from *the necessary additive*, from the given form, in order to find the original form of being, and with it the possible substrate of all matter./

The Categories must be *free* procedures, or forms of thinking.
We must apply them to themselves in order thus to find their *original* genesis.
We must distinguish the form and matter of the Categories – activity and object, or better, possibility and actuality.
It is only by being applied that they can be found – They produce themselves – One believes to have [found] their producer and repeatedly finds them [the Categories] themselves.

[8] Literally: "something put together": *das Zusammengesetzten.*

13. Necessary free effects of *life* on the *Something* in the I – that's what the categories are.

14. What reflection *finds*, *appears* already *to be there* – property of a *free* act – Reflection *finds* the categories that appear already to *be there* – that is, their possibility (*form*) and, so far as that goes, their necessity (*form*) is in the I and through the I, their *actuality (matter)* is only in the reflection.

*   *
*

UNDETERMINED PROPOSITIONS

15. Philosophy should not answer more than it is asked. It can generate nothing. Something has to be given to it. /Analysis/. Philosophy orders and explains it, or what comes to the same thing, it shows it its place in the whole – where it belongs as *cause* (1) and effect (2).
But what is actually its proper sphere of activity?
It cannot be a learned skill. Philosophy must not depend upon objects and information that must be acquired – upon a quantity of experience – otherwise every science would be philosophy. But if these are sciences, philosophy is no science.

What could it possibly be?

It deals with an object that is not learned. But all objects must be learned by us. – Thus, it deals with no object. But what is learned must be distinct from the learner. What is learned is an object – thus the learner cannot be an object. Could philosophy perhaps then deal with the learner, that is with us, when we learn about objects?
Philosophy, however, is itself in the learner. So now philosophy becomes self-observation. Aha! How the learner begins via this operation to eavesdrop on himself. He would thus have to learn about himself – because by ["]learning["] we mean absolutely nothing but intuiting an object and impressing it along with its characteristics upon ourselves. It [the self] would thus become an object again. No, philosophy cannot be self-observation, because it would not then be what we are after. It is perhaps a self-feeling. What then is a feeling?

/Philosophy is originally a feeling. The philosophical sciences conceptualize the intuitions of this feeling./

/It must be a feeling of inner, necessary free relations. Thus philosophy always needs *something given* – it is *form* – and yet *real* /and ideal at once,/ like the original act [*Urhandlung*]. Philosophy does not admit of construction. The borders of feeling are the borders of philosophy. Feeling cannot feel itself.
That which is given to feeling appears to me to be the original act as cause and effect.
The distinction of philosophy and its product – the philosophical sciences.

What then is a feeling?

It can only be observed in reflection – the spirit of feeling is then gone. The producer can be inferred from the product in accordance with the schema of reflection.

16. The faculty of intuition. No special drive grounds intuition.
Intuition is divided for feeling and reflection. Without application it is one. Applied, it is *tendency* and *product*. The tendency belongs to feeling, the product to reflection. The subjective belongs to feeling, the objective to reflection.

/Relation between faculty [*Vermögen*] and power [*Kraft*]/

Feeling and reflection together cause intuition. It is the unifying third thing – that however cannot enter into reflection and feeling – because substance can never creep into accident, synthesis can never quite appear in thesis and antithesis. /Thus an object arises out of the interaction of two non-objects. Application to the original act.
Feeling appears to be first – reflection to be second. Why?

17. In *consciousness* it must *appear* as if it went from the limited to the unlimited, because consciousness must proceed from itself as limited – and this happens through *feeling* – without consideration of the fact that *feeling*, regarded abstractly, is a progression from unlimited to limited – this inverted appearance [limited to unlimited] is natural. As soon as the absolute, as I want to call the original ideal-real or real-ideal, appears as accident or halfway, then it must appear inverted – the unlimited becomes limited and vice versa. /Application to the original act/

If feeling is there in consciousness and it is supposed to be reflected, which [reflection] is caused by the drive to form [*Formtrieb*], then a mediating intuition must precede, which itself must be produced by a preceding feeling and a preceding reflection, which however cannot enter into consciousness – and the product of this intuition now becomes the object of the reflection. This *appears* now, however, to be progression from unlimited to limited [from reflection to feeling] and is *actually* precisely a reversed progression.
Of course, "unlimited" is used in a different sense in the two cases of feeling and reflection. The first use [for feeling] is more appropriately called "unlimited," or "*undetermined*" – "*independent*" would be a better term for the second use [of "unlimited" for reflection]. The latter use indicates causal connection and the ground of this may well lie in the fact that the second act seems to be caused by the first act – that is, it is a reference to the first act – On the other hand, the former use [of "unlimited"] indicates the determination of reflection and is thus a reference to the second act – which strikingly illustrates the inner connection of these two acts.
But from where does the first reflection that generates the middle intuition get its material – its object? In general, what is reflection? It will be easy to determine, like each half of a sphere when one has the one half as *half*, and the sphere as divided. For then it [reflection] must be just the opposite – because only two opposed things exhaust *a sphere in our sense*, or constitute one. The sphere is the human being. The half is feeling.
So far we have discovered that feeling contributes to intuition, that it provides the tendency, or the subjective, that it corresponds to reflection, [which is] half of the sphere of the human being – In *consciousness* [it is] a progression from limited to unlimited, but *fundamentally* [it is] the opposite, since something would have to be given to it, and this thing that must be given to it would appear to be the original act, as cause and effect.

18. Theoretical and practical philosophy – what is that? Which is the sphere of each?

19. Reflection finds the need of philosophy, or of an assumed systematic connection between thinking and feeling – because the need is in feeling.[9] It searches through its material and finds nothing but itself and itself

[9] That is, it is a *felt* need.

alone, unchangeable, as something firm to support it, – that is, without material, mere form of material – but properly understood, its own form, thought, indeed, as without actual matter, but nevertheless in order to be *its* form, [thought] in essential relation to matter in general. Because otherwise it would not be the pure form of *reflection*, which necessarily presupposes a material, because [reflection] is the product of the limited thing, of consciousness in this sense – in short, of the subjectivity of the subject, the accidental character of the accident. This is the original act, etc.

It is this contingency that reflection, apparently alone, delivers to satisfy the need [of philosophy]. For this reason the category of modality finishes with the concept of necessity. Now the alternation of control starts. The original act connects reflection with feeling. Its form as it were belongs to reflection, its matter to feeling. It [the original act] occurs in feeling – it is styled in reflection. It is not possible to present the pure form of feeling. It is merely unity, and form and matter, being composite concepts, are simply not applicable to it. Reflection can present its [reflection's] pure form, if one calls its partial function in community with feeling "form," and carries this name over to its abstract efficacy. Only *in* feeling, so to speak, can reflection display its pure form – a new datum of the all-controlling alternating relationship between opposites, or the truth that everything presented through reflection is presented according to the rules of reflection and must be abstracted from these in order to reveal the opposition.

As its contingent contribution, feeling now gives reflection the material of intellectual intuition. Just as feeling had to help reflection display its (feeling's) first forms, reflection must also cooperate in order to have *something* at all for itself to work on – in this way intellectual intuition arises. This in turn becomes the material of philosophy in reflection. Now reflection has a pure form and a material for the pure form – that is, [it now has] the unchanging, firm hold that it sought, and now the prospect of a philosophy as a *thought*/systematic (tautology)/connection between thought and feeling is inaugurated.

Now how do we find the material determined, the object that is not an object, the area of the alternating control of feeling and reflection?

The connection between thinking and feeling must always be there – we must be able to find it in consciousness everywhere – but how do we find it systematically?

We have learned the procedure of reflection with matter in general from the pure form of reflection – Reflection now has a determinate matter – with which it will therefore proceed in the same way. This determinate matter is intellectual intuition. It is divided according to the law of the original act. It separates into its two parts – into feeling and into reflection, because it is put together from these. The synthesis of this thesis and antithesis must be one, an absolute sphere, [with] border and sphere of both, since it is a synthesis; but we are in the determined matter, so that it must, cannot be other than, the human being or the I. The human being thinks and feels – it limits both *freely* – it is determined matter.

/This would be Fichte's [notion of] intellect. The absolute I is this determined matter before the original act occurs in it, before reflection is applied to it/

Thus we have observed the most natural path in our deduction of philosophy – The need for a philosophy in consciousness – apparent progress from limited to unlimited – reflection upon that – apparent progress from unlimited to limited – results of this reflection – results of the feeling of this reflection – reflection upon these results according to those results – Discovered connection, or philosophy.

1. 2.
Feeling ———————— Reflection
4. 3.
Reflection Feeling

Back and forth direction.
Sphere exhausted —— connection there.
This is [the] basis of all philosophizing.

1. /So/ 2.
An *apparent* given ——— Why?

Therefore 4. /Thus/ 3.
That which is presented in the answer —— Something found in us

The connection between "So" and "therefore" is *mediated through* and *in* the subject – the sphere – the absolute or relative absolute.

20. However, before the aforesaid matter is divided it must be placed in opposition – the intuited thing can be placed in opposition to the [faculty of] intuition – nothing further can be opposed to the intuiting being. Here reflection and feeling are at their limits – Moreover the intuited thing can only be opposed to intuition as a part to a whole.
Everywhere we must encounter the synthesis of feeling and reflection, to which nothing more can or will be opposed.
If feeling is *something*, then reflection is *nothing* and the human being is the synthesis, and vice versa. But both can occur only in reflection thus necessarily in that which is something – in the half that is *just* reality – Thus both times the nothing is a nothing – thus a something – This is a deception of reciprocal interaction.
Reflection is nothing – if it is something – it is only *for itself* nothing – So it must thus be something then. Feeling is nothing, if it is something *in* reflection -/Apart from this reflection, *as it were*, it is nothing./

> /*In* this reflection feeling must always be something and reflection nothing/

If in reflection reflection is something and feeling is nothing, then in fact it is reversed, so that feeling is something and reflection is nothing. But both should occur in *reflection* – Consequently the one [feeling or reflection] always would have to take place in another reflection, if the other [reflection or feeling] were to occur in another [reflection]. The apparent consequence, or the real reflection would ground the cause [,] the ideal reflection. The latter [ideal reflection] would appear free, if it were the former [real reflection] – isn't it that the former is simple consciousness, the latter is reflected consciousness.

21. Intellectual intuition is not to be divided immediately into feeling and reflection. Rather into

Subject and object.

Feeling supplies the subjective, reflection supplies the objective in intuition.

22. Feeling and reflection are one in the original act. Here arises an original need to set up an opposition. A feeling of reflection, a reflection of feeling. Both drives operate in one. They cannot posit anything beyond themselves. Their efficacy is limited to their spheres. It becomes

a reflection in itself – a satisfaction of this need in itself – a reciprocal interaction of the I with itself – [that is] *apparently mediated*. This is intellectual intuition. It stands in reciprocal interaction with the original act, namely in reflection, in the sphere of the original act. The I encompasses them both. In the I they are one. In reflection they are divided.

> /The original act is the *unity* of feeling and reflection, in reflection. Intellectual intuition is the unity of feeling and reflection outside reflection. Granted, since everything that is thought is reflection, intellectual intuition will also be thought only in the forms of the original act – but we must abstract from that here. Originally intellectual intuition is prior to the original act. It grounds the original act – it is reversed secondarily. It is a similar relationship to that between pure and reflected consciousness.

Feeling also, as always, first gave rise to it [intellectual intuition] – if one may otherwise still separate that which is unified – [Intellectual intuition] gave the original act the "something" and life in relation to the something – the object and subject. The original act adds, so to speak, the nothing, life in relation to nothing and the relation of the whole – or with one relationship [it adds] relationship in general, as a half. Here it appears clearly that they are divided only in the sphere of the original act – fundamentally – in the I – they are one. Neither is without the other – they stand in reciprocal interaction.

> So it becomes clear that subject and object are precarious/apparent/ accidents.

In order to form an absolute reality [in relation to the I]/in contrast to the relative reality and negation of the mere original act/ intellectual intuition and original act must coincide – By itself alone one is neither real nor ideal – it can, however, be both –

> /Intellectual intuition alone gives *mere reality* – however, in reflection this is as good as nothing – It is supposed to be for reflection and is not – that is, it does not allow of an opposition – Consequently it is nothing for reflection./

The application of the original act to intellectual intuition occurs through drive in general. Because drive in general is the union of both known

drives taken together in the original act and in intellectual intuition, or in the absolute I. Through this a joint striving is produced – the determinate declination [*Deklination*] of both drives.
The first application of this is the finding of their mutual connection in the I. The original act cannot go further here, because through its drive it is aimed merely at intellecual intuition.

Product – Absolute I

The second application is to itself. The intellectual intuition is divided –

Product – Subject and Object

23. At first, as we know, the original act constitutes itself. Then on the strength of its self-constitition it must turn to the "Something" [cf. #20]. But we have just seen the original act first constitute itself as the opposite of intellectual intuition, then progress to intellectual intuition – all on the strength of the drive of the original act.
Perhaps both should be one. There [on the one hand] only half presented, abstractly, in reflection for reflection; – relatively real – Here [on the other] absolutely real – whole – in reflection for the I.
  There, original act, in relation to itself.
  Here, original act, in relation to the absolute I.
There, only as half, here as whole – there relatively real – here absolutely [real] – there as form alone – here as form and matter at once – namely, through drive.

/About drive? The drive to be I – the first. I is I. That is drive, and everything/

That which is *something* for the *original act alone*, is subject and object for the original act in the I.

/I *want* to call the original act alone a relative original act, and the original act in the I an absolute original act./[10]

Intellectual intuition is also something.

[10] Cf. #39, where Novalis changes his mind about this.

Experiments.

Subject. Object. Limits. ——— One intuition Several intuitions All intuitions. ——— Undetermined intuition Determined intuition Exclusive intuition. ——— Possible intuition Actual intuition Necessary intuition.	In intellectual intuition.

24. The absolute original act can perhaps be presented this way.

Ich
Matter —— Form.

We can find nothing formal here that does not already lie in the pure form – because here form [*diese*] is self-constituting in the determined indeterminate thing – in the I. The forms of thought remain as they are and it is only their genesis that is here cast in a new light. As pure forms of thought they must be discoverable in this first, absolute thought.

*

25. It may be reviewed once more – that the original act stands in reciprocal interaction with itself. Its relative first act, its relative constitution, is originally the second act, its relative second act, the progress to the

something, is originally the first act. The latter is originally absolute, the former is relatively absolute – but for it alone it must be reversed. The relative point of view always turns the thing around – it is a progress from the limited unlimited to the unlimited limited, or from the apparent unlimited /because it limits itself and thus notices no compulsion, no barriers/ to apparent dependent /dependent namely upon this self-limiting/ The dependent is dependent mediately, through itself – The medium is that limitation through itself. In this area deception of the imagination or reflection is unavoidable – in presentation – because one wants to present what is not reflection through reflection and precisely through it never arrives at what is not reflection – one hastens to demonstrate that black is white. /That which makes the limitation through itself, so to speak, into nature, the absolute I, is that from which the dependent thing and the self-limiting thing are both derived – it is the actual independent thing and the actual unlimited thing.

/More soon about how the dependent thing is ascribed to the subject and the self-limited thing to the object./

26. Investigation of the absolute original act.

27. /Feeling is matter in the I – Reflection is form in the I./

28. The dynamic Categories ground the mathematical Categories in spite of the fact that they must precede them in reflection. Upon closer investigation we will find the absolute Categories everywhere in the deduction of the merely formal. The merely formal/relatively formal/ *reveal* the first [Categories] only in reflection.
It is easily surmised that this translocation of the merely formal Categories does not remain without influence on their *content*. Their content, however, is nothing but that which they order. The absolute that is their ground must be concerned with the mere form. Now the mere form must conform to the absolute – The absolute was their content – their content was nothing, however, but what they ordered. What they order, however, is determined through nothing further than the order [imposed by the Categories] – nothing but simply "the ordered," that which is referred to the order. If it were further determined, then it would also have to correspond to another order – because this "ordered" is only for this ordering – they

are inseparably united. This other ordering must be an absolute in the actual sense, since the first is already a relative absolute.
The First Concept of the ordering, then, will be

Synthesis: absolute, and applied to a determinate matter,

absolute I.

The relationship of that which is ordered to the first ordering – inseparable, exhaustive correspondence – alternation.

Thesis: Alternation between matter and form.

Relationship between the relative absolute and the actual absolute – exclusion, reciprocal. Antithesis.

The absolute Category is related to the merely formal in such a way that the thesis of the formal is the synthesis of the absolute – etc.:

Synthesis – Thesis
Thesis – Antithesis
Antithesis [is] Synthesis,

Absolute
Category of Relation.

	/Correlate/
Thesis. Determined matter –	Succession
Antithesis. Determined form.	Exclusion
Synthesis Undetermined I.	Together at once

/The undetermined I alternates absolutely in itself/

Absolute
Category of Modality.

	/Correlate/
Thesis: Possible matter	non-matter
Antitheses: Necessary form	non-form
Synthesis: Actual I	contingent I

Absolute
Category of Quality.

Thesis: Formless matter.
Antithesis: Matterless form.
Synthesis: Real I.

Absolute Category of Quantity.

Thesis: Divisibility of matter.
Anthithesis: Wholeness (*Allheit*) of form.
Synthesis: Unity of the I.

29. In the genuine table of the Categories to be displayed at this point modality will precede relation, quantity will precede quality.

30. In reflection, matter is one with object, form one with subject.

31. At this point, further observations on the Categories and the connection of the whole.
Drive. Time and space. Intuition. Feeling. Representation. Consciousness. Faculties of the soul.
Reflection and representation are one.
Still, in the preceding everything is deduced in a very confused way.
But we now have a firm hold.
The I is the synthesis of intellectual intuition.
The original act is mere form of reflection, only insofar as it presents itself in thesis, antithesis and synthesis. Its substrate, as life, something and nothing, contains the pure presentation of feeling or of matter in relation to form alone.

To be posited through a non-positing – is pure *feeling*.
Non-positing though a positing – is pure form of reflection
or
Positing determined through non-positing
Non-positing determined through positing –

That is the purest presentation of feeling and reflection.

The undetermined as such, which is both positing and non-positing and also is neither, simply unites them in itself – it is their unconditional unity. Thus we see the pure form grounded in this absolute original act.
Both drives together are unsatisfied in intellectual intuition – whence their need – feeling needs form in its endpoint -/Form for vision, as it were/ reflection needs matter to be able to be form. They are nothing, both nothing, without the drive to be an I that unites both in itself, that is both but also neither. Now they are both something. They have an absolute ground of their relation.

/What still needs to be brought up is that the form of reflection rests merely in opposing something – the apparent non-positing in the relative original act is actually only an opposing./

/The feeling of the Not-I arises first in empirical consciousness. How? We will see./

The original form [*Urform*] of the absolute original act [*Urhandlung*] determines or grounds, as we have now discovered, the pure form of reflection.
Thus in this way the I determines the form – but how does it determine the matter? Because the I provides equally for its children. Its form is relinquished – its matter, so to say, is thoroughly conditioned and conditioning – Consequently it makes its matter into conditioned and conditioning. But pure matter without form can no more be conceived than the pure form of reflection without matter. One can abstract from it – but that requires imagination – and so we speak of *pure* matter and *pure* form.

On the empirical I

32. How does the absolute I become an empirical I?
The drive to be an I is at the same time the drive to think and to feel. Both manifest themselves in matter and in form – against one another. Now reflection has obtained *its determinate manner of acting* (its determinate material), and feeling has obtained its determinate form. *To* each other, both appear to be independent. The need of their drives is satisfied – they do not know how – that is, it does not lie within their spheres. (That they are independent *from* one another proves for each that they are independent in general.) Both appear to themselves to be dependent only

on an I – and neither notices hereby the influence of the other through that [with which they are] identical.
Thus there are two I's here – neither absolute – The I of feeling is the matter – the I of reflection is the form. Both feel their dependence. Feeling proceeds from the undetermined, which it is without knowing it, toward the determined, which for feeling is undetermined – hence from matter to matter – from determined to determiner – that is – it mistakes itself with and in itself. This deception arises from the dependence upon the I that is unrecognized by feeling, as the determined and determiner, upon the I. Reflection proceeds likewise toward form – it progresses from what is in its view dependent, form in general, which really is independent, to what is in *its view* independent, but *actually is dependent*, *its* form, or the form codetermined through matter, from the original form to relative form, from form to form – [Reflection] elevates its particular relation to the absolute I, contrary to the I – feeling does this also – Thus there are two mediated I's at hand – the I that is felt and the I that is thought. The absolute I goes from the infinite to the finite, the mediated I from the finite to the infinite.

But how does the absolute I arrive at the finite, where it then is a mediated I, according to its own laws?

The absolute I is at once both a united and a divided thing.
Insofar as it is divided it must have an empirical consciousness – in short, it must be a mediated I. The divided I must nevertheless be bound – namely, through the drive to be an I.
The I must be divided in order to be an I – only the drive to be an I unifies it – the undetermined ideal of the pure I is thus characteristic of the I in general –
But the divided I is that which is divided, that is, according to the laws of division – thus according to the laws of the pure I – However, if there is no pure I, then neither are there any laws – consequently there is always a pure I. It is the unity of the totality [*Allheit*] of form and the divisibility of matter.
We are I – consequently identical and divided – consequently a mediated and unmediated I together. The mediated I is indeed the divided I.
The pure I is only divided insofar as it is one, and is only one insofar as it is divided.

This is, however, the famous conflict within the I – which constitutes its character – which is already to be found in the absolute original act – and which is nothing but a necessary deception of the mediated I alone – that wants to stop being mediated and thus strives against itself. The conflict is, as conflict, merely in the mediated I and is necessary precisely because it is not originally a conflict – one need only pay heed to the inverted order [*ordo inversus*] of the mediated I – because this is the actual ground of the contradiction [cf. #36].

33. Which of the two mediate I's is object or subject? That of reflection – why? Because matter is thesis and form is antithesis[11] – the mediate I of feeling is no I – it is a relation of matter to matter -/a negation, for reflection/.
The I of reflection has, however, the form of the I, therefore it also has necessary, if not intentionally, reflected content – Thus it is subject – and the I of feeling is object. If the former is I, then the latter is Not-I. Here reflection becomes what feeling is – feeling becomes what reflection is – they switch their roles.

In the I feeling is ideal and real and so also is reflection.

Contrasted with one another feeling is ideal and reflection is real.

Viewed singly feeling is real and reflection is ideal.

The ideal separated from the real, that is, abstracted from the I, is subjective – consequently the ideal feeling and the ideal reflection are subjective – therefore the product of the ideal reflection is [the] subject. Now we might have discovered the reason in the I for just why it is [a] subject. It must be subject in order to be I – and the reason for just why it must be subject, if it must be mediated, lies in the abstract relation of feeling and reflection in opposition to each other, and the necessary consequences of this [relation].
What is the case in this relation, must be other outside the relation, and among two possibilities it must be *the* reality that it was *not*, [when it was] *in* the relation – ideal there, real here.

34. Are matter and feeling, reflection and form one[?] – Yes, because it is in [that which is] identical – in the I. Relation to form – relation to matter – are in *absolute* unity [*Eins*] with the related – No relata, no relator; no relator, no relata. This is also the I's provision for its children.

[11] But compare #39, where Novalis chastises himself for this claim.

Absolute matter – absolute form
What is absolute matter? – Determined and determining matter.
Absolute form.
Determined and determining form.

In absolute matter, matter is substance – determined and determining – accident. In absolute form, form is accident – substance determined and determining.

35. In the I material and form are one with feeling and reflection – Outside the I they are not-one – [Being] outside the I can only occur in the mediated I – consequently matter and feeling, form and reflection are separated in the *subject*.

[36.] General Rule.

What is one in the absolute I is separated in the subject according to the laws of the absolute I – or more generally – what holds of the absolute I holds also for the mediated I, only inversely [*ordine inverso*].

/Reversed Categories./

Determination of the *object*.

37. It must be possible to find a *specific sort of deduction* in the I.

38. The absolute original act occurs in the following order:

Absolute I.
Absolute form – absolute matter.

Its categories are as follows:

Synthesis.
Antithesis.
Thesis.

The relative act of the form –

Thesis
Antithesis
Synthesis.

And thus the mere forms of thought as well.

The absolute original act has neither thesis, antithesis nor synthesis. It resembles only the form of reflection. For reflection, however, the original act begins with the synthesis and ends with the thesis. Here also the subject and pure I [are] visible – The latter proceeding from infinite to finite – the former from finite to infinite /from thesis to synthesis/.
Thesis and antithesis must be exactly the same in the absolute Categories.

39. The Categories are grounded only through the absolute original act. There is only one sort of Category. There is no relative original act in the sense that we believed previously [#23].
The absolute or determined form is thesis, antithesis, synthesis – its application to a possible matter are the Categories. These are divided into two sorts, namely the dynamical and the mathematical.
The mathematical are grounded by the

Identical I.

The dynamical are grounded by the

Absolute I.

In the original act there is neither thesis nor antithesis. In it there is only a determined and an undetermined – Unity and manifoldness. From this arise the Categories.
Thus the mathematical [Categories] appear to be related to form – reflection – the subject – and the dynamical [Categories] appear to be related to matter, feeling, the object.

/For the I, form is a manifold; for form, form is a manifold oneness [*Mannichfaltiges Eins*]./

That was a false concept, when you made form into antithesis, matter into thesis [#33].

/Synthetic procedure is according to the manner of the pure I – analytic procedure is according to the manner of mere form/

Is there a pure I, or are synthetic judgments possible a priori! is one and the same question.

*

40. The Categories are thus analytic forms – Forms of thought of the subject.

41. Now we can determine the categories more exactly. First the object, however.

The real separated from the ideal is objective. Matter considered alone, that is, object. Feeling would be relation to the object. Reflection would be relation to the subject. The subject is, however, the mediated I. The medium must be that through which the subject ceases to be the subject – but this is matter and form, feeling and reflection, subject and object in alternation. Here the roles are exchanged – object becomes subject – subject [becomes] object. *For the subject* is a complete contradiction here – it sublates itself – Thereby it is nothing – so that here the absolute I is postulated – Now everything is set right. If the subject does not postulate the absolute I, it must lose itself here in an abyss of error – this can only happen to reflection – thus only to a part of the subject, the merely reflective part. This loss is a deception, as every elevation of a part to the whole is a deception; the subject remains what it is – divided absolute and identical I.

The subject is a divided I; inverted, it looks as follows:

Matter – Form
I. / Subject/

What is matter for the absolute I, is form for it [the subject] – form – matter. They never come together – because I is I. What is matter for the subject, is form for the absolute I, what is form for the subject, is matter for the absolute I. Naturally, it is for the absolute I, because it is subject – *both* – and for that very reason also *neither* – and for that very reason also *one*. Here from the italicized words one can quite clearly perceive the pure I. The pure I is everywhere and nowhere – It can never be obtained from itself – If the subject seeks it in the unlimited, the I is in the limited and so forth. /Sophistic of the pure I/ Here I must remark that the subject is actually being anthropomorphized here. The pure I and the subject – both are One and divided at the same time. They are both free and dependent – from and on what? themselves and their not-selves, and therein lies the real freedom – It is an alternating freedom, a mediated freedom. Thus the eternal struggle for freedom – the opponent is constantly sought where it does not exist – consequently it can never be found.

Object can thus only be opposed to subject in an unreal way, that is, without reference to the pure I – matter and form are possible objects for the subject. The pure I contains the possibilities of thought and feeling.

The subject [contains] the actualities of thought and feeling. Both together [contain] the necessity [of thought and feeling].
When the subject thinks, the pure I feels – when the subject feels, the pure I thinks. The subject is only subject, however, in relation to an object – the subject cannot, as it nevertheless must, set up anything except the object in opposition to itself. For the subject the object is what the pure I is for the observer. – It transfers everything that it knows of the pure I to the object – the pure I on the other hand transfers everything that it knows of the subject to the object – the object is the vehicle of both accidents, insofar as it is the one substance. The object, however, is in itself nothing but alternating absolute and identical relation of the pure I and the subject. In the pure I a possibility must correspond to [the object], in the subject or mediate I, an actuality must correspond to it – that is, in the former case a faculty, in the latter a power [must correspond to the object].

What can [the power] be called?

The object, as its correspondent, its substrate, contains or is the image of pure being on the one hand, and on the other, it is the image of the subject.

/Faculty of intuition. Power of intuition. (power of imagination)/

/This power is thus that which unifies all faculties and powers for the subject./

The object is that which is generated from matter (feeling) and form (reflection), to which this faculty in the pure I and this power in the subject correspond – or through which it is freely produced. The drive to be an I that feeling and reflection already united previously [# 22, 33] probably then grounds this faculty and this power – Intuition drive.

*

42. /Faculty of feeling, faculty of reflection, faculty of intuition – power of feeling, power of reflection, power of intuition, drives as well.

43. /Exhibition of the Categories. Object. Subject. Empirical consciousness. Time and space. Application of these three faculties,

drives, and powers to the deduction of the whole. Deduction of the subject and object. Unification of the whole./

(Whether an act is still possible

Absolute I
Not-I – mediated I –
and How?)

The intuition drive /what is a drive?/ thus operates on the object. It is a mere direction toward two sides, that is *something*, and the two sides are united in a third – The unification of absolute extremes and for that very reason itself absolute. It is the product of both together.
The pure I is not possible without subject, nor is the subject without object [possible]. All these are inseparably united. The object is formed matter without further relation.

Pure I.
Feeling in general – Reflexion in general.
Subject.
Feeling in general – Object. – Reflection in general.

The order of feeling and of reflection is completely arbitrary.
There is only an object for the subject. For the pure I *alone* there is nothing.

/Reason is a product of the intellectual power of vision./

It has an object only because it is a subject. Without a subject the object is nothing.

Genesis of the Drive.

[44]. The I is absolutely One – the subject is divided absolutely – Interaction of the I in itself – It wants to be One, it wants to be divided. In the pure I alone both are absolute – the character of the absolute is: no change – no opposition – no *continuation* – stasis – rest – identity – Its character must be a manifold in relation to the subject – activity conditioned by rest.

Yet the subject, the *ordine inverso* of the I, must have the character of the divided, the continuing, the active – in relation to the object its character must be that of rest conditioned by activity, oneness [conditioned by] manifoldness.

/The character of pure act is this unconditioned alternation in the I/

The activity of both divided things in the subject is separated, as long as the subject is not related [to the object], because since the subject is composed only of them [both divided things] they must both be active if the subject is active. – As soon as the one activity is related to another in an object – then it can be nothing other than a striving. A striving to be one – through intellectual power of vision – which unites subject and pure I in the object – Striving towards rest – but precisely for this reason an endless striving, so long as the subject does not become a pure I – which will not likely happen as long as the I is an I.

This would be the drive, and indeed, the drive to be an I.

A continuation in itself is a drive. Now since every activity is a continuation, there must be a drive in both members of the subject because they are active – these drives must thus be the drive to think and the drive to feel.

45. What are the parts of the subject.

The parts of the absolute I,
1. The pure I / or the unconditioned, identical alone/
2. The divided I / the conditioned, divided alone/
The subject is the pure, the divided, I
/this illuminates the particular relationship between object and subject/

Both are one in the absolute. Here we discover – that the subject continues on in itself in that it goes into the object – from self to self – only taken together from itself, to a part of itself – namely to the pure I. The subject is *at once* whole and part. – Hence its descent from the absolute I, or from itself.

Subject and absolute I are one.

Thus we always see the pure I as outside – the pure I is the object. It *is* in us and we see it outside us in one and the same moment.
Its laws are ours – our laws are its. They are separated merely through the intellectual power of vision – and this separation is deception insofar as the subject is in one and the same moment now a viewed whole and insofar a part, [then again] not a viewed whole and insofar again part. This self-deception connects the being of the I – or is absolute.
Reflection, feeling and intuition are always in one moment drive and power – as well as faculties.
Reflection is a faculty, intuition a drive – feeling a power. *Like everything*, they are only distinguishable *in the* faculty, *through* the power and *mediated by* intuition, and only distinguished insofar as they are distinct.
Faculty and power are subjective. Drive is objective.

Subjective and objective are
both
either – neither
in the absolute I or in the simple subject
if one may put it thus.

Every further separation occurs in the sphere of the absolute subject. It would be a verbal separation – for us there is no meaning in it.
The absolute subject must be set up in opposition to the absolute I – here the movement is not *outward*, but *inward*.
We could have again [had] absolute matter and absolute form – absolute object, absolute subject – pure I, divided I – feeling, reflection – Only an object can be opposed to the subject.

In.	the absolute I
mediated by.	pure I
Through.	divided I.

In.	the divided I
mediated by.	object
Through.	subject.

46. The I with the members, form and matter, is the point of empirical consciousness, toward the top of the pyramid is the transcendental. Actually we have always remained at the point [of empirical consciousness] – only

through intellectual power of vision have we viewed something of the transcendental – actually we have here only felt the need for the transcendental – and have drawn the pyramid-image that extends itself behind us in an inverted direction – necessary deception of the object that finds itself.

This point is everywhere in us – everywhere where thesis, antithesis and synthesis are, that is, where we ourselves are.
Thus philosophy is – sophistic of the I – transcendental *image* of our consciousness [cf. #49].

47. I think – I feel – already with this the absolute subject's inner relationship – whole and part at once – is expressed. Both, reflection and feeling, are faculty and power, depending on whether the subject feels or thinks. If it feels, it is object, pure I – if it thinks, it is subject, divided I. The unity that accompanies it everywhere, that it is *there* completely, *where* it is – this is the highest, most essential character of its subjectivity.

Thus the subject has
three drives.
Drive – to intuit – the vision-drive.
Drive – to think. The thought-drive.
Drive – to feel. The feeling-drive.

Three faculties.
Faculty of vision.
Faculty of thought.
Faculty of feeling.

Three powers.
Power of vision.
Power of thought.
Power of feeling.

48. But what does that mean? Where is it? Time and space.

Now the positions are still undetermined. However, in order to be really in the subject, that is, in that which is simply determined, the places must be determined – then they must be determined in the pure and simply determined thing, that is, *in* the subject. The subject must determine the places in virtue of its subjectivity in general. Through the drive to be an I it is absolute subject – through the vision-drive and its faculty and power.

/Particular subjectivity and subjectivity in general./

Thus every determination of place must lie in intellectual intuition.

/Being-in-connection [*Verbundenseyn*] through being-separated [*Getrenntseyn*] – time. Being separated through being in connection – space./

We already have the determination of the place itself, but only a particular determination or property of it – we are seeking its accidents. Until now it is determined simply through itself – absolutely – now it has still to be determined, as *absolute*. This can only occur according to the manner of the absolute I. It must interact with itself. But it is not the absolute I – consequently the accident will be the particular determination of that which is already determined through the absolute I in general – that would be form, consequently it would have to be forms of intuition. Intuition is, however, the reciprocal determination between pure and divided I – consequently it must have two forms – one in relation to the pure, one in relation to the divided I. Because the pure I is a mere divided thing, the relation to the pure I must be

A being-separated mediated by being-in-connection,

[B]ecause the divided I is merely a connected thing, the relation to the divided I must be

A being-in-connection through a being-separated.

The separated-being in the connected [being] is *space* – the connected being in the separated [being] is *time*.

/Form is thus that which is determined for the subject, that which is determined through the absolute I in general – Material [*Stoff*] that which is determined through the absolute I in general, insofar as it is determined in particular. All material is formed by it, all form is materialized by it. In the pure I all is separated, since all material is formless, all form [is] without material.

[49.] Abstraction means transposing oneself in the pure I – to separate what is not separate, but what must be separated in order to be separate – the form of pure activity of the subject.
If the subject reflects upon the pure I – then it has nothing – in that it has something for itself – if on the other hand it does not reflect upon the pure I – then it has nothing for itself, in that it has something. The "for itelf" means for itself *only*, for *its particular subjectivity*.
/The theory of the subject must be a *particular* one – One could call it a theory of the ideal – the theory of the relation of a particular subject to the universal object or pure I, the theory of the absolute.
The ideal is simply the relative subjective in relation to the absolute, or simply insofar as it is the particular. /It refers to time./
The real is simply the absolute subjective in relation to the relative or simply insofar as it is the absolute. /It refers to space.[/] Both arise from the interchange of the particular subject with substance and accident in reflection, mediated by intuition through feeling.
In the ideal the relative is substance, the absolute is accident; in the real it is the opposite.

/Substance [is] the determinate in general. Accident [is] the particular determination.

The latter [is] form, the former [is] matter./

The pure I is never a whole – neither is it the particular subject. Its self-sufficiency makes it a part. It is only a part, if there is a part. However, it posits a part, consequently it must be part and partitioner – hence whole and part at the same time [cf. #45].
We feel ourselves as part and are for that very reason the whole.
/No transcendental language for applied philosophy/ It contradicts itself because it grounds a contradiction – a necessary deception. Transcendental philosophy is sophistic – but in what sense?

/Seeking of the extreme in the other extreme, the thesis in the antithesis, both in the synthesis, is sophistic.

Thesis and antithesis set in opposition to each other is synthesis/

50. The particular subject is in time insofar as it is a particular subject, that is, insofar as it thinks, feels and intuits at once – the pure I is in space,

insofar as it is the pure I, or substance in the particular subject, that is, insofar as it is felt, thought or intuited.

51. Morality, natural rights and politics become the three practical sciences – whose basic principles will be drawn from the preceding.

For the particular subject, morality is its relation to itself insofar as it is universal subject, grounded by the vision-drive [drive to intuit], conceived by its faculty, begotten by its power.
Natural right, – established by both drives, the feeling-drive and the thought-drive and their faculties and powers –
Politics. Established by one or the other drives, etc., exclusively.
Natural Right: Relation between the ideal and the real, in which the real, the pure I, is merely necessary accident; where the particular subject thinks, feels and intuits itself as particular subject.
Politics. Relation between the real and ideal in which the ideal, the particular subject, is merely necessary accident, that is, where it thinks, feels and intuits the pure I or real object as pure I or real object.

Morality – Categorical.
Natural right – Hypothetical.
Politics – Disjunctive.

52. We will see later that the particular subject opposes the pure I, or matter in general as particular matter, or what is the same, as formed matter – that is, how every opposition in the I occurs in accordance with the procedure of the absolute I *in* the I and not a genuine opposition, but rather a synthesis of the thesis and antithesis opposed – an entering in, an entering under in itself – nothing out-going, but rather a process of going in.

53. One can also call the absolute I the

Absolute synthetic I.

It is the synthesis of the I insofar as it is not an actual synthesis – yet must be so called for the purposes of the analytic I, because analysis, in that it is analysis, can only be set in opposition to synthesis.

This synthesis is absolute sphere without boundary

– all other syntheses are relative spheres, that is, sphere and boundary at once. It contains the possibility of boundaries in general, in the analytic I. The analytic I in general fulfills the synthetic I.[12] The latter [the synthetic] is the sphere of the analytic – its one and all. The synthetic I is the necessary substance – the analytic I is the possible and actual [substance] – the former [the possible] in relation to that [synthetic I], the latter [the actual] in relation to itself [analytic I].
The analytic I has Actuality/power/ in virtue of its own [*Seiner*] [actuality and power]. It has Possibility/Faculty/! in virtue of it relation to the synthetic I – It has Necessity / Drive/ solely in virtue of the synthetic I.

/Drive is categorical, necessary, simple and real. Faculty is hypothetical, possible, divisible and *negation*. Power is disjunctive, actual, creative and bounded./

In order to be an *I* the analytic I must have drives, faculties and powers.

The actual synthetic I must actually be called

simply I –

the predicate synthetic contradicts it – it is an addition of the representing, analytic I. The analytic I becomes the sphere of the synthetic. The synthetic I, as we now understand it, is a product of the analytic I.

Thus

The analytic I is established by the I and consists in a positing of itself through an opposition. It posits itself for itself, in that it posits an image of that which establishes it and thus reproduces the activity of its establishment.

/The analytic I must be totality in divisibility. Deduction of the several empirical I's./

54. God is I. /Infinity – Totality in divisibility/ He changes with the *infinite* personality identically and absolutely. Analytic I is [the] person.

[12] This could also be translated with the subject and objects (as I have translated it) transposed, and might make just as much sense. I have simply translated it as it literally stands: "Das analytische Ich überhaupt erfüllt das synthetische Ich."

To worship God in spirit and in truth – theoretical infinite striving toward God – practical striving toward God – this *alone* [is] duration in general – in relation to this personal duration – this alone [is] unity in time – ideal, morality, highest good.

Morals break down
into religion and ethics.

Dichotomous division in general. /The one branch simple postulate.

God created us in his own image [cf. #119].

/Synthetic I is a simple, relative postulate./

55. I must invent the elements of the mathematical sciences for myself.

56. What are the philosophical sciences.

57. Beauty, sublimity, etc.

58. Critical physics. Vice. Criminal law. History. Medicine.

59. Positing is a determined being. Being, a determined positing.

Identity of the unconditioned and the conditioned is I-ness [*Ichheit*].

I is everywhere, where this sort of extremes exists
Mere analysis – mere synthesis are pure forms of I-ness. What separates analysis and synthesis is the I – what unites them is the I – because analysis and synthesis are here also applied to the representation of analysis and synthesis. They are applicable to *everything*, therefore also to these representations – They are not actually applied to themselves, but rather only to their representation. They establish [*begründen*] their representation – but are not it. They are not their representation – this means that as *mere analysis* and *synthesis*, they are not [their representation] – because otherwise they are their representation, because they establish it.

60. Now I must proceed further with what has already been discovered – through application the elementary propositions must become clear.

61. Their *possible* relation is form – their actual [relation], matter – their necessary [relation], I.

62. I now seize upon a new idea:
Modality and quality are one.
Relation and quantity likewise.

63. The analytic I is the I with consciousness – the synthetic I, [is the I] without consciousness. In the synthetic I the analytic I intuits itself. The intuiting I is its own intuited thing – the synthetic I is, as it were, a mirror of reality.

> The image is reality for the I that is conscious of itself – for abstraction in the self-conscious I, [it] is the pure form of reflection – the medium of reality, negation alone – [it is] nothing at all for the I, or [it is] image of original being.

The analytic I alternates again with itself – like the simple I – in intuition – It alternates image and being. The image is always the inversion of being. What is to the right of the person is to the left in the image.
We are the analytic I, because the *we-being* is the analytic I. That we are we – no philosophy can ascend higher.
Why we are we – that is self-explanatory and as a question, contradictory.

64. There is nothing to be done with the object, it is a *medium*, nothing else. The actual object, to whose investigation we now proceed, is the image of the analytic I. Our current study will approach the image as image, that is, as object – it will consider the analytic I as object. As mentioned, the image in and for itself is the inverted surface of the object – However, because we engage our description of the image as analytic I, it will again come out to the right, if it is to the left in relation to the object – thus we must present the left in order to get *the pure character of the image* as image alone; on the other hand, in order to get the analytic I right for ourselves, we must describe what we see.

65. Application of the forms of thought to themselves.

The categories are
Simple,
Divisible.
Exhaustive,

Real,
negated,
bounded.
categorical
hypothetical, inclusive,
exclusive,
possible
actual
necessary.

66. Pure form must also be pure matter – both together [are] the conceivable I.

Matter is – feeling and intuiting – form, reflection alone.

67. Singular and plural. The former – quantitative form of the I – the latter, relational form of the I; or better, the former [is] *relative* unity, the latter [is] *relative* plurality.

68. Systematic. Encyclopaedic. Prophetic.

69. The Categories in general contain possible matter – actual form, necessary I or both together necessarily.

Kant established the possibility, Reinhold the actuality, Fichte the necessity, of philosophy.

70. Everything rests on three relations –

Synthesis. Relation to the cause. Necessary.
Thesis. Relation to itself. Possible.
Antithesis. Relation to effect. Actual.

71. God – nature – I.

Synthesis. God is the simple I.

Antithesis. Nature. Synthetic I in the forms of intuition.
Thesis. I, analytic I, in regard to the synthetic I, or the object bound up with the forms of intuition.

72. God. Necessary.
Nature. Actual.
I. Possible.

73. Thus insofar as we are actual we are nature. Everything actual in us belongs to nature.

Thus the empirical I is in God mediated by the subject through the object.

74. Philosophy, like everything in the I, is an actual, thus a conditioned thing, mediated by a possible thing, related to a necessary thing.

I *ought* always to be I.

For the simple I to be related to the object is a must [*ein Müssen*] – [to be related] to the object, mediated by the subject – an ought.

75. <The simple I is an idea. The analytic I, a concept, the synthetic I, a feeling.>

76. We must explain the unconditioned by way of the conditioned, the conditioned by way of the unconditioned.

77. The analytic path must be synthetic, and vice versa – it just depends upon which end one adopts.

78. The analytic is conditioned through a synthesis, the synthetic through an analysis. The effect here is the cause there. Space is as big as time, that is, they stand in alternating unity [*Wechseleinheit*]. Eternity *a parte post* and *a parte ante*. The former an analytic path, the latter synthetic [cf. #153]. That synthesis and analysis stand in these relations – that is the simple I.

/The I is merely the highest possible expression of the genesis of analysis and synthesis in the unknown.

/The unknown is the holy nothing for us./

/The surrender of our I-ness – Not being through being is our theoretical goal; enlarging of our I-ness – or being through not being – [is] our practical goal./ They must contradict each other, in order to be in the I./

79. First conditioned principle schematized in the first form.

(Synthesis)	Nothing.	I.
(Antithesis)	Life.	Object.
(Thesis)	Something.	Subject.

Second conditioned principle.

Synthesis.	Life.	Object.
Antithesis.	Something.	Subject.
Thesis.	Nothing.	I.

Third conditioned principle.

Synthesis.	Something.	Subject.
Antithesis.	Nothing.	I.
Thesis.	Life.	Object.

*

80. For antithesis here it is better to say

Analysis.

81. Every Category alternates with itself according to this schema. There are only nine of them – in three classes, in the following order.

Modality.
Relation.
Quantity.

82. Quality is the pure form that is in all three and alternates with itself in the original act – It is the schema of [the original act].

83. Quality is the prototype of the Categories – as the unknown is the prototype of the I.

/The tree grows according to its prototype./
/The prototype is the determinate cause of a determinate effect/
/I am that, that wants to be an I./

/We can find our being only in our willing./

/The prototype is relative. In the synthetic sequence it is cause – in the analytic sequence, effect./

/The representation of the representation of the limits of the Something has the most extremely simple matter – indivisible matter – Consequently *none at all*, since all matter is divisible – Thus nothing is the limit of representation. But representation is composed of feeling, reflection and intuition. – Consequently this is also the limit [of representation]. However, they all three limit each other – consequently this is not a true limitation, but only an apparent one.

/What is apparent is where the part represents the whole./

They [feeling, reflection and intuition] are, however, *in* the I, consequently the I limits them and nothing would be the I – they depend upon [this] Nothing. It remains no less true that they limit only themselves, therefore the I, the limitation, and Nothing would depend upon them [feeling, reflection and intuition]. They are dependent insofar as they independently posit themselves – limited, insofar as they posit themselves in a limited way – but also the reverse – [they are] free insofar as they posit themselves unfreely, not free insofar as they freely posit themselves – They posit themselves freely only in reflection, that is, in the accident – and so substance, their threefold effectiveness, is restricted – They posit themselves unfreely likewise in reflection alone – ergo partially for possibility, hence in this [in possibility], they *are* not free.

/Acting is the expression /the utterance/ of being, of reality of the I, Thought is the expression /the utterance/ of not being. The latter is always limited, conditioned; the former is unlimited, unconditioned. Acting and positing – being and thought.

Character of pure action.
Form of positing.
The acting I.
The thinking I.

84. Infinite transposition of the forms of thought.

Divisibility of matter.

85. From where does a determinate direction come, anyhow? Every utterance of being, of freedom, of the acting I, is a determination – nonfreedom – here, the effect is that which is opposed to the cause.

/The direction in positing from feeling to reflection and from there back – from synthesis to analysis and from analysis to synthesis -/

But why does the synthesis start for us? Because we are synthesis. See absolute subject – particular subject – that posits a universal object in opposition to itself [see #49]/

/That which we *posit first* is original; in the acting I, it is the second thing/

/The infinite judgment is that which exhausts – in the parts of the I./

86. Theory must start from the *conditioned* and from thence also return. Its unconditioned is only that which exhausts – totality. Its conditioned is the simple, not the identical. One is not identical. One is that which is determined through totality. Plurality is an interruption of continuation – the result of an act of freedom. Possibility is the act of freedom in modality. Exclusion is the act of freedom in relation. <*Power* corresponds to the act of freedom – It is set up as these acts are set up.>

87. Faculty.
Drive.
Power.

The Practical proceeds from the free, to that which is conditioned, though not through alternation, to the not-free, and should from thence return again to the free. The free should have causality in the not-free – the not-free should be free. It can do this all at once. Striving is only infinite because time is infinite /infinite [is used] here in the theoretical sense/ the not-free must *be* free, or act freely, in every moment. To *posit* freely is theoretical freedom.

88. Why free action and moral action are one – In this way there is only one unconditioned – consequently they must be one and the same, since both are unconditioned. Until now "moral" has been taken only in an inhuman sense, and has been astonishingly restricted. From a theoretical perspective, nothing is free in this way. Thus the morality of an action cannot be determined from principles at all.

Theoretical freedom.
Practical freedom.

The former [involves] causality and *all* dependence like unity upon totality – subject causality – object dependence.
The latter – causality in the subject – dependence in the subject, because the subject is, as subject, an unfree thing.

89. Practical I -/practical thesis -/
Theoretical I -/theoretical antithesis./

The practical I is a postulate of the theoretical I for theoretical use – and consequently [is] only a theoretical I, thought practically – a moral God – a Nothing – a contradiction. It borrows the idea of the unconditioned, the purely free, from the practical I and treats it necessarily as only a changing thing.
The practical I commands pure and simple. If its efficacy is presented, that is, if it is reflected upon, [this efficacy] must be found to be theoretical. Already the commanding expresses a theoretical efficacy. The conflict of the practical and theoretical I.

/The Categories can have a theoretical and they can have a practical reference./

90. The quantity-act is the first act within the theoretical I. /"First" here means belonging to it alone.
For relation and modality, the theoretical I must borrow the thesis and synthesis from the practical I – categorically, necessarily – for quality [it must borrow] the negation or possibility of its own presentation or positing.

The practical I.

91. It is, because it acts. Thus activity grounds being.

We find the practical I in the theoretical I – for we are the theoretical I – because we *are*.

Are we? Yes – precisely thus are we the theoretical I.

Do we act? Yes – precisely thus do we find the practical I in the theoretical.

The theoretical I is determined in intellectual intuition for itself.

92. The possibility of being divided lies in the theoretical I.

93. Existence – reality. /Identity – empirical unity of quantity should not be confused/

94. Praxis – real prototype.
Theory – ideal prototype.

95. The I seems to be the first here. In the completed theory, it is the last thing – The theory proceeds from [the I] – and returns to it. It closes the theory of theory as well as beginning it. It begins the theory of praxis, as well as closing it. The closure of [the theory of praxis] is the beginning of the theory of theory – Its concluding proposition is the beginning proposition of theory. The theory of theory is one with the theory of praxis. Only it is reversed.

The theoretical I.

[96.] The theoretical I searches for a simple I. It is quickly convinced that the attempt, which it nevertheless is driven to, to attribute its parts to the I, is impracticable – that it would become an I that was impossible in practice, thus a theoretical I, again. It feels itself to be incapable of positing such an I – the part feels that it is a part. Even in this case it opposes the doable in this case to that which is doable – that is, it makes itself *in this case* into a theoretical I, and [makes] something else into a practical I – and thus strengthened, it can posit a simple I and complete itself by surrendering itself. The suspension of its efficacy is its highest efficacy.

Being through not-being is theoretical freedom.
The theoretical I is thus *in itself* free.

<Now we can strike the I – free theory – free praxis [are] both in the I for the reflecting (theoretical) I.>

The I, without predicate.
The I with a predicate.

I should be free, says practical freedom. Theoretical freedom says I must be free.

/Politics is already grounded in the concept of the Ought for the practical I/

97. The completion of theory includes praxis in theory – and the I becomes a theoretical I through a not-I – a stranger, namely the practical in the theoretical. The theoretically practical arises from a surrender [*Entäußerung*] – Being [arises] through a not-being.

/No opposition is possible in the practical – Thus being can be opposed to not-being only through a play on words. Not-positing is an actual opposing ["oppositing"]./

/Positing is a *real* opposing – Positing is thus also a not-positing – so also a real opposition. An opposing is a not-positing – and so also a real opposing, and thus also a positing./
Everything can thus be observed in three ways. The object of the first is the thing – the object of the second is the simple observation – the object of the third is the double observation – nothing more.

1. Representation of the object.
2. Representation of the representation [in] 1.
3. Representation of the representation [in] 2.

98. /Emergence expresses in its ambiguity the highest philosophical truth – the surrender of the I, in order to complete itself – thus it is clear how, through its emergence, it emerges. It finds *itself*, *outside* itself. This finding becomes a finding out – a finding in reality, in theoretically determined reality, which is the only one there is for the I.

Theory leads us only to a theoretical I – that must be practical in order to be theoretical.
The completion of the theory of theory will show us the limits of the practical and the theoretical in the I, it will show us why *here* the I must be a theoretical I, and there it must be a practical I – in order to be completed in its parts – in order to be an I through the alternate completion of its parts.

The I that is thought/posited/ is a completed theoretical I – and the I that is not thought, but is *acting* is a completed practical I. Both must emerge from the theory of the theoretical I – or both must be able to be systematically thought – because the I is an I – a completed theoretical I, as well as a completed practical I – and because the theoretical I necessarily must come to its opposition according to the laws of its freedom.
/If the one – is an I – then the other is a not-I – [that] is what the theoretical wants – but that the theoretical should be the not-I is what the practical wants, and insofar as the practical is in the theoretical, the theoretical must relinquish its freedom in alternation [*Wechseln*] – and make itself into a not-I, and precisely thereby complete itself.

99. The practical is a longing. If it were not a theoretical I, it would have no causality – it would not be an I.

100. There is a practical not-I.
There is a theoretical I.

101. Praxis is what *drives* theory to surrender of itself – because praxis contains the possibility of all drive – [it is an] acting being because it acts –

102. Without praxis theory is incomplete, without theory, praxis is incomplete – that is, if both are an I.

/The I is the indivisible subject of all predication./
/The predicate is to the subject as the cause to the effect, etc./

103. Theoretical I.
practical I
Theoretical I.

This is the highest principle of the theory – that concludes as the theory of theory with the first principle of the theory of praxis

Practical I.
Theoretical I.
Practical I –

and this ends with that first principle of theoretical theory.
The theory in general is completed – or thus theory becomes theory.

104. In theory, practical theory *follows* theoretical theory.

/Every rooster is master over its own droppings./

In praxis, theory follows praxis, or theory is subordinate to it.

105. As soon as we speak of the *I* we are speaking of the theoretical I.

106. What is called *ought* in practical theory is reality in praxis – praxis can exist only in reality – because it is an activity.
Practical theory must therefore be sharply separated from praxis – They are *essentially* different.
The former can only have a theoretical use – regulative – not constitutive.

107. Actual praxis can absolutely not be grasped.
The path that we now take up again is simple.
We again divide the product of the first analysis, of the practical and theoretical I, or the second synthesis, unite them again, and so forth, until we arrive at the last principle that forces us to turn around, and so we reverse ourselves (the way is already prepared) – because we have stepped into the realm of the practical where all is one, and immediately – unmediated activity. This reversal grounds the analytic path for theory. Actually, it does not *ground* it – everything is free – praxis is only immediately present in the analytic process.

/It is to the right of the observation of the image/ – the image is to the left – and the original is to the right -/

108. My ethics [*Moral*] must further my system. Through my ethics, I must make my system necessary to every empirical subject.

/Who does not believe is damned/

[109.] For the practical I, God is in the theoretical [I] – for the theoretical [I], [God is] in the practical [I].

110. Eternity is the totality of time.

111. The practical I is *the absolute I* – or becomes it after the completion of theory.

112. As practical I, the I is merely necessary to complete the theory. /It appears to complete a part through its whole – but then the part would

become a whole and the whole would become a part – In order to prevent *this*, it must complete a part through the other and thus make them into *essential parts* of the whole.

113. The reason why the three original propositions stand in the order that they do, with the thesis beginning in the first proposition, is that in the theory of theory the synthetic process is determined through the analytic, synthesis [is determined through] analysis, and in practical theory analysis is determined through synthesis. Then the form of the unconditioned proposition on its own produces

original form and original material.

Thesis. practical I.
theoretical I. Synthesis.
empirical I. Antithesis.

Material proposition.	Formal proposition.
Antithesis. practical I.	Synthesis. theoretical I.
Synthesis. theoretical I.	Thesis. practical I.
Thesis. practical I.	Antithesis. theoretical I.

114. What is determined alike in both determined propositions must be in the original propositions – Thesis – practical I – Synthesis – theoretical I – Antithesis – both together – empirical I.

The *first* part must be what posits itself merely as *first part* – and then the other must be the second [part], which, however, also is determined, as what posits itself as the second [part].

115. The opposing of itself outside itself is immanent – the part is opposed to the whole. Thus the opposing [to] the theoretical I is immanent – synthetically and analytically immanent.

116. The original proposition is clear only after the completion of the system.

117. *Time* is the condition of all synthesis.

118. The original proposition is the nine-part proposition determined in the manner [shown] above.

119. God – Nature – I.

God created man in his own image [cf. #54].

120. Synthesis and analysis is logical. A *real* synthesis and analysis is an impossible object.

121. Freedom and morality are characteristic only of the empirical I. The I is only an empirical concept – i.e., only for the empirical I – empirical unity and identity.

122. *For God* we actually proceed in reverse.

From age to youth.

123. Totality is – a generic concept.

124. *Unending* and eternity – mere time representations.

125. Time for practice – space for theory.

126. God is neither free nor moral.

127. Beauty and sublimity.

128. Our chronic talking – the garrulousness of our century – that is its basic mistake and characteristic.

129. *Apparently* we are going *forward*.

130. Philosophy is merely for theory – language – thought – it has a merely regulative use – but this is not to be despised.

131. The theory of the sign – of the image.

132. Philosophy must only correct the mistakes of our education – otherwise we would not need it.

133. History told backwards.

134. Philosophy of humanity.

135. The species becomes the individual – from our perspective. The human being becomes more and more personal – the species less and less personal.

136. Humanity flourishes and blooms, withers and dies, at the same time.

137. The All-giver. Fate. *The rhapsodic.* Fortune. The study of fortune. Conversation.

138. Immanent drive. Transcendent drive.

*

139. On the use of the categories.

140. Ten. 9. 12. Line. Point. Dimensions.

141. 7 colors. 4 Elements. On the construction of numbers up until now.

142.

God.
Nature.
Person.

I	Nature.
Nature	I.
I.	Nature.

143. On the different transpositions of this proposition.
How can T[hesis] A[ntithesis] S[ynthesis] be applied to it?

144. The first proposition allows of absolutely no transposition – it is above all transposition.
<God is absolute thesis, antithesis and synthesis – insofar as this refers to sphere.>
Nature is also thesis, antithesis and synthesis – but [is] all three relatively – here the latter [synthesis], as medium – limit.
I – also only in a different way. These two relations exhaust all – they are immediately unconditioned.
Nature, as synthesis, is conditioned only by the unconditioned/God. Or [nature,] as absolute relative, as antithesis, is conditioned only by the person, that is, by the absolute relative – as thesis [nature] is conditioned by both at once – by God and I.
Thus if we call antithesis form, nature is conditioned *mediately* only with respect to *form*. Because as thesis [nature] is mediately conditioned with respect to form also.

/All matter is – nature. All form – personality./

The person is, as antithesis, conditioned by God alone. As thesis, by nature alone, as synthesis by both at once.

/What is distinctive arises from form – antithesis – the person/

145. God.
Nature – I.

Here is neither right nor left. Both limbs are completely alike. If we freely posit all thesis as right, and all antithesis as left, then nature must stand as right, and I, as left.

[146.] The oriental way of writing is the natural one if it is written with the right hand. Our way is painterly, pictorial, artificial – the former row moves away, the latter row approaches. The former [is] subjective – the latter, objective.

147. If the higher [proposition] always precedes, then in the proposition of nature the synthesis must lead – thus:

S[ynthesis]	Nature.
Th[esis]	I.
Ant[ithesis]	Nature.

In the proposition of the person,

Ant[ithesis]	I.
S[ynthesis]	Nature.
Th[esis]	I.

148. The mediate determining thing is always on the right. Here mediate means the highest mediate.

149. Here the highest division results in an unmediated conditioned thing and a mediately conditioned thing.
<Nature must rise above God to the person. The person [must rise] above nature to God.>

150. God.
Nature-God – personal God.

151. Spinoza ascended as far as nature – Fichte to the I, or the person. I [ascend] to the thesis God.

152. God is the sphere of all analysis and synthesis – a theoretical and practically necessary concept – the latter a feeling – the former an idea. /Relationship of the necessary feelings and ideas./

153. Transcendent nature is at the same time immanent – thus also the immanent person is at the same time transcendent – and also the reverse. Nature, however, as we have seen, is part immediately, part mediately conditioned. Similarly with the person – both in different ways. What is here immediately conditioned is there mediately conditioned and also vice versa.

They are one and the same being – only reversed. They correspond down to the finest detail.
Pictorially they are like two pyramids that have a single tip

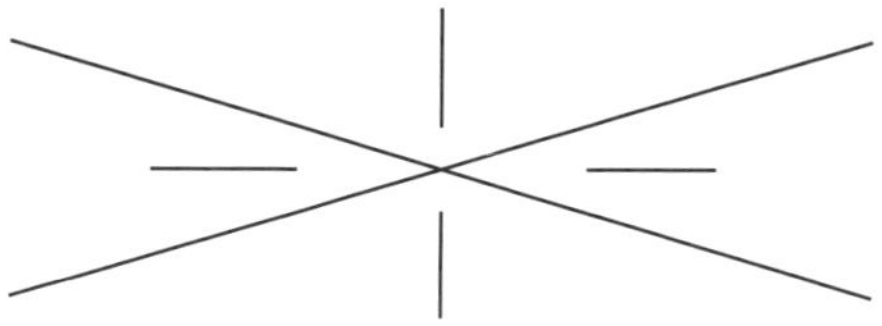

[a]

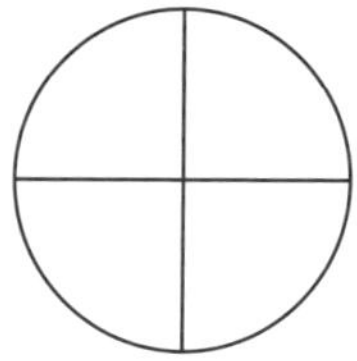

[b]

They are like a single line. *In one direction* it is the image of nature – *in the other* [it is] the image of the I.

/Eternity *a parte ante* and *parte post*. Synthetic, analytic path – *image in general* [fig. [b], cf. #78].

154. Mathematics appears to be the science of pure forms of space in the empirical I's faculty of form or reflection. Space and time are one, only reversed – like nature and person.

155. The elements of mathematics must be found prior to mathematics in the theory of theory.

/The doctrine of science [*Wissenschaftslehre*] must ground mathematics. It proceeds *toward* – [mathematics] proceeds *away from* – subjective – objective./

/Transcendence and immanence are one – only reversed/

The form of the transcendent person is space – of the immanent person, time. Hence their inseparable unity.

156. What remains after all abstraction of form in nature or of the mediate conditioned is the pure concept of nature or God – thus if we abstract from all matter in the person we then come upon God as well – because God is in both the last and the first.
<For nature God is the first, as unmediated conditioning thing; the last as mediate conditioning thing – for the I it is the reverse.>

157. Because God conditioned mediately, he conditioned immediately – thus speaks nature.
Because God conditioned immediately, he conditioned mediately – thus speaks the person.

/Matter is thesis – Form [is] antithesis/

Nature: Because there is matter, there is form
Person: Because there is form, there is matter.
In the pure doctrine of form/doctrine of science/ form must lead; subjective. In the applied [doctrine of form] matter [must lead] – objective and subjective at once. Similarly in the pure doctrine of matter, matter [must lead] – only objective.

The first is the science of [the] antithesis.
The middle is the science of [the] synthesis.
The last is the science of [the] thesis
Thetic. Synthetic. Antithetic.

Thetic and antithetic together is analytic. What is called pure science arises from an analytic arm [*Glied*]. What is called applied science arises from a synthetic arm.
Pure form and pure doctrine of matter are one, only reversed – originally so to speak, namely *for* God.

Synthesis, as limitation, is a *free* restriction, boundary – an application of the unification to that which is unified. Pure science deals analytically, that is, through analysis with synthesis – Applied science on the other hand deals synthetically, through synthesis, with analysis.

158. Science remains science. Consequently by pure science is meant only this much: that it proceeds from the *unmediated conditioned*. The pure doctrine of matter proceeds from matter, from the concept of nature, toward the mediately conditioned. The pure doctrine of form proceeds from the mediately conditioned, from the concept of the person, into and beyond the immediately conditioned. Expressed popularly – Everything goes as far as it can – both are one, in reverse directions.

*

159. Pure doctrine of nature is pure doctrine of the person and the application, or the synthesis, grounds it – even if it would appear as if pure science grounds applied *science* – which is in fact the case when we speak of *science*.

> /Synthesis and analysis are one, only reversed. – Praxis and theory also, only reversed./

Pure and applied science are one, only reversed – that is, always, what is here immediately conditioned is there mediately [conditioned], *etc.* Indeed, because nature originally leads, *for us*, that is in science, nature and matter always lead; the synthesis of analysis – the nature of the person.

> /God is, as it were, an absolute analytic member – or contains their spirit, that which is essential to the thesis, antithesis, and synthesis, inseparably. God is all three, without being One – and indeed, he begins with the presentation of thesis and ends with the antithesis. Father, spirit and son. The son is pure personality. Jesus.
> /Spirit of synthesis – creating power, creator of nature/
> /With this we can make nothing more/
>
> Triune God
> Spinozist God
> Personal God.

160. 1. Absolute Triune God
Triune Nature. relative
Triune Person. relative
2. Nature. Synthesis.
divine nature.
personal nature.
3. Person. Synthesis.
Natural person.
divine person.

161. /Synthesis is always an *Idea*. Thesis is a feeling – antithesis is reflection. An idea can never be a *something* – an actual thing – it is a necessary thing. Antithesis is the possible. Feeling is the actual./

162. There is a simple – a twofoldness – a threefoldness.

1. Doctrine of science in general. 2. pure (immanent) – 3. applied (transcendent) doctrine of science. 4. Theory of God. 5. Theory of nature. 6. Theory of the person.

163. Nature becomes transcendent insofar as it descends – the person [becomes transcendent] insofar as it ascends.

/Synthesis, as border, species, sphere./ Spirit – image – imagination -etc./

164. Where does the synthesis – the antithesis – the thesis begin?

165. *One* science must determine the original order. (Thetic) doctrine of science.

Two [sciences] must determine the form.
Analytic – Synthetic.
Three [sciences must determine] the matter.
The particular thetic – the particular antithetic – the particular synthetic.

166. The meaning of the synthesis in the thetic – the analytic and the synthetic – likewise of the thesis and antithesis in these three sciences.

167. The spirit is creative power. The Son is pictorial power – matter – form.

168. All synthesis is in a certain way a deception of imagination – solely subjective.

169. What is powerful in us is what appears not to be God, and for that very reason is – Line.

All synthesis is

Simple
Twofold
Threefold

Analysis also:

170. Monadic./God./
Dichotomous./Nature/
Trichotomous./Person/

171. What determines form must be matter – what determines matter must be form. That which determines [is] exactly the opposite of that which is being determined.

172. Thesis and synthesis should be one – only in different ways.

173. Positing an opposition *through being posited* is analytic – Positing through opposing – synthetic – both arms of the dichotomy. The former *descends*, the later *ascends*. The *monas* is the point that begins and ends them. The former begins *discernibly* [*sichtbar*] bipartite and ends *as* synthesis; the latter begins as synthesis – and ends discernibly as analysis.

174. Thesis, antithesis and synthesis – each is composed of 2 parts – therefore each can be constructed from its 2 opposing parts. Thesis is a proposition that is related to antithesis and synthesis – Antithesis and synthesis have a common characteristic, relation to the thesis – taken together this is the thesis – the generic concept.
It is the same with the antithesis and synthesis and we see from this three generic concepts arise. Each is the generic concept of the other two.

/Procreation. Man and woman./

175. How are the three distinguishable? Because here they would be one. It must be an act of freedom – to make what one wants the thesis, antithesis or synthesis. It depends on which generic concept one reflects upon.

176. Synthesis is the general in the particular. Thesis and antithesis are the particular in the general. Thesis is the particular from which one proceeds – the determined – Antithesis is the particular, toward which one proceeds – that which is to be determined. Thesis is the subjective – Antithesis [is] the objective.
Thesis and antithesis are the endpoints of the line. The line is the synthesis.

177. The arms of the dyad are accidental/particular/ and doctrine of substance/general/.

178. The method of our sciences. In the monadic – diadic – triadic —

179. Definition of the crooked line.

180. Doctrine of science is triadic. The *monas* that deals scientifically with substance and accident – yields the sciences of elements. The doctrine of science follows these – that consists of three parts – and here [these] create the other sciences principle – matter – and form – method -.

181. The monadic begins with the *monas*. The doctrine of substance begins with substance – the doctrine of accidents with accidents. The thetic with the thesis – the antithetic with the antithesis and the synthetic with the synthesis.

182. On the *dimensions*.

183. Theory of the sign. Geometry.

184. What is a sense? Homogeneity of nature with the person. The person in reverse is nature – Nature in reverse is the person.

185. Presentation in space of that which is thought.

186. The doctrine of substance deals with the general. The doctrine of accidents deals with the particular. Both refer to nature. The triadic refers to the person.

The particular must always be twofold. The general [is] always a *divisible* simple thing. Simple twofold-ness [is] the character of the first – Twofold simplicity the character of the other.

The thetic begins with the thesis – the antithetic [begins] with the antithesis – the synthetic [begins] with the synthesis.

187.

Thesis God.	God.
Antithesis <I.>	Synthesis Nature.
Synthesis <Nature>	Antithesis I.
Antithesis Nature	Anthithesis Nature
Synthesis God	Thesis I
Thesis I	Synthesis God
Synthesis I	Synthesis I.
Antithesis God	Thesis Nature.
Thesis Nature	Antithesis God.

188. God is thesis and synthesis at once. Nature is antithesis. The human being and nature make up the last. It must be completely like God, that is, through opposition. It must correspond fully to [God] only in a reversed way.

It is the painter's image of himself.

189. Hypothetic. <3 1 2>
<2 2 3>
<1 3 1>

*

190.

God.	God.	Synthesis is simple: combining and combined at once – absolute sphere.
I.	Nature.	
Nature.	I.	

1 1	2 2	3 3
2 3	3 1	2 1
3 2	1 3	1 2

Concept of the monadic synthesis.
Thesis and antithesis
Concept of the substantial synthesis, thesis and antithesis

In the doctrine of the general: the common characteristic of the twofold particular – subordination of the lower under the higher.
In the doctrine of the particular: the antithesis. the particular

likewise of the accidental synthesis, thesis and antithesis.
Concept of the thetic, antithetic and synthetic thesis, antithesis and synthesis.

characteristic in the particular – subordination of the particular under the other particular: e.g. the *blue* foxes – of the same under the same.
In the thetic: the combined things, as such, without relation.
In the antithetic: the combined things, as such, in relation to one arm.
In the synthetic: the combined things, as such, in relation to 2 arms.

191. Concept of *crime* and *punishment*.

192. Thesis is, in the monadic, – simply God alone.
Antithesis ———— God as creator.
Synthesis ———— immanent creative divinity.

Thesis is in the doctrine of the general – the simple general.

(Original genus or God)

Antithesis ———— the general related once. ———— In the doctrine of the particular *One* particular
———————— several particulars.

In the thetic is the thesis. The simple without relation – antithetic. The simple in relation to one arm. – in the synthetic. The simple in relation to two arms.
Antithesis is in the thetic. The related without relation – in the antithetic – the related in one relation – in the synthetic – the related in twofold relation.

On the monadic – and dyadic and their method.

193. Doctrine of science.

/The doctrine of the subject is the doctrine of accidents. The doctrine of the object is the doctrine of substance. The former [about] the person – the latter [about] the doctrine of nature./

Thetic (substance.) – Doctrine of the good; – antithetic (subsistence [*Accidens*].) – Doctrine of the true; – synthetic (subsistence.) – Doctrine of the beautiful.

194. Monadic / Hypothetic / Doctrine of religion.

195. The person is, as object, *particular*; as subject, a general thing. Nature is, as subject, particular, as object, general.

196. Every *thinking* person will always find truth – he may start *wherever*, and proceed *in the manner* he wants.

197. It is not merely the faculty of reflection that grounds theory. Thinking, feeling and intuition are one.

198. The thesis is a representation without an express reference

199. Intuition. Representation of intuition. There is no more – to be sure, the last is divided. Everything that corresponds to the object in the subject, or the object in general, is intuition. The subject is representation. The felt, thought intuition, the reception of it, is representation.
Intuition and representation are the necessary accidents of the person. The intuitions are not free. The representation, however [,is]. /The person is likewise merely immanent –/ The human being only feels free where he *feels* himself as causality – in the manifold – in the representation – in the particular, or subject – in the moving away from.

200. Completed human being – To be a person – that is the vocation [*Bestimmung*] and the original drive in human beings.

201. The triad contains the laws of representation – the line – *away from*. The diad [contains] the laws of intuition – the line – *toward*.

202. Method in both sciences.

203. Feeling and imagination are the types of personal powers of nature – Intuition is the common characteristic. Understanding and reason are the types of personal powers – representation is the common characteristic [cf. #218].

204. The concept of thesis – antithesis and synthesis investigated according to the Categories.

205. Everything is nature insofar as it can become an object. Object is antithesis – nature is thus antithesis. Person is thesis without relation to nature – synthesis in this relation.
Synthesis is nothing but thesis in relation to antithesis. /Intuition is antithesis[,] representation – synthesis.

206. Actual philosophy is dyadic. Applied philosophy is triadic.

207. The doctrine of substance (antithetic) moves *toward* – the doctrine of accidents (synthetic) moves *away*. The latter is subjective – the former, objective./ Monadic – thetic/ The latter goes from representation to intuition – the former from intuition to representation. The synthetic must stop with the antithesis that is no longer related, that is, with the original intuition. The antithetic [must stop] with the last synthesis that is no longer opposed, that is, simply with the thesis. The former [synthetic] ends in an unconditioned intuition – the latter [antithetic] [ends] in an unconditioned representation.

/Antithesis is the medium of change of the one into a manifold/

208. From the unending, every *determining* judgment is an unending one, in the sense in which every negation of a particular in the particular [thing] is called an infinite judgment.

209. This last intuition and representation is *Monas*.

210. Unification of intuition and representation – reciprocal causation – They are inseparable – always *together*.
God cannot be the quintessence of all intuition for us – any more than could the most general oneness of that which is conceived.

*   *

*

Group II: 211–287 (winter, 1795 to February, 1796)

211. <Intuition consists of feeling and imagination. Feeling consists of senses. The sense of feeling – the sense of sight. Imagination [consists] of sensations – the sensation of pleasure – of displeasure.

Feeling – Sensation – Imagination/
Concept – Idea – Power to act.>

212. Feeling is twofold – outer and inner sense. The outer is again the sense of feeling in the strict sense – and the sense of sight. The inner sense is again the sense of feeling in the strict sense – and the sense of sight. Imagination is exclusively productive. It corresponds either to outer sense or to inner sense. There [in outer sense] it is creative and pictorial – and here [in inner sense] likewise. Reason corresponds to [imagination]. Reason contains its laws. The understanding corresponds to feeling. Feeling, understanding and reason are in a way passive – which is already shown by their names – imagination on the other hand is the only *power* – the only active one – the moving one.[1]
So it must also be that only one is productive – all four are always together – they are one – only for us to separate through itself.

213. There is a faculty of representation and a faculty of feeling – [there is] no faculty of imagination. A faculty is passive.

214. They always work together – and this makes up the empirical consciousness. The human being lacks full consciousness if one piece is missing.

[1] The German words for these aspects of the mind are *Gefühl* ("feeling"), *Verstand* ("understanding"), *Vernunft* ("reason"), and *Einbildungskraft* ("imagination"). Novalis' point is that only the word for imagination contains the term *Kraft*, which means power.

215. There is only imagination – feeling and understanding. Intuition and representation are just the names given to feeling and imagination [together] and concept and imagination together.

216. Until now chemistry has taken the analytic route – the synthetic route must be tried once. Prime matter [*den ersten Stoff*] is taken to be that which can no longer be divided. That is an endless toilsome route – for its completion it must certainly also return to an absolute thesis or synthesis.

217. A theory of intuition must ground the sciences.

218. Power. Space. Time. Division of the sciences. /Our nature is immanent – our reflection [is] transcendent. We *are* God – we think as individuals. If transcendence becomes immanence, it is the idea of divinity – that is, if representation becomes intuition – then we are in the realm of the divine I – Imagination, as intuition, is God. Feeling is nature – Understanding is the person – personified psychology.
If reason is called the *laws* of imagination, insofar as [the imagination] can be saddled with being *lawlike* at all, then philosophy is actually nothing but the theory of reason. Logic would be the theory of the understanding, or of representation. Universal [*allgemeine*] doctrine of nature – theory of intuition. Every science in the realm of intuition arises from a principle of reason, and according to logic's rules of form and the universal doctrine of nature's rules of matter.

/Form is a mere relation bound to neither space nor time/

/Space is the determinate infinite – time is the indeterminate finite. Time can only be measured by space, space can only be measured by time. Space involves intuitions – time [involves] representations.
The subject, which as representation is called the I, is a power at rest, a stable, simple, changing thing that does not change.
Intuition and representation are one. The former [is] the relation of the imagination to sensibility – the latter [is] the relation of imagination to the understanding.

219. Previously an absolutely simple thesis was sought – now [we seek] an absolute synthesis /for chemists the former is simple, the latter is

composite, matter./ Thesis is the residue of that which acts – the simple basis. Absolute synthesis – absolute thesis – the former is the imagination as such – the latter is the imagination itself in *opposition* to its product – or in relation to the product. The subject is thus only an idea – it is only that which is set in opposition to the representation or intuition, absolutely nothing more. But the subject must necessarily lack causality – just because it [the subject] is only a residue. To what extent will the subject, that is, the product, be able to relate to itself? Basically, never. How can one speak of freedom? Or how can causality be ascribed to the subject at all?

/In a certain respect our thoughts are also spatial./

Reason is actually understanding applied to the original relations – or to the nature of the imagination. Imagination consists of sensibility and reason – combined, both must be creative and formative powers. They cannot determine the representation of the imagination – the imagination must determine their representations.

/The idea is the concept of concepts./
/The image is the intuition of intuitions./

/The concept of *one* concept is impossible – *One* concept can only be *intuited*. An intuited concept is a sign. *One* intuition cannot be intuited – it can only be conceived. /A simple concept is an impossibility – likewise a simple intuition.

The differences of representation and intuition.

Concepts and sensations correspond. Sensation is to intuition, as concept to representation.

/Sensation appears to be subjective – feeling objective/
Representation – Intuition – Sensation – Concept. /Space – Time./
/Idea. Power. Image. Sign./
/*Matter. Form.* Life. Spirit. Movement. Activity./

220. How can the empirical I project its *own image* without assuming an objective medium. /Division of the imagination./ Sensibility and understanding correspond in detail – because they are one in three.

221. /Thesis – Antithesis and synthesis in the *Conclusion*.

222. An object has several forms and thus also several [types of] matter.

/Objective matter and form in general.
Determinate types of its being. Determinations a priori, sensuous determinations – arbitrary determinations./

/Categories. Particular [power of] imagination.
The imagination of the understanding. The particular understanding of this imagination and the particular reason of the [imagination].
We would do better to call that understanding the faculty of representation.
The faculty of intuition divides into the formative power [*Bildungskraft*] – and into the *general* and the *particular* – the former [is] form, the latter [is] matter – as when in the faculty of representation, understanding yields matter, and reason [yields] form.
/Sensibility seems to me to be the particular/
<Purposiveness [seems to be] the general./>

223. The faculty of representation contains the unity [*das Einfache*] of form and the manifold of matter – the faculty of intuition contains the unity of matter and the manifold of form.

[224.] *Space – time*. Conditions of all material.

Concept of succession. *Rest – motion*.

225. Matter [*Materie*] and spirit correspond in the smallest detail – one is like the other. Both have pure causality only in the other.

226. Space is a *concept*. Time is an *intuition*. The first is proper to all intuitions, the last [is proper] to all representations.
It is as impossible to think of space without time as it is to think of an intuition without a representation. /Instead of *representation*, thought/

/Time is the form of space in the imagination./

Space and time are the most general material and form. /The most general material can become form in another area./ The most general form [can become] material in another area/.
Space is the condition of that which is moved – Time the condition of the movement.

/Matter is thesis – that is, that which can be thought without essential relation. Form [is] antithesis; that is, that which cannot be thought without essential relation./

/Difference between material [*Stoff*] and matter [*Materie*]. The latter is the substrate of intuition – the former is the substrate of representation.[2]
/Categories are nothing but the relationships of the object in general with the imagination, faculty of representation, and with the faculty of intuition./
Why dichotomous oppositions everywhere?
Mobility is proper to matter [*Materie*] – activity is proper to material [*Stoff*] – from it arises motion. Form is either form of matter or form of material. Material and matter are product: to be noted are 1. product and 2. its form. In matter the product is that which endures and the form is that which changes – in material the product is what changes and the form is what endures. The enduring thing is the simple, the changing thing

/Everything is recognizable through opposition/

is the complex [*Mannichfache*].

/An image is a represented intuition.
A sign is an intuited representation./
/Symbolic formative power [*Bildungskraft*]. Imagination./

What are representation and intuition?
/There is no absolute form, and no absolute material [*Stoff*]. They all condition each other alternately in the circle./

The material/ of the representation (of spirit) / is the enduring. Form is the changeable – the former is the simple, the latter [is] the complex. The material of matter is that which endures, the form is that which changes. The form of the enduring in matter [is] space – the form of the changing in matter [is] time.

[2] Since Novalis makes recurrent use of this distinction throughout, I henceforth translate *Stoff* by "material" and *Materie* as "matter." Cf., e.g., #245.

The material of that which endures in matter is the durable itself (*durability*), abstracted from its necessary condition. The material of that which changes in matter is *mobility*.
The material of the spirit is the enduring, whose material is identity – [and whose] form [is] determinability.

/Material is the enduring, form [is] the changing/

The form of spirit is thus that which changes. Its material is activity – its form [is] manifoldness.

227. What is material and form?

Form is the necessary predicate. Material [is] the subject.
Form is the condition *of every subject*. The subject is *everything* from which one proceeds – *what* is asserted of [*the subject*] is a predicate. –

228. A is a – contains the absolute or total form – it asserts the thing itself completely – but does not teach us to recognize anything – it is the real form or the form of material, as such – without reference to something else. Identity is the form of all material. The material of all form, of which nothing more or less can be said than that it *Is*, that is, is its whole [*sein Ganzes*].
Matter *is* – original material – matter is matter – original form – pure form. The material of matter is matter – its form is durability.

229. Form is antithesis. Material – thesis. Material is self-supporting, enduring. Form is related, changing – the ground of negation – like material, the ground of reality – form *can be excluded* from the sphere of things. Material cannot – this is clear in the case of *thought*.

230. Matter has its material unmediated from the imagination – its form from spirit, hence mediated by the imagination. Therefore the latter [the form of matter] is simple, enduring – the former [the material of matter] [is] changing.

/The unmediated product is material. The mediated [product] – form/

What can be thought alone is material, what must be thought in relation [to something else] is form.

> /Why the proposition "a is a" contains – the *pure* form – because here there is actually no predicate, but only the predicating action – is *pure*, material without form. The purest form is thus the material of form. The purest material is the form of material. /This is only uttered facetiously.

Form without material is the purest form – material without form – the purest material. Rest is thus characteristic of pure material – motion is characteristic of pure form.
Pure material and pure form, however, are only parts. Because the actual material and the actual form consist of the pure and the empirical part. The empirical part of material consists of two relations: of the relation to form and the relation to pure material.

/Distinction between condition and form/

Pure material is the condition of empirical material. Pure form is the condition of empirical form. Empirical material consists of the necessary relation with pure material and the necessary relation with form in general – the latter can be called formality. Material is thus, *qua* material only, formless. But because material is a relational concept with reference to form, actual material is never alone, it is only *thinkable* alone; as such it is thus still

/How can thought divide what God has joined/

relatable [*beziehbar*], formable, determinable. Real relatability and ideal relationlessness [*Beziehungslosigkeit*] are thus the conditions of material. Pure form is also only a partial condition of actual form. This [actual form] consists likewise of pure and empirical form. Pure form is relating without a relational ground – *simple action*. Empirical form – relating to a relational ground in general – is causality. Action and causality are thus the essential conditions of actual, or *absolute*, form. The former is ideal, the latter is real. What does this mean?

231. Matter has its material unmediated, its form mediated. Its material is part pure, part empirical. The pure material of matter is without

form – formless material – the empirical material of matter is formable material. The pure form of matter is motion in general. The empirical form is mobility.

232. Pure matter – empirical matter. The latter consists of matter related [to something]. The former consists of unrelated matter. That which is unrelated is ideal. The material of the ideal is pure and empirical. The pure material of the ideal is simple being – the empirical [material of the ideal] is manifold being. Pure form [of the ideal] – [is] sphere – the empirical [form of the ideal] – [is] manifold sphere of being. Related matter also has twofold material and form: pure material [of related matter] – [is] unmediated being [given] through the imagination – empirical material [of related matter] – [is] being mediated through spirit. Pure form [of related matter] – [is] the condition of related matter's pure material. Empirical form – [is] the condition of related matter's empirical material. Pure matter and empirical matter are conditions of matter in general.

/Everything in general has a pure and an empirical part, or an ideal and a real part. Both are one – pure and ideal – and empirical and real./

Spirit in general is pure and empirical spirit. Pure spirit has twofold material and form.

/Spirit is what matter is not, and is not what matter is./

The pure material of pure spirit is – being – the empirical material [of pure spirit] is – relational being (presence [*Dasein*]) – or manifold being – The pure form [of pure spirit] – [is] sphere – the empirical [form of pure spirit] – [is] relational sphere or manifold sphere – The pure material of empirical spirit is being through the imagination.
The empirical material of real [= empirical] spirit – [is] being mediated through matter; the pure form [of real = empirical spirit] – [is] the essential condition of being through imagination – the empirical form [of real/empirical spirit] – [is] the essential condition of being mediated through matter.

/Pure spirit and pure matter are for the possibility of thought. Empirical [spirit and matter] – [are] for the actuality of thought – possibility of thought – pure thought (*ideal*) – actuality of thought – empirical (real) thought./

/The forms of empirical matter appear to be space and time – the forms of empirical spirit [appear to be] synthesis and analysis. The forms of pure matter and of pure spirit contain the *thought possibilities* of space, of time, of synthesis and analysis./

/The materials of empirical spirit are reason (ideas) and understanding (concepts). The materials of empirical matter – [are] elements and *drives*. The thought possibilities of this are contained in the materials of pure spirit and pure matter./
The ground of this division must lie in pure and empirical thought – what, then, is pure and empirical thought?

/Categories. Material and form – their difference from matter and spirit must lie in the theory of thought. (Material and form is the pure part – matter and spirit the empirical part) Natural science. Criminal law. The beautiful. The good. Politics. Imagination – symbolic formative power [*Bildungskraft*]. Representation. Intuition. The sciences. Method./
/Thought is the pure part of representation, perhaps – feeling is the pure part of intuition, perhaps – then why is it possible to think and feel separately? (It only appears to be the case.)/

Observation of ideas and elements and concepts and drives and their intersecting analogies. The forms of spirit and matter are manifold simplicity – the materials [of spirit and matter] are the simple manifold. Pure matter is pure material for spirit. Empirical [matter] is empirical material for [spirit], since pure spirit is the pure form of that pure material, and empirical spirit is the empirical form of that empirical material.
Relative to matter, spirit is form – relative to spirit, matter is material – or rather both are themselves form and material – it just depends on which of the two we reflect upon, which we take to be subject or predicate.

233. Pure and empirical thought. <The pure part is always representation, the empirical part [is always] intuition> – or the pure part refers to the pure part of intuition and of representation – and the empirical [part refers] to the empirical part [of intuition and representation]. Simple or pure intuition is representation – simple or pure representation is intuition. They thus mutually ground each other. Intuition without representation is the pure part of representation – representation without

intuition is the pure part of intuition. This shows the intimate connection between intuition and representation – and the confusion [*Täuschung*] [of representation] with the pure part.

/Intuition and representation appear to be identical in the pure part? <All intuition is material – representation is form.> The former [is] object – the latter [is] subject. The pure part is representation – the empirical part [is] – intuition. Representation is the relationship [*Verhältnis*] to the subject – receptivity. Intuition [is] the relation [*Beziehung*] to the subject or the relationship to the object – spontaneity.

The subject is the substratum of representation, the active thing insofar as it is affected. The object is the substratum of intuition, the affecting thing insofar as it is active. Subject is the changeable enduring thing – object [is] the durable changing thing. On the one hand [in the subject] the predicate or the form is the changeable. On the other [in the object] the predicate or form is the durable.

The predicate is the material. The subject is the form. The absolute subject is the predicating thing – the relative subject, of which [something] is predicated, is the object.

I am relative subject, object, intuition, when I predicate something of myself – but [I am] at the same time absolute subject, insofar as I also predicate – I am active and passive at the same time – like object and subject. The predicate is form for the relative subject. The relative subject is form for the predicating subject – because every object is a predicate of the absolute subject. Only the unmediated predicate is form – the mediated [predicate] is material – the predicate of the predicate is the mediated predicate. Thus, the form of form is material and the material of material is form.

Form and material are actually relative concepts – /Analysis./ /Subject is synthesis/. As soon as something is predicated of both, they are transformed. Form is the sphere of the predicate – material [is the] sphere of the relative subject – in whose concept is already contained a necessary predicating [*Prädicirung*]. All material is possible form – all form [is] possible material. Material and form are interchangeable concepts [*Wechselbegriffe*] – the one presupposes the other and postulates it.

234. Thesis is the pure part – the relative subject. Antithesis [is] the relation of the empirical part to the predicate – synthesis [is] the relation to the pure part or to the relative subject. The relation of the predicate to the subject [is] antithesis. Relation of the subject to the predicate [is] synthesis – the former [is] form – the latter [is] material – both relations occur together and are one in this respect. The first relation occurs inward – the second outward. The former occurs from the general to the particular – the latter from the particular to the general. The general consists of the particular, the particular [consists of] the general. The particular is the form of the general – the general [is] the form of the particular. For the absolute subject material is that from which it proceeds – [For the absolute subject] form is that toward which it proceeds. First in [this] alternating relation is material – the identical – the enduring in precisely this sense./ But there is nothing that is absolutely enduring/ (pure and enduring are in this respect the same.)

> /It seems to me that a kind of principle of reciprocal determination, a pure law of association, must have to be the highest fundamental principle – a hypothetical principle./

Universal [*allgemeingültige*: universally valid] philosophy would presuppose the *fixation* of so-called subjectivity, that is, [it would presuppose] a *free* fact, or the assumption of a hypothetical, free principle. One's philosophy can be called true just as certainly as something can be called beautiful.
The purest representation is intuition – pure intuition [is] – representation. The purest subjective is objective – pure objective [is] – subjective. /Principle of beauty – grounds representation and intuition./ In intuition, en route from the particular to the universal, we must come upon representation – In representation we must come upon intuition.

> /Represented intuition, and intuited representation constitute the essence of imagination./

(Pure) force is the material, (pure) effect [is] the form of the imagination. Material and form *kat exogin* are always pure – they are related things – without relation – relatable. To be sure, everything relatable is in the realm of *actuality*, or imagination, including that which is already related. Possibility, actuality and necessity are one. [The concept] *Actual* relates to intuition – *necessary* relates to imagination – *possible* to representation.

The ground of the concept of possibility lies in representation – [it] is thus the real thesis. The concept *actual* is grounded in intuition and is the antithesis, since it is a relational concept – [the concept] *necessary* is grounded in imagination and is the synthesis – *possible* is a twofold relation in the third – it is nothing but an oscillating (*Schweben*) between *necessary* and *actual*. The thesis of these three concepts is that from which one begins – antithesis is that toward which one proceeds – and the return to the point of departure is the synthesis. Thesis is the relative subject. Antithesis is its relation to a predicate. Synthesis – [is] relation of the predicate to the subject. Thesis is material – antithesis [is] the form of material – synthesis [is] the material of form. For absolute subject, thesis is at once material and form – antithesis – form – synthesis – material. The concepts of material and form are not applicable to the concept of thesis.

Thesis consists of an immanent relation – antithesis of a thesis and an unmediated transcendent relation. Synthesis, [consists] of thesis, antithesis and a mediated transcendent relation. Thesis, antithesis and synthesis are the empirical (or already related actions) forms a priori – they are the determinations of material in general a priori.

Thesis: material is simple, immanently related. Antithesis: it [material] is immanently and transcendently related. Synthesis: it [material] is immanent, immediately and mediately transcendently related.

These are the empirical forms of material in general and the empirical material of form in general.

Material and form in general are pure material and form.

[The term] Pure[3] thus expresses the character of mere relatability, the representation [expresses] the mere possibility of a relation, the mere receptivity – the character of the relative subject as thesis. The character of the thesis is pure.

/Spirit and matter are thus 1. pure (immanent). 2. immediately transcendent. 3. mediately transcendent, or transcendental.[4]/

[3] Novalis usually does not indicate mention, as opposed to use, of a term or concept in these passages at all. Indeed there is a consistent conflation of use and mention in this text that might be seen as a hallmark and/or flaw.

[4] This is the Kantian distinction between transcendent (outside the possibility of human cognitive experience) and transcendental (having to do with the conditions of the possibility of that experience a priori). For Kant, the former can never be an object of knowledge, while the latter can be discovered, or uncovered, through "critique."

Material is the related – form the relation.
The predicate is not the form – but only the form-giver, because via it [the predicate] the form, the *relation*, occurs.
Form – condition of material – material – condition of form – pure material is form – pure form [is] material – the connection between power [*Kraft*] and effect is form – relation. Power and effect are the related. Form comes from material and proceeds toward material – It is the movement – material [is] the moved.
Form is /pure/ power. Material [is] /pure/ effect.

Power and effect.

1. Thesis: pure power. 2. Antithesis: effect in general. 3. Synthesis – power in general.
Effect is immanent and immediately transcendent power. Power in general – immanent, immediately and mediately transcendent power. Pure power is immanent power. Pure and empirical are set in opposition to each other. Material and form are simply empirical concepts a priori. There is no pure material or form.
Material in general is [the] related. Form in general is relation.

What do *pure* and *empirical* mean?

What kind of concepts are these? Pure – that which is neither related nor relatable. The forms of the relatable are the empirical forms a priori. The concept *pure* is thus an empty concept – that is, a concept to which no intuition corresponds – a concept that is neither possible nor actual, nor necessary – everything pure is thus a deception [*Täuschung*] of the imagination – a *necessary* fiction.

Truth – fiction or illusion.

The imagination has two products – the true and the illusory. One excludes the other – negates it. Both are identical – illusion is illusion – truth [is] truth.
Truth is the form of illusion – illusion the form of truth.

/Illusion is spirit. Truth is material/

Illusion is that which is opposed under the form of the posited – It seems [*scheint*] to relate, and does not relate. It seems to be the related and is not. Truth is the whole – illusion only the fracture – the half that seems to be the whole and is not – the former [truth] [is] the positive, the latter the negative quantity.[5]

/Every thing is a whole composed of intuition and representation – one of these alone is half the reality of the thing. The more reality I posit in the one half, the less [reality I posit] in the other – that then becomes the negative quantity. Every thing is positive and negative quantity; because it is indeed not the not that it is – What it is not, it is not – i.e., it gets determined and not determined/made determinable and not determinable by being and not-being, by positing and not-positing. It cannot become determined to be what it [already] is; what it cannot be determined to be is what it is. Determination that contradicts its being, is illusion – determination that does not contradict [its being] – [is] truth.

(Representation without intuition is illusion and vice versa. There are concepts and ideas but no mere representations. There are sensations and perceptions, but no mere intuitions. Both are mere illusion. Illusion is, however, necessary everywhere – since illusion is everywhere half – only the half of a whole is illusion – but since everything cannot simply be halved, illusion is everywhere. The illusion in our cognition arises from the elevation of the half to the whole – or from the halving of the indivisible, of that thing whose *being just consists in* the composition, from the unnatural (immanence and transcendence), or from rounding off and division.

Thus illusion arises
1. from the elevation of the part to the whole.
2. from the degrading of the whole to the part.
3. from the dividing of the indivisible.
4. from the combining of that which is not to be united.
(from action and omission)

Illusion is the contradictory, that which is excluded from the determined thing – the determinable – the sphere of illusion is thus the determinable and thus that which is excluded by an actual determining – everything

[5] This passage plays with the cognates *Schein* and *scheinen*. To capture this play *Schein* should be translated "appearance" to match *scheinen*, "appears." I have had to sacrifice style for philosophical content here, since Novalis clearly intends the term *Schein* to refer to an illusion or fiction. The term "appearance" has been the standard translation of the German *Erscheinung*, which has a quite different meaning, especially since Kant, who opposed *Erscheinung* or appearance to *Schein* or illusion. Novalis is well aware of this opposition.

that is determined by a determining – thus also relations are excluded herefrom, and thus are not illusion. Intuition and representation *alone* are illusion. All thought is thus an art of illusion. Illusion is the only ground of all form and all material.

Illusion and truth together constitute only one actual reality.

Illusion is the original form of truth, of original material. It is truth related to itself – reality is for reality only through relation – form – illusion. Reality knows reality only through relation, form, illusion – negation. /The form of being is not-being – the form of not-being [is] being./ The relation of not-being is being. Consequently truth is existence – the form of illusion, of not-being – and illusion [is] the form of existence.

This is pure form and pure material. Related and relation.

All material of thought is material of illusion – *Urform* – all material of feeling likewise – and so also with the forms – that is the pure material and pure form.

There is a form of illusion and a material of truth – negation and reality. Both together constitute empirical material and form. Illusion gets its material from truth – truth [gets] its form from illusion. Illusion is negation – truth – reality.

/A thing gets negated on the border, on the surface./

One can make two claims about every thing – a priori – it is – and it is not – The first is pure material – the latter is pure form. Simple relation is pure form – simple related [is] pure material.

The empirical forms a priori are already twofold relations – namely of something to something.

a = a	-Thesis	Empirical
b = a	-Antithesis.	Forms of truth -
c = a + b	-Synthesis.	Reality
-a = -a		Empirical forms
-b = -a		of illusion,
-c = -a + -b.		negation.

The principle [*Satz*] of identity is a principle of truth – reality. The principle of contradiction – principle of illusion – [is a principle] of negation. The principle of sufficient reason lies in both of the preceding [propositions] – thesis – antithesis – synthesis.

The principle of identity is characteristic of illusion and truth. The principle of contradiction expresses their relation to each other. The principle of sufficient reason or better, of excluded middle, – [expresses] the relation of both to imagination or to their common sphere and opposite sphere. From this it appears that antithesis [is] actually the twofold relation of both relata – synthesis, [is] the fourfold relation of both relata to the imagination or the absolute subject and to each other. Thesis has no quantity – I can say 1 or 0, both are thesis. Antithesis is the twofold relation of two particular spheres – merely insofar as they are particular. Synthesis [is] the fourfold relation of isolated spheres to each other and to the common sphere. An actual contradiction can occur only between *same things* – different things cannot be opposed to each other – the universal not the particulars contained *in it*, the immanent product not the produced – those are objects [*Gegensätze*, literally: things standing against each other] – contradictions [*Gegensätze*, literally:*propositions* opposed to each other] are only possible between illusion and truth. Contradictions, with respect to their quantity, are illusion – with respect to their quality, truth – with respect to their modality, illusion, – with respect to their relation, truth.

235. Every antithesis consists of two propositions – the first and second antithetical proposition – the oscillating relation.
Every synthesis consists of a closed relation – or a fourfold relation – the four relates to circulating right or left.

So synthesis can

1. proceed from a /the one contradictory proposition/ to b – the other contradictory proposition – from b – to c as the common proposition – and from c to a.
2. from a to c – from c to b – from b to a.
3. from a to b – then from a to c – then from c – to b.
4. from a-b + a-c + b-c.
5. a-c + a-b + b-c.
6. a-c + a-b + c-b.
7. c-a + a-b + b-c.
8. c-b + b-a + a-c.
9. c-a + c-b + a-b.
10. c-a + c-b + b-a.
11. c-b + c-a + a-b.
12. c-b + c-a + b-a.

236. These are the forms of empirical synthesis – that can only be distinguished with respect to content insofar as one begins; proceeds from the particular, from the contradiction, or from the universal, the common proposition.

/empirical refers to space and time/

237. a negates -a[,] + however also posits it, insofar -a is [the] actual contradiction of a +. It is also the same with -a.

Every negation is affirmation [*Position*][6] – every affirmation [*Position*] [is] negation. Truth negates as well as illusion, it negates illusion.
Illusion is the reality of all form. Being is the reality of all material. No being, no illusion – no illusion, no being – they are counterspheres of the absolute common sphere – the two halves of one ball – the form and material of the ball – both are nothing without the other –

Illusion would therefore be absolute form –
Being – absolute material.

Neither is recognizable without the other. Every product has material and form. Negation has form and material just as much as reality does.

/Being expresses a total relation, Having expresses a particular relation. Being is a relational concept that relates to material and form in general. Having is a relational concept that relates to the *particular* (further determined) material and form. Material and form in general lie in the determination.

238. Material and form are the most universal relative concepts – the product a priori of the relative imagination – Being and illusion [*Schein*] are the most universal concepts – the product a priori of qualitative imagination.

/Reality and ideality are opposed to each other – Affirmation [*Position*] and negation./

Determinability and determinedness are the most universal concepts – the product a priori of modal imagination.

[6] I translate *Position* as "affirmation," to avoid the ambiguity of the English and to underscore the opposition to "negation."

Whole and part are perhaps the most universal concepts of the quantitative imagination.

*

239. The originary is eightfold – in the form of *affirmation* [*Position*].

<1. Thetic. /in the Categories of relation.>
<2. Antithetic. /in the Categories of quality.>
<3. Synthetic. /in the Categories of modality and quantity.>
<The synthetic forms from c on contain the empirical concepts of modality.
The synthetic forms from a on – [contain] the empirical concepts of quantity.> [Cf. #235.]
The form of negation is the same.

If we refer these eight forms and materials to the imagination, then twelve forms and materials arise.

The imagination is

1. *in general* exclusive, exhaustive, limiting, necessitating.
2. in particular real, ideal, active, passive, possible, actual, simple, multiplex [*mehrfach*].

real – limited. determinantly determined –

*

240. Unity – totality – in order to have totality we must start from a unity and this is the imagination. Totality is the product of the imagination. Unity is the product of totality – the *unending determinant* [thing].

241. The quantitative and qualitative imagination refer to the commonality [*Gemeinsatz*] – the relative and modal [imagination refers] to oppositions [*Gegensätze*].

242.

power

being illusion

1. passive relationships between being and illusion – themselves.
2. active relationships between being and illusion *through* power – material and form.

3. active relationships between power and the products – determinability and determination.
4. passive relationships between power and products – whole and parts.

243. Activity – passivity.

(Negation. Affirmation [*Position*]. Reality. Ideality.)
(Substance. Accidents. Causality and dependence.)

244. The being of representation is form – the illusion – [is] material.
The being of intuition is material – the illusion – [is] form.

*

245. The material of representation is the manifold – the form [of representation is] the one.

The material of intuition is simple – the form [of intuition] is manifold.
The *whole* intuition is the material of represention.
The whole representation [is] the form of intuition.
Intuition is thus material – representation [is thus] form. Both are nothing without the other.
How is pure science possible in the human being – or how is the human being what it is?
What is matter? It is the material of the representation of intuitive material in general.[7]

246. What does that mean? The whole intuition is [the material of representation – *qua* intuition, it is not that material of representation]. It is also not [the material of representation] itself – They [intuition and the material of representation] are divided in the strictest sense by their identity. What is the connection between the two? how can intuition be called the material of representation.
There must be mediating faculties, etc., that in virtue of their identity belong to both, have something from both.

Intuition – Representation.

[7] Cf. #226, where Novalis defined "material" [*Stoff*] as "the substrate of representation" and "matter" [*Materie*] as "the substrate of intuition." Making the substitutions we get the (nearly impossible) formulation: "[Matter] is the substrate of representation of the representation of the intuitive substrate of representation in general."

/Material, form. Being, appearance. Whole, part. Determination, determinability. Activity, passivity. Reality, ideality. Affirmation [*Position*], negation./

The imagination is the binding mediator – the synthesis – the *power of change* [*Wechselkraft*].

power of change
power is change – change is power.[8]

247. Rule – game. Material – form. Being – appearance. All such propositions are interchangeable propositions. Philosophy will be the working out of all contradictions. It is the endpoint of the line – as the simplest whole – the sphere of the line will be determined by the endpoints.

Line in general – determination in general – thesis.
Half determination – an endpoint – an insight point – antithesis.
Whole determination – Both endpoints – Whole – synthesis.

Genetic determination.
Universal determination.
Particular determination.

First: expression of the power of thought [*Denkkraftäußerung*].
Second: expression of the power of thought, or action.
Third: thought-action.

Power of positing
power of insight
particular power of positing

The whole – power of identity. That which is identical in the whole is the particular determination – that is, *its* essence – its existence in general does not belong to [the whole], to its identity – Identity is a *subaltern* concept – being-posited in general cannot be identical – It is everything or in fact nothing.
The moment one wants to call it identical as opposed to particular and universal, the concept of the positing receives its *sphere*, the thesis becomes synthesis – the endpoints are – universality – particularity.

[8] *Wechsel* also means "exchange," as in exchanging currencies or alternating electric current. This is also part of the sense of Novalis' claim about the role of the imagination.

Being-posited in general, insofar as it is supposed to be that, is not to be posited in opposition to anything, since in that case it would lose its nature.
The nature of a thing is in the strictest sense its identity.
In a broader sense – [the nature of a thing is] both its particularity and its universality.
Nature in general is the quintessence of all things as such.
In contrast to art – the state of a thing that comes into being for its own sake without subjective causality.
In contrast to the person – Everything that is not-person.
Meanings of the word nature.

248. Power of change [*Wechselkraft*].

Activity – passivity.

> /The human being is a particular, a universal, and a simply posited – a sphere.
> The universal is what is not determined, but is related – the product of the power of insight [*Einfallskraft*]. The possibility of the particular sphere;
> /The present does not allow itself to be fixed. The *before* and *after* determines or relates the present moment – hence that which is affected is not a present passive participle, as actual passive thing it is never present to determine./

Difference between relation and determination. To relate is an act of the power of insight. To determine – [is an] act of the particular power of positing – the former is ideal – the latter [is] real.
Intuition and representation must be distinguished in the strictest way.
The imagination is everything to everyone – Through *relations* to each other both are *determined*. Relation is the one act of production – determination is the other act.
The imagination is the power of creation in relation to intuition – [the imagination is] the power of presentation [*Darstellungskraft*] in relation to representation – I could call intuition "matter."

> /The universal can only be expressed at all with the particular and the particular can only be expressed at all with the singular./

*

249. Power can only be expressed through the product.
What is science? It is the the totality of concepts of an object, ordered according to an idea.
Difference between matter and the material [*Stoff*] of representation.
1. Theory of intuition. 2. Theory of representation.
What can language contain for reality?
Relation of language to intuition, power of thought, and imagination.
Written – spoken – thought language.
Language is material and formal appearance.
Sign – image. The concept prevails in the sign – intuition prevails in the image – language or conceptual image.

/Freedom signifies the state of the *oscillating* [*schwebende*] imagination./

/Law must be the product of *freedom*/

We only ever think and see *the product*.
All transition – all movement is the efficacy of the imagination.
All determination is product.
Relationship is a consequence of a relation – of a suspended [*ruhend*] [concept] – relation [is a consequence] of a moved concept.
Substance is the quintessence of the positable *reality* of an object.
Accident is the negatable reality of an object.
Analysis of the concept of cause and effect / consequence, causality./ (occasion, opportunity etc.)

250. Language: Connection of the particular sensuous material of thought with sensuous signs. The sign is a hypothetical intuition, determined by a representation.

[251.] All causality demands a sphere. The sphere is, however, only possible through opposites [*Opposita*] – Sphere is thus the form of causality – all causality is in the imagination. Consequently the imagination must have a sphere. The opposites of this sphere are, that which is posited in opposition in general, and the posited thing in general. Both are fundamentally one. The sphere is posited in opposition to the endpoints – the imagination to the sphere and so forth.

/Tower of Babel/

What kind of image of thought [*Gedankenbild*] can language give of *nature*. Should all philosophy therefore have to be necessarily *one-sided*.

All *reality* [*Wirklichkeit*] has a before and an after – both are possibilities – After *is* possibility. Before was possibility – But in them everything is at the same time.
Self-activity – *Genius* belongs to *philosophizing*.

252. Ontology – Philosophy – Aesthetics – Logic – Dialectic.

253. Only the particular in general is dichotomous.

254. What are the Categories? Space – time?

What is reality?

255. *The power of procreation.*

/Woman = representation – man = intuition./
Unmediated, mediated products.

256. Consciousness – sphere of representation.

Space – sphere of intuition.
Time – common sphere.

257. Instead of the power of insight – the power of interruption [*Unterbrechung*], since we are always in line with that with which the universal sphere can best be compared. Indeed, intuition and representation appear to me to be separated in the strictest sense, but insofar to be one – that both are [in?] the same line, but in opposite directions. This circular line is as large and as small as one wants, it really depends only on the unending divisibility and division of it.

258. Are material and form real [*reele*] concepts and contradictions?

259. Affirmation [*Position*] – negation.

Reality – ideality.
Being – Appearance.

260. *Philosophical power.*
Difference between power and reality. /in general what is reality?/

261. Its [reality's] direction is at once centripetal and centrifugal. But immanence [is] the characteristic hallmark of the imagination. Material

is only for representation, matter is only for intuition. Form, like time, is common to both. "Formed" refers to a subaltern relation.

262. Power of poetry [*Dichtungskraft* = also "power of invention"].

263. The circle can be interrupted at any point – the pole of intuition and representation can be placed and displaced at any point. Imagination manifests itself as insight[9] and inhibition [*Hemmkraft*]. Intuition and representation are in themselves static. Their interruption[10] first gives them reality – that is, insofar as reality consists of an identical mixture of intuition and representation.

Power of freedom – free power.

They must be interrupted, however, otherwise they *are* not.

264. Analogy with the circular line is *surface* [*Oberfläche*] – perhaps form. With the sphere [*Kugel*] – material, perhaps – content of the surface. The latter for matter, the former for spirit. /From this absolutely no conclusions can be drawn./

*

265. *Costs*. 2. Memos. 3. *Survey*. 4. All sorts of questions – fund for the disabled – coal – *debtors* –

266. Every determination of a branch involves the determination of power, and of the other branch. Three theories appear to me to arise from this:

1. Theory of intuition. 2. Theory of representation. 3. Theory of imagination.

267. What is form? Passivity of one sphere with respect to another. Material and matter: Activity of one sphere over against another.

268. On concepts: intuition and representation.

[9] *Als Einfalls* – the German word also has the sense of an interruption – something coming into one's mind.

[10] *Unterbrechung*. The German also has the sense of disruption – for Novalis, of a "breaking in" to the circle of intuition and representation.

269. Determinability – determinateness.
Being – appearance. Affirmation [*Position*] – negation.
Reality – ideality. Activity [*Thätigkeit*] – enduring [*Leiden*]. Activity – passivity. Motion – rest. Simplicity – manifoldness. Durability – changeability. /Mobility./ Substance – accident. Causality – dependence – universal – particular + whole – part. Freedom – necessity. Form. Material. Matter. Spirit. Power. Facility [*Vermögen*]. Drive. Sign. Image. Space. Time. Consciousness. Sense. Feeling. Sensation. Concept. Idea. Synthesis. Analysis. Representation – intuition. Capability. Beautiful. Good. Right. Vice. Virtue. Science. System. Method. Spontaneity – receptivity /*Hofbauer's Logic.*/ Desire. Inclination. Habit. Will. Inclusion – exclusion. Immanence – transcendence. Relationship – relation. /*Dictionary of Kantian Philosophy.*/[11]
Constant – interrupted. *Same – dissimilar*, or *different.*[12] One – divided. Change. Sphere – /passivity of the undetermined/ ending – unending. Absolute. pure. empirical. Representability./ Indeterminability / Subject. Object. qualitative. limitative. quantitative. relative. modal. symbolic. Purpose – means. Judgment. Idea. Concept. Condition. *Degree*. Action. Application. Possibility of language. Thing. Being [*Wesen*].

Philosophical language primer [*Sprachlehre*].
Synonymistic
(Grammar)

270. Opposite of power – weakness.

Difference between power and activity.
One says – activity of the imagination.
active – Inactive power.
/strength [*Macht*] – speed [*Geschwindigkeit*]./

[11] Possibly a reference to Carl Christian Erhard Schmid's *Wörterbuch zum leichtern Gebrauch der Kantischen Schriften*, already in its fourth edition in 1798 (ed. N. Hinske [Darmstadt: Wissenschaftliche Buchgesellschaft, 1976]).

[12] Although "similar" and "dissimilar" better capture the related roots of the German *gleich* and *ungleich*, I have preferred to use "same" and "different" respectively, to capture Novalis' philosophical sense, which has to do with identity and non-identity claims, not claims about similarities and dissimilarities. His explicit identification of *ungleich* with *verschieden* (= "different") here is the cue.

Should only the empirical power be capable of activity or inactivity. Inactivity is enduring.[13] Inactive power is sublated, negated power – it always presupposes more power that strives to oppose [it].
Activity is power without resistance.
How can speed augment power?
/Strength is a *relative* concept that refers to the object of which it is predicated or to which it is opposed, and stands in quantitative relationships to it./
Centripetal force increases with speed – is it in the body or is it attractive power? /Magnetism. Electricity./

271. Positive – *negative* power –
the latter – *sublated* [*aufgehobene*] power.

272. What constitutes a theory? The universal and the particular, and their interchange. Philosophy should contain the universal of all particulars – it goes from particular to universal. Other sciences [go from] universal to particular.

Every science can go from below up and from above down – the first – [is] synthetic – the last [is] analytic.

All philosophy, as science, can go in both of these directions.

Fichte has taken the analytic route following a synthetic principle. I take the analytic and synthetic way at the same time – I observe every step forward and backward – Only, I have to develop more purely the synthetic *Categories* – then I can classify every universal concept more certainly and precisely – I borrow the expressions, names, from analysis – from empiricism.

273. Widening – tapering *pyramids*. Sphere – consisting of 4 pyramids, two united at the base and two at the tip – converging. The outer sections belong to both halves.

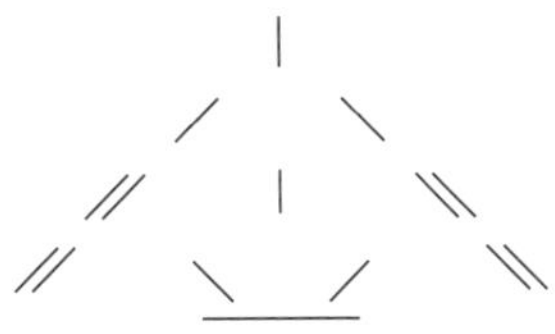

[13] *Leiden*. The sense is of undergoing something passively. "Suffering" is the literal translation, but carries a too negative connotation in its ordinary English sense.

better still:

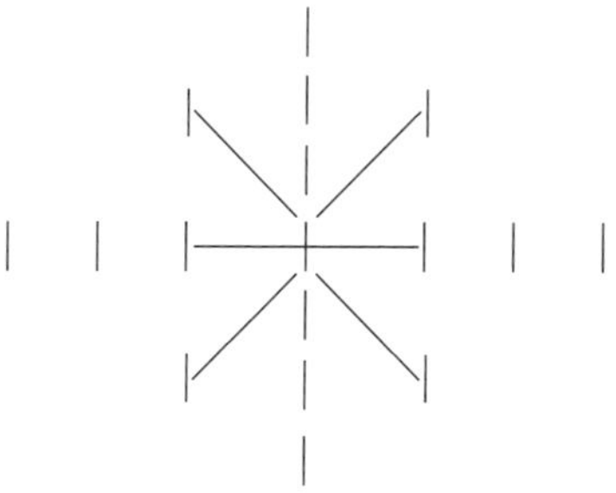

This is the sphere [*Kugel*] of science. The sphere of the actual rotates in an area of a circle – since it moves in a circular line.

274. Form is passivity, separated from its outer and inner possibilities. A crooked line is also a line that presents the possible relation to a material – or the passivity of the material of the line.

275. On the concept of surface – no essential concept of line.
Space determined by one dimension is line – by two – [is a] surface – by three [is an] actual space.

276. The power to think the *universal* is philosophical power. The power to think the particular is poetic power. The universal is the pure and simple already posited – the particular is the relative [*das Beziehungsweise*] posited – or, the former is the sphere in which something is posited – the latter, [is] the sphere that is posited *in* the former.
The former is a being-posited – the latter is a positing.

/Being expresses the relationship of the whole to the part, and of the part to the whole./

Totality and partiality oppose each other.

277. Every totality consists of two parts in a certain respect – of the positive and the negative – of the determined and the undetermined – of the real and the ideal – of the like and the unlike.

1. Of two single things.
2. Of one commonality and one single thing.
3. Of two common things.
   etc.

278. How many original oppositions can there be?

1. Affirmation [*Position*] – negation.
2. Whole – part.
3. Conditioned – unconditioned.
4. Cause – effect.

/pure – empirical./
/being – appearance./
/substance – accident./

On the application of these concepts to a material. This problem is answered by the application of themselves to themselves in the whole. Their application itself is a fact [*Factum*]. The factual can only follow from a fact – experience only [follows] from experience.

/Affirmation and causality considered together in one thing produces the concept of existence [*Daseyn*] (of identity)/

Nothing can be posited in fundamental opposition [*entgegengesetzt*] to a fact – opposed in the pure sense. The opposites themselves together are a kind of opposite of the fact. There is nothing to oppose and to set up against the fact itself – But its appearance, or the fact in relation to the opposites – this is the object [*Gegenstand*]. This [*Gegenstand*] is set against the *opposite* [*Gegensatz*].[14] The sphere of the object and the sphere of the [opposite][15] become related to each other in the sphere of the fact. The fact is object insofar as it is related to the opposites. Thus the object must be determinable utterly only with respect to the opposites – or only a determination of the opposites can be predicated of it as object. Its [the object's] concept can be exhausted by the relations of opposites. Its reality is thoroughly determined by the opposites.
If one proceeds toward a theory of positing, then one must begin with a concept of positing – with the undetermined determination. If this concept is exhausted by the opposites – we observe it in the application,

[14] Novalis here is exploiting the various German words compounding *gegen* or *entgegen* ("against") with verb forms: "gegen*setzen*" or "entgegen*setzen*" means "to posit in opposition"; *entgegenstellen* is "to set or pit something against something else"; the ordinary term in German for opposite, *Gegensatz*, takes on a more technical meaning for Fichte, given his notion of positing (*setzen*), and so too, Novalis is suggesting, does the ordinary notion of an object or *Gegenstand*, as something that *stands* (from the verb *stehen*) against or in opposition.

[15] Novalis writes *Gegenstand* twice here, where he clearly means to write *Gegensatz* the second time.

or in the opposition, relation – then there emerges the first empirical opposite – form – material and matter – and only now, in the opposites, we get – *forms* of thought, etc. – and the difference between material and matter follows easily.

Now we find that thought contains the thought form, or *thought* possibility, of the freedom of the fact. Freedom in the sphere of the form is thought – positing or positing in opposition. Freedom in the sphere of fact or of matter – is imagining. Freedom in the sphere of material or of the object – is setting up [*stellen*] or setting up against [*gegenstellen*], feeling. /Positing and positing in opposition –, setting up and setting up against are the same/.

Matter is the object without *intentional* reference to the opposite – the quintessence [*Inbegriff*] of its affirmation as cause. Material [is] its affirmation as effect.

The application of the factual concept a priori rests again on the fact as appearance.

The concept of application is already an empirical concept.

The opposites contain the forms of determinability. Their application lies in their affirmation. They are posited according to their own laws[16] – they are, before they are – that is [they are] a priori, outside the sphere of time. Their being posited in time can therefore only occur apparently – that is, they contain the ground of *all* positing and sublation originally – formally – thus also their own positing and sublation. They sublate themselves as soon as they are applied to themselves – this, however, is only an apparent negation – they are thus grounded in the fact. They are therefore in the sphere of the fact, insofar as they sublate themselves – they are in their own [sphere] insofar as they posit themselves.

> /I *am not* insofar as I posit myself, but rather insofar as I sublate myself – I am not, insofar as I am in myself, [insofar as] I apply myself to myself./

Every same sphere excludes that which is the same. Different spheres *limit* each other.

Same and different are not set against each other, they *are* simply posited in opposition to each other – insofar as they are related to each other in a

[16] "Sie werden nach ihren eigenen Gesetzen gesezt . . ." Novalis is playing with the notion of positing and, more literally, position, that is contained in the German word for law, *Gesetz*.

common sphere – They are posited in opposition to the whole as partial *concepts*, or set against the whole as parts.
All reflection relates to an object. An object as such, however, is determined by the original oppositions. I can thus think only a determinate thing – the undetermined is only thinkable as opposite, but insofar as the opposite is an object, it is already determined by itself.

/Opposite – appearance/

The object presupposes an opposite. The opposite can only come into reflection as an object. Every opposite, insofar as it becomes an object, that is, insofar as it is reflected upon, thus presupposes yet another opposite, and so on. The undetermined is thus the substrate of the opposite, or better, its logical possibility or sphere.

/The sphere of the object [is] determination – the sphere of the opposite [is] indetermination. The former [is] law, the latter [is] freedom/
/Freedom is the product of law (of the object)
Law [is] the product of freedom (of the opposite)./

I say product, but [it is a] reciprocal product – relation.
Determined and undetermined, however, act like same and different.
The determined does not determine itself – it excludes itself. The undetermined determines itself – because it limits itself.
Every concept of opposition contains two objects – the determined must be twofold – the undetermined must be twofold in order to be *identical*.

/A twofoldness belongs to the unity of consciousness/

The different, e.g., must be twofold in relation to totality.
The concept of the same, however, must here be the opposite of the different – and in this regard leads the way, so to speak, – unnoticed, as soon as one reflects upon [the concept of] *same* and thereby makes it into an object, – different becomes opposite and likewise seems to precede [same].
This is also the case with determined and undetermined. One is opposite and object of the other, according as one passes from one to the other. The transit [*transitus*] produces the transformation.

The adversity of the fact of reflection occasions both./ Adversity in the literal sense of the Romans, where it means turning *toward* and turning *away* from/

Every object posits – every opposition sets up[17] – if we attribute the particular nature of the fact to the ladder[18] – object and opposite are ladders – neither active nor passive. Activity is, however, attributed to them – because, pressured by the natural laws of reflection, this [activity] must be *posited* somewhere; and so one resorts most easily to the ladder and attributes [activity] to this – all activity belongs to the fact.

But whence the possibility of this philosophical reflection? /The *most rule-governed play* of ideas is *true* philosophy/

It all depends on the arrangement, the quantitative, scientific form – If I go the pure way of method, then I can use whichever concepts/words/ I want to fill the spheres.

279. If one only reflects upon one's relation to the opposite in the object, one reflects upon the form of the object – one reflects upon [the object] as appearance of the fact, then it is twofold – material and matter. In the first case, when one reflects upon the form and [the form] thus becomes object – one reflects upon the fact – If the opposite becomes object and thus the object becomes opposite, then one reflects upon the content of philosophy. If one reflects upon the object itself, pure natural philosophy is obtained.

280. With the four opposites it is as with determined and undetermined. They are not actually opposites – but rather the part which is reflected upon is object, and meanwhile the other is opposite – Together they are, as parts of a whole, either object or opposite, according to whether one reflects upon them both at once or upon the sphere of the fact that is common to them both, which then becomes object and thus must be judged according to the *laws* of the object.

17 German word play is at work: "Jeder Gegenstand sezt [*sic*]" – jeder Gegensatz stellt . . ."
18 *Leiter*. Novalis is suggesting that the object and its opposite are active in the sense that "leaning on" something else can be said to be active.

The object is determined by the opposite – the opposite by the object. Both are in themselves [*allein*] undetermined. They thus mutually determine each other.

/Eternity *a parte post* and *a parte ante*/

The expression – undetermined – a concept of determination – it is not an opposite of an opposite, but rather [it is] the object and opposite of the opposite and *determined* object – sublated through the concept of determination that already lies within it. The undetermined basically contains a determination through the mere concept of determination – it fails to express what it ought to express. It should entirely negate determination.

/*real* sublating can become nothing – only ideal – the object cannot [be sublated] from the object, but only from the opposite, and vice versa./

For us there is *only* negation, an undetermined, an unconditioned, etc. It is only appearance – objectivity of the opposite, oppositionality of the object.
Conditioned and unconditioned.

/Schema of the concept/

Possibilities of the object and of thc opposite in general. This must be the Categories –
Their original relations.

281. Totality and partiality – causality and dependence – these concepts are derived from the original relationships of the fact to the ladders.
We can only judge the fact as *object* – but every object has an opposite – real – ideal fact.

282. We find only one object and one opposite.

/No object of the object in general, etc./

Their being in opposition is only explicable if the object can be an opposite and the opposite can be an object.
Every object presupposes something – thus has its opposite originally – the object in general presupposes opposition in general.

/In general the universal presupposes in general the more universal, etc.
/Presupposition is a most welcome expression. Positing must be used in that sense, since it expresses: I posit [something to be] the case. It is the act of hypothesis – actuality and necessity conditioned by possibility or actuality and possibility conditioned by necessity or necessity and possibility conditioned by actuality. In short, the act of the second member of the relation.
To presuppose means to posit in opposition an act prior to existence, an anticipation, needed by the object – because the positing agent first becomes possible through a positing – this positing is, however, originally the same. Through this positing in opposition *existence* (significant etymology of this word) first becomes possible, actual and necessary.
The object – *emerges* through an [act of] positing in opposition.

Positing is the original act. Positing in opposition is the producing act of the opposite. To posit in opposition out of [is] the producing act of the object. From [the side of] the opposite it means, it is posited. From [the side of] the object [it means] it arises out of it.
Both expressions have many features.
To emerge expresses a self-bringing forth, a causality that is self causality, a passivity through its own activity.
To be posited is: a foreign dependence, a passivity through foreign activity. One cannot say, the proposition posits itself. The object posits itself mediately through positing in opposition. But positing and positing in opposition are one.
Here the freedom of spirit entangles it in apparent contradiction. The concept of activity already contains merely the data of the concepts – positing, positing in opposition, emerging. All concepts of movement, all verbs / in the most authentic sense: *Words*/ embody the passage [*transitus*] upon which everything rests.

/Verb, subject and predicate or noun and adjective – these are the materials of the *Elementarphilosophie*/[19]

283. The object posits itself in that it emerges – there are not two unmediated corresponding acts, but rather the [act of] opposing is the medium.

[19] A reference to Rheinhold's adaptation of Kant.

[The object] is only an object insofar as it has emerged, that is, insofar as it is posited *out of* in opposition[20] – or has posited itself. As the firm point from which one starts it is called the object.[21]
Objectivity, or the possibility of the becoming an object, *excluding real objects* – is the essence of the opposite. It becomes an object as soon as reflection turns upon it.
The turning of reflection [upon it] can be called *intuition* – and it is the genetic act of the object.
The opposite is determined only by the object and vice versa – The following proposition lies within it:

> Since only the object is the sphere of the determined, the opposite can only be determined as object. If, however, the object should become determined, as it already is, this can happen in no other way than that it is transposed into the sphere of the opposite, that it becomes the opposite – undetermined.

But undetermined is only an abstraction – since it is at its basis also determined because it is a concept – the object abstracts from its basic conditions – [the object] is determined as opposite – All determination is abstracted from – and there remains – schema – *mere sphere*.

284. Since reflection is also an object, all intuition of the object is a particular [intuition] – since it goes from object to object.
Of course the intuiting agent becomes opposite – and in order to be quite precise – one must say: intuition is a relation of opposite to object. The relation of the object to the opposite is naturally – a turning away – a withdrawal, actually – an abstraction – reflection – and this would thus be the genetic act of the opposite. But nothing is [to be] confused here – causality with dependence – activity with product – the causality of the intuiting lies in the opposite – that [causality] of reflection in the object.

/Reflection is a very expressive term/

[20] "*Ent*gegengesetzt." Here Novalis is making philosophical hay of the German prefix *ent-* in *entgegensetzen* ("to oppose," or "to posit in opposition"). The prefix has no one fixed meaning, but it often means, roughly, "out of." He is emphasizing the emergent nature of the object, as arising out of an opposition.

[21] "Gegen*stand*." Novalis is emphasizing the term *Stand* in the German word for object: *Gegenstand*. It is literally that which stands firm when posited against another thing or even itself.

Intuition and reflection are *particular* acts. Fact in general is the sphere of their totality. In order to be genuine opposites [*Opposita*] of reflection – each must have a homogeneous and a heterogeneous feature.
Their common characteristic is – activity or direction in general / adversity/.
The particular [characteristic] of intuition – being posited in the opposite – the particular [characteristic] of reflection – being posited in the object.

/However, I prefer to call reflection idea. Unrealizability, necessity, unity, unendingness of the idea can easily be developed from it/
/Idea and intuition are thus related to each other as opposite and object. The causality of intuition lies in the idea, the causality of the idea – in intuition./
/ending and unending relate to each other just like determined and undetermined, conditioned and unconditioned, etc.

Unendingly determined is without determination in the most general sense – since unending is also a concept of determination – unendingly determined [things] cannot be further determined – it is then undetermined for the determining power, since it is indeed unendingly determined – freedom is sublated.
Freedom is the substrate, the sphere of the opposite, the idea.
The *opposite* of all determination is *freedom*. The *absolute* opposite is freedom – It can never become an object, as little as the opposite as such [can ever become an object] – Every substrate of the opposite can become an object, but it is therefore not a real opposite. It [the opposite] is actually not itself any determination of the opposite, even its determination as opposite. [The opposite] has actually no sphere, since it excludes all spheres. All words, all concepts are borrowed from the object – objects – and therefore they cannot secure it [the opposite]. Its essence is namelessness – therefore every word must drive it away. It is a non-word, a non-concept.

How can that which is only a voice produce an *echo*?

But inasmuch as we determine, we gain something from it [the opposite], since it is *everything* – and only in the All do we determine. If, however, it is All, then it must also be the determined – insofar as it is the Not-determined.

The determined, or the object, is, however, a twofoldness – a posited-in-opposition-to – Insofar as we make *all* objects into objects, the opposite of this object must be the particular opposite in general. The universality of the object and the particularity of the opposite are actual opposites. Object in general, as well as opposite in general, can express totality and particularity – whereby, however, one thing is at bottom expressed. Because, as totality, the concept actually contradicts itself – it is not one in itself. Every object excludes every opposite – but both thereby lose the concept of divisible determination – they are only to be considered as limited to their heterogeneous marks.
Reciprocal determination is their common mark.
active causality / determinately determined / the individual mark of the object.
passive causality / determinedly determinating / the particular mark of the opposite.
If reciprocal determination becomes object and if this is opposed, then nothing can be posited in opposition to it, since out of that another object would arise that is already contained in it – the law of nature demands – an object should be produced outside the states of the object, a sphere without sphere – the object resists its demand – the object is found – the idea or *reflection* is the new object – negation of the *power of nature* – impossibility has become possible. The stasis of satisfaction is interrupted and precisely thereby satisfied. Contrariness to nature is nature, the particular mark of the opposite – active passivity is the only possible opposite of reciprocal determination, as object. Reciprocal determination as object is not complete – nothing more remains but that which can never become object, the particular mark of the opposite – but this opposing is markedly different from all remaining opposites. All remaining opposites could become posited *out of* in opposition – but not this one – at least not in the usual manner until now – until now the satisfaction of the drive to posit in opposition out of was *static* – now it will be interrupted.

/The concept of progressing lies in the interruption, of activity, as in all verbs/

The individuality of the opposite expresses the word reflection very well.

Now I see that in general, ["]to posit in opposition to["] already contains the proper concept of intuiting and reflecting – that these already lie in the concept of activity, that intuiting *arises* out of reflecting, reflecting out of intuiting, object out of opposite, opposite out of object – that the identity of the object for itself must be derived from its contrariety.

Reciprocal being and reciprocal determination are one.

The possibility of striving against itself is factual and for that very reason already the most evident proof of the twofold direction of activity.

[285.] We have seen what the particular mark of the opposite in general was. Active passivity, or determining determinability must thus be the appearance of freedom in the realm of the object. Because it [the appearance of freedom] should be the absolute opposite of the sphere of reciprocal determination. However, no opposite is possible here – in the actual sense – because opposite itself is a relational concept – But here all relation should be abstracted from – thus an opposite without an object should be here – This is, however, nothing else but the particular mark of the opposite. This is indeed also a determinate thing – but insofar not reflected upon and it is determined and made into an object so that it takes the place of that which is sought, of the absolute opposite, takes over the function of freedom – and with this the possible concept of freedom is given.

It [freedom] is nothing but the opposition of the whole to the part, for us.

/Because the object is only posited in opposition to – reciprocal determination, as the whole[,] but is here the object, consequently the part must here be the opposite to that which is posited in opposition to.

Transition from homogeneous to heterogeneous, or from [what is] common to [what is] unique / universal, particular / is a kind of freedom –

From unique characteristic to unique characteristic, heterogeneous to heterogeneous – [is] the other kind of freedom.

/The object is determiningly determined free, the opposite is determinately determining free./[22]

[22] "Der Gegenstand is bestimmend bestimmt, der Gegensatz bestimmt bestimmend frey." Novalis is capturing the point that the opposite is "actively passive."

/Object and opposite can have unique and common characteristics. Object can be opposite, insofar as it is determined by exchange and thus vice versa. In the sphere of reciprocal determination both are mutually determinable, and actually determined.
Every object can be opposite and every opposite can be object to a certain extent only, namely insofar as they have a common sphere.
However, how have their heterogeneous characterstics been able to be determined? Merely insofar as both stand under the law of reciprocal determination.

286. The concept of freedom already lies within the concept of activity. Determined and undetermined activity is not pure activity. Activity must be negated only through itself, if it is to remain pure activity – not narrowed by any concept. But it [activity] is our object – consequently determiningly determined – the opposite of this object is none other than the determinately determining. We would have determined activity as object.

287. Freedom as object is equally easy to determine.

*   *

*

Group III: 288–372 (February–March, 1796)

Principal Rule

288. Everything, irrespective of whether we reflect upon or sense it, is an object and so stands under the *laws* of the object. The opposite itself is an object insofar as we reflect upon it.
If the object in general is an object of reflection, then it also stands under its [the object's] laws. It is determined by the opposite. If reflection turns from the object in general to the object's opposite, then it only rotates, it has again *one* object before it, but a particular one – and so we discover that the particular object was the *objective* opposite of the object in general.

289. What holds for the object *in general*, holds for *every* object.
Opposing the object in general there is an opposite, which we became acquainted with as the particular object. [See #284–285.]
But how can the particular object be presupposed by the object in general, but of course not as object – the object in general was the particular object. The aforementioned particular object must therefore not have become a kind of particular object, but rather nothing other than the particular, or opposite in general.
What holds of the opposite in general, holds also of every opposite.

/Intuition relates to the object from the opposite./ Reflection [relates] from the object back to the opposite. Reflection is returning intuition. Feeling refers from [the] object to [its] opposite and is called returning sensation./

Intuition and reflection appear to be in the object and are in the opposite. Feeling and sensation appear to be in the opposite and are in the object.

290. Reflection brings presentation of the object – sensation brings presentation of the opposite.
Presentation is also object – but what kind of object?
What kind of opposite does it have –
Objectness is the common characteristic.
The particularity of presentation is that the common characteristic in it is an accident.
The particularity of its opposite, as object, is that the common characteristic in it is the substantial.

/Herein lies the law of reciprocal determination./

Presentation and *object* – each has both substance and accident.
The particular is the substance of *presentation*, the universal is the substance of the *object* – the universal [is the] accident of presentation – the particular [is the] accident of the object; that is here only posited in opposition to [*gegengesetzt*] and in opposition out of [*entgegengesetzt*] the presentation.

/Positing in opposition expresses the activity of the object, whereby the opposite and thus the *object itself* emerges.
Positing in opposition out of expresses the activity of the opposite, whereby the object becomes unmediated object and the opposite itself becomes mediated.
The former is thus the shibboleth of feeling and sensation – the latter [is] the act of intuition and reflection.

291. Presentation has the alien, hence particular determination of the object as the substance of its concept; as accident [it has] its determination, thus the universal determination as object in general. *Presentation* is thus the opposite of the object in general, if [the object] is reflected upon. Object in general has the common characteristic, object-ness (universality) as its substance – as accident [it has] the particular characteristic, particularity.

/Universality determination of totality – particularity – determination of partiality./

This shows why the object in general is determiningly determined, [and the] opposite in general is determinately determining.

/Presentation is determinately determining/

Investigation of the concepts substance and accident. /Their relation to intuition and reflection, feeling and sensation.

/Object – subject./ The subject observes and reflects – the object feels and senses/

292. Reflection is also sensation. Idea is thus more suitable.
This is why intuition and feeling are so closely related – because both are outward-going acts – and so also sensation and concept [are closely related], since each is a returning act. The opposing [*entgegengesetzte*] relationship is between intuition and sensation and feeling and concept. That is, [intuition and sensation] go from opposite to object, since [feeling and concept] go from object to opposite.
State [*Zustand*] superbly expresses the most real essence of what was just now called opposite.

State [*Zustand*] and object [*Gegenstand*].[1]
Practical – theoretical philosophy – inner reciprocal determination of these spheres.

/Practical reason must lie in nature/

How is philosophy capable of presentation?

/Substance – the self-active, accident – the alien active – the former, the active [part] of the concept, the latter, the passive [part of the concept]./
State – universality (Accident) of the particular (substance) –
Object – particularity (Accident) of the universal (substance).
2 – Unique feature [*Eigentümlichkeit*] (Accident) of the common [*des Gemeinschaftlichen*] (substance).

1. Common feature [*Gemeinschaftlichkeit*] (accident) of the unique feature (substance) and so forth.

[1] Again, the reference is to the German word itself: *zu* (= "to" or "toward") + *stand* (= "stand," or "stay in a place"); *gegen* (= "toward," or also "toward in opposition to") + *stand*.

293. Categories. /Science of nature/

There must be forms of reflection, because thought – is conceiving and sensing. They must therefore have the character of suffering[2] and of form, and they must be twofold. We can retain the division of mathematical [Categories] that are grounded in intuition, the causality of conceiving, and the dynamical [Categories] that are grounded in the causality of feeling.[3]

294. The Categories are fourfold.
They contain 1. The form of intuition.
2. The form of the concept.
3. The form of feeling.
4. The form of sensation.

Every one of these forms is threefold – they consist 1. of the relation of reflection, 2. of the relation of desire or striving after, 3. of the relation of the whole, or of both acts [of reflection and desire] at once – of the proposition no. 2 – of the opposite of no. 1, of the common proposition, or of the proposition of reciprocal determination.
The mathematical Categories are the forms of intuition and the forms of the concept.
The dynamical [Categories]: the forms of feeling and [the forms of] sensation.

1.
The form of intuition
Category of quantity.

*

[2] *Des Leidens*, literally: "suffering." The character of passivity or receptivity, in other words.

[3] A reference to Kant's table of Categories, which contains twelve Categories divided into four headings, the first two of which (Quantity and Quality) Kant calls the mathematical division, and the second two of which (Relation and Modality) Kant refers to as "dynamical." The first he says "is concerned with objects of intuition" while the second "is directed at the existence of these objects (either in relation to each other or to the understanding)." *Critique of Pure Reason*, AA B110.

295. Intuition is

Act of opposition (state) to object.
/common unique feature – acting through suffering – determined determining/

It is a single positing – this act is categorically determined by the two strivings of intuition and feeling.
1. One / *intuition*/ unity – / *feeling.*/
2. It is a progression – interrupted by one – double reflection – once (concept) – From determining determinate, as effect, to determined determining thing, as cause, back – once (sensation) from determined determining thing, as effect, to determined determining thing, as cause, back – however, here the causality in the point of reflection is apparent both times.

Two /concept/ plurality – /sensation./

3. A whole /intuition and concept together/ totality – /feeling and sensation together/ Here is a free effect of the state and the object opposing one another, with respect to the form of intuition – reciprocal determination or reciprocal being – their mutual striving back and forth confront each other – and become confused with each other – the reflection of the concept that actually should have return to the opposite, is stopped – it returns to the object – the reflection of sensation returns to the opposite – Thus a double-branched whole emerges – that is for that very reason a whole – that is, "a" was,[4] as no. 2 above says, reactive until the point of stoppage /determinately determining power/ apparently having become active through the object – now it [reflection] regains its old features and a negative, active power, a foreign power instead of its positive active power, is restored to the object. The same thing happens to the state. The foreign power of sensation, which was originally positively active and became apparently negatively active in the opposite, driven back by the point of stoppage, regains its old direction and with it its positive activity, and the state is restored to an actual (substantial) positive, active power, the power of sensation, instead of its *apparent* (accidental) positive, active

[4] Apparently a reference to the identity statement discussed at length at the very beginning of the notes: "a is a."

power of the concept – through this arises the concept and intuition, the feeling and sensation of the whole – because object and state are, as it were, deceived. 1. The *object feels* the *whole*, that is, the state determined by the object, as it were, outside itself. 2. The subject observes the whole also – the object determined by the state – as it were outside itself – both reflections set up this unified act, *as always*, together – and thus the synthesis of quantity is accomplished. /This synthesis provides the model for all future [syntheses]/ [cf. #297].

> But how is it that the Categories can be presented like this? Because reflections – conceive all states and objects and the laws of reflection must be applied to every state and object – because they really become it.

/*Power – state – object*/ (The Categories must determine themselves. Power – state – object.)
But how is it that it is *quantity* that is hereby determined? That can be discovered only after the other Categories are developed.

296. From the preceding, the analogy of the Categories of relation and of quantity – and of quality and modality.

> similar, insofar as there are only 2 and 3 Categories?

*

297.2. Form of the concept. Category of quality.

1. Reality /feeling/ affirmation [*Position*] – /intuition/
2. Ideality /sensation/ negation /concept/
3. Limitation /feeling and sensation/ limitation/ intuiting and concept/

3. Form of feeling. Relation. Reciprocal determination.

1. essential – accidental. /intuition and feeling/ (substance)
2. efficacy – effectedness /reflections/ (cause)
3. Exclusion – *Conceiving*. /Tendency[5] and reflection at once. (Sphere)/

[5] Cf. #16 and 17.

4. Form of sensation. Modality. /Reflected activity of the object, positively active, particular universality. /Meaning of the universe/

1. The merely *formal* activity of the object that is returning from the state constitutes both, for intuition and feeling, as *determinable*, negative and positive, and *facilitating*.
2. *Actuality*, for concept and sensation, first arises through sensation that has become negative – which presupposes an *actual* state and *actual* object – discloses – actuality – activity in general. (Unity of the object)

(Feeling and intuition must operate together like concept and sensation in order to produce something./ no. 3 can always be expressed by a verb – just as the branches of the Categories of reflection in general./ "Actual" expresses both relationships, of the object and the state in a common sphere.)

3. Necessity arises /for all 4 apperceptions/ out of their unification /by the reflections/ and their relation to the form of sensation. This relation shows the strict dependence of this form upon the whole, upon object and state, feeling, intuition, concept and sensation – [it shows] the determinate determinability, possibility of this form. The faculty becomes active. The activity [becomes] facilitating – reflecting form [is] joined with striving material – Drive [is joined] with activity – Power arises – /for intuition and feeling/ Necessity – for reflection.

/Concepts of coercion, compulsion, etc./ Are nature and the force of law. The former [i.e., nature] in relation to the tendencies – the latter in relation to the reflections. Must be – [is] the character of the former – Ought to be [is] the character of the latter.

298. There are doubled twofold, threefold, and fourfold Categories.

1. The forms of reflection in general in relation to the tendencies. Modality and quality– /relation and quantity.
2. The forms of tendencies, etc.

---

a. The forms of objects /relations to the object, in alternating relation
/quantity and modality.
b. The form of the state – /relations to the state –
/quality and relation

α. The form of the object alone. — Eclectic Categories – because here the rest must be parceled out.
β. The form of the state alone.
γ. The form of the reciprocal determination alone.

The fourfold ones are the ones that are familiar.

299. The familiar Categories arise through reflection in general, which [reflection], to be sure, is induced by experience/intuition/and need/feeling, by [reflection in general] relating each of the 4 apperceptions, as the 4 possible kinds of objects in general, once to the tendencies, once to itself, and once to both together, by confounding the branches of the drives and reflections /cf. a. and b./.

I. The forms of the object alone. /Relation and modality.
Dynamic
and
II. The forms of the state alone. /Quantity and quality.
mathematical
Categories.

300. Where and how the activity of the state and the object breaks off / Sensation and reflection must always arise together. Because every reflection presupposes the other – It is one act of rupture. This will better help explain the synthesis of quantity and the rest.

Appropriate meaning of the word = *Inhalt* [content] – /To contain, relation – relate. To withhold, etc.[6]
Transcendent activity of drive and of reflection.

301. How does a relating to two things arise at the same time? It is a relating to their common sphere. Synthesis is a relation of power, or activity as of the common sphere of state and object. Reciprocal determination is nothing other than activity. The change lies in the essence of the active being.
Activity is only conceivable between subject and object.
The reflected object and state transforms its nature – it is no longer the mere object and state. It is reversed. Each appears to be what the other is. There is one mere object and state, and one reflected one.
The mere object is the active thing. The reflected [object] – [is] the inactive thing; and it is also the same with the state. /The active is passive returning [*rückleidend*] – The passive [is] active returning [*rückthätig*]./
Reflection is twofold – every act of reflection is predicated upon an inactive object and state together – the concept of the former – the sensation of the latter. An active object and state is posited in opposition to this. Object is – reflected object and state. Subject [is] – both [object and state] apart from reflection – in the tendency.
The activity of the object and state stand in mutual interaction. Both reflections happen at one moment – as do both tendencies. / About the essence and properties of activity./

/*Experience* of the most universal is called a priori [experience]/

Feeling is – passive activity. Intuition – active activity. /passive power is understood as active returning – active power is passive returning./
Every object is state – every state [is] object. Sensation is thus active activity of the object, which relates itself as state (which it has become through feeling), to itself as object. Concept is thus – passive activity of the state which relates itself as object (which it has become through intuition) to itself as state.

[6] The German words *Inhalt* ("content"), *enthalten* ("to contain"), *Verhältniß* ("relation"), and *vorenthalten* ("to withhold") all contain *halten*, "to hold, keep, support, maintain."

Transposition [*Versetzen*] is thus a more appropriate expression for the inner efficacy of the identity of object and state. Every product of activity is identical.

302. True – derivation from *to continue*, *to last* [*währen*] – perception [*Wahrnehmen*, literally: "taking to be true"] – to grasp steadfastly. /To take – is active receptivity./

303. Activity is the actual reality. /Neither object nor state is alone, to be thought *purely*. In reflection the opposite is mixed in already even through *striving* – desiring – because both are identical acts. The concept of identity must contain the concept of activity – of the exchange within itself. Two things posited together are the highest sphere to which we can raise ourselves.

> /God is unending activity. Nature is unending object, I – [is] unending state. All three are abstractions. All three are one. They are not divided, as in itself in reflection, which is constituted out of all three./

What Is, is through activity. Insofar [as] object and state are – they stand under the laws of activity, that is, they are active. Activity is original power [*Urkraft*] of the accident – it is the unending accidental. State and object are the unending substantial. Activity decomposes, as *situation* [*Stand*], originally into two parts – real–ideal – or positive–negative – or active–passive. The rule also holds for activity: that it can only be perceived in *combination*, not *alone*. It [is] always in relation to object and state.

> /it is foolish to want to obtain a resolved product by an act of solving – [to want] to separate what is bound by an act of binding. What is to be separated – must be bound together – what is to be bound together – [must be] separated. This yields the impossibility that lies in general in the nature of such things – to retain a so-called pure, simple product – because every product as such can only be set up in that which is *dividing*./ All that is separated is perceived in that which binds together – all that is bound together is perceived in that which separates./

*

304. Activity is separated –

1. Activity of opposition.
2. Activity of the concept.

The former befits the object, the latter [befits] the state. Form and figure arise out of both together.
Limited activity can only be limited by activity. That which limits is the object – that which is limited – [is] the state. Negating activity is the activity of the object. Asserting [*ponirende*] activity – [is] the activity of the state.

/The *material* belongs to the cause, the form of the effect [belongs] to the thing caused./

Causality *in the particular sense* is thus to be ascribed to the state – Effectivity [is to be ascribed] to the object.
Insofar as both are inseparable, each is cause and effect of the other. But this is linguistic confusion. Action and passion, reaction and affection correspond to each other. The activity that is first is for us the causal [activity].
Insofar as the object is active – that is, opposes (reacts) – then to that degree the state is inactive, affected [*afficirt*]. Insofar as the state is active, acts, then the object behaves passively. The object reacts to the intuition that proceeds from the state and the state is affected. Action and affection are thus mediated causes and effects for each other. In reflection of the concept affection becomes object – [affection] thus reacts and the active state is affected all over again.
Where the object formerly was is once again state – and where the state formerly was, the object now steps in. The state acts upon the feeling that proceeds from the object and the object endures [the feeling]. Reaction and passion thus behave as mediated cause and effect. In sensation feeling becomes state – thus [state] acts [upon the sensation] and the opposing object again endures [sensation]. State has become what object was – object [has become] what was state. From this it is clear that action and affection, reaction and passion are *one act* – that action can become affection, affection can become action, reaction can become passion and passion can become reaction.

/Further it is shown that when the state intuits, the object senses – and when the object feels, the state conceives./ In the first case feeling is naturally already presupposed, just as intuition is [already presupposed] in the second case. But hereby, how unified the ground of their inexpressible connection is can easily be reckoned. Here the path to the unity of consciousness opens before us.

305. Should not the object in general be reflection, but the state be tendency?
Sensation is the act of the object becoming the state, and of the state's becoming an object.
The same for concept.
Intuition and feeling – are acts of the state and object as such.
The difference probably lies in the fact that intuition and feeling are the universally determined acts of the state and object – Sensation and idea, however, contain the transformation of these universal acts into particular [ones]. The former determine nothing particular, and the latter [determine] nothing universal. From this can also be established the difference of reflections.
Reflection negates the universal activity and posits the particular [activity]. Tendency negates the particular [activity] and posits the universal activity.
The activity of the tendencies is in and of itself universal – through the activity of reflection that is inseparably bound up with them it becomes unmediated, however, or due to the *stoppage*, a particular determined activity. All particular [activity] expresses an action and affection or reaction and passion, depending upon whether it is a particular of the object or of the state.

/mere intuition and mere feeling are just as inconceivable and unrepresentable as sensation and concept without intuition and feeling/

/presentability, or conceivability is the criterion of possibility of all philosophy. We can think and order only the particular determined thing./

Here we obtain an extremely important division of the object and state.

1. Object and state of the tendency;
2. Object and state of the reflection.

The first is the universal – undetermined determinable – simply determined.
The second is the particular – determined indeterminable – conditionally determined.
The first can only be *cognized* in the second – the second [can be] *grounded* only through the first.
The object of the second is the state of the first, the state of the second the object of the first – that is – the object of the concept is the affected state of the tendency, the state of the concept is the reactive object of the tendency. The object of the sensation is the passive object – the state of the same [i.e., of the sensation] – [it is] the active state.
One sees from this that in reflection state and object alter their essence.
The object of reflection is active and therefore affected – the state of [reflection] is reactive and thus passive.
Both are determined as particular – consequently we can set forth the following rule:
The universal state is active and affected. The universal object is reactive and passive. The particular object is active and affected – the particular state is reactive and passive.

/One may not think of object and state as to a certain extent divided, like the a. ___ b., but rather as changes in the identical./
/Activity and being are thoroughly identical [*idem*]./

The *concept* of activity is an expression of the original relation of accidentality – of the identical as object and state. Activity can be excluded but *will* not be *excluded* from their pure concept – from the concept of their sheer substance.

306. Activity is change. Change is unthinkable without state and object. It consists in the displacing of identical activity. Every thing is object and state. State with regard to its outside – object in regard to its midpoint. The outside is the intuition. The inside is the subject reflecting – upon the midpoint. Hence the manifoldness of the first and the unity of the second. One sees from this why the intuiting subject is the active affected [subject] – [and why] the conceiving subject – [is] the reactive passive [subject].
If the outside becomes passive, then the object, because of its elasticity, becomes pliable – it feels. But it springs back again for this very reason – it senses.

307. Affirmation [i.e., positing: *Position*] and negation of activity.

308. Object, as state, is the particular state. State, as object, [is] the particular object. Both are plainly different. Universal and particular activity. Power of the state – power of the object. The power of the state is the power of the particular object [*Objekt*] – the power of the object is the power of the particular subject. State and object [*Objekt*] are identical, as object [*Gegenstand*] and subject. The former is the universal, the latter the particular – in both.

309. The subjective object [*Gegenstand*] (there is no objective one) as well as the objective state, that cannot be subjective, are now easier to determine. Now we have both original concepts of accidentality of original substances [*Ursubstanzen*].

310. The power of the identical – or the being of activity consists in the exchange – in being through positing and in positing through being. Where [the power of the identical] has an effect, there is substance – substance is the sphere of its being. Accident [is the] sphere of its positing. Where it is, there is reality – affirmation [*Position*]. It switches eternally between state and object. It proceeds at the same time from state and object – at the same time from object [*Gegenstand*] and object [*Objekt*].[7] State and subject are both active and affected, as object [*Gegenstand*] and object [*Objekt*] are both refractory and passive. Both are thoroughly one act – that, however, appear to be opposed to each other in a twofold manner.

311. Concepts of the active, affected, refractory and passive.

312. /Being is a relative concept – ground of all relation./
Intuiting and sensing or belonging to and sensing are One *act*, as standing against (feeling) and representing. Belonging to representation, however, and standing against and sensing are One *essence*. Intuition and sensation are One *Fact* – feeling and representation. Intuition and representation [are] One *product* [*Produkt*] – feeling and sensation. Effect of the essence is the product – effect of the act – [is the] fact.

[7] Novalis is introducing the distinction between *Gegenstand* (as before, literally, "standing against" or in opposition) and *Object*, only to argue that they are both parts of one activity, affirming (= positing), and of one being.

/Every determination requires two oppositions./

The active is only active insofar as it is affected, [it is only] affected insofar as it is active. The refractory and the passive behave in just the same way. The state is simply active – the subject [is simply] affected. The object [*Gegenstand*] [is] passive, the object [*Objekt*] [is] refractory. State and subject act together and object [*Gegenstand*] and object [*Objekt*]. Action and affection are *one act* – like passion and refractoriness. Refractoriness and action are, however, one essence, so also are passion and affection – concept and sensation are the products – intuition and feeling [are] the facts.

*

313. Action and refractoriness give rise to intuition.
Passion and affection – [give rise to] feeling.
Refractoriness and affection [give rise to] representation
Affection and refractoriness [give rise to] sensation.
Working on something [*Hinwirkung*] creates facts.
Repercussion [*Rückwirkung*] [creates] products.

In accordance with the prior claim that only one determination can occur through two oppositions, the fact is only

determinable in the product –

The product is the sphere of the determinable.

314. What becomes positive from the object [*Gegenstand*], becomes negative from the state. In the object [*Gegenstand*] the positive becomes negative again and the negative becomes positive in the state, and so they switch back again. The positive comes from the state and the negative originally comes from the object [*Gegenstand*].

315. Activity begins in the state.
It always ends in the object.

316. Intuition and representation move outward – they are transcendent, so to speak – feeling and sensation alone are simply *immanent*.

317. Intuition is the universal, like feeling. Sensation [is] the particular, like concept. Intuition is the universal state. Feeling is the universal object. Sensation [is] the particular state – Concept [is] the particular object. Intuition is the relation of the universal state to the particular state. Concept [is] the relation of the particular state to the particular object. Because intuition precedes – the universal object suffers – since action gives rise to passion, as refractoriness [gives rise to] affection – [the universal object's] suffering refers to the particular object – it feels – [I]n the repercussion of the concept, sensation, which is a relation of the particular object to the particular state, also reacts. What is different in these manifold relations is that the relation of the object begins at the same time with the relation of the state and works this way, when the latter works that way – (one increases as the other decreases, and one decreases as the other increases.)

/The universal in the particular – the particular in the universal./
/Consciousness must be simple and unending./
/I almost believe that it must be all the same, if one ascribes to the object what I ascribe to the state./
Reason contains the forms of the inner, as sensibility [contains] the forms of the outer – space and time/

Action and passion are as inseparable as north and south; and so too [are] affection and refractoriness. Refractoriness is the inseparable relation of action – affection – of passion. Opposition and being affected order themselves absolutely according to action and passion. Affection is a negative suffering, passion is a positive suffering. Action is a positive activity – Refractoriness is a negative activity.

Negative suffering is the character of sensation.
Positive suffering – [is] the character of feeling.
Positive activity – [is the character] of intuition.
Negative activity – [is the character] of the concept.

Thus we see – that a. 1 and 3 – and b. 2–4 make up a unified act – and that a. and b. are again also one act, but a compound one.
We already know that what is united according to the essence is divided according to the act and [is] united with one branch of the opposite. According to the essence the state thus has the character of the active

and of the affected being. [According to the essence] the object [has the character] of suffering and of resisting. According to the act the procedure of the state is that of acting and the procedure of the object is that of suffering.

The universal state intuits.
The particular object senses.
The universal object – feels.
The particular state represents.

This yields that the universal state is representable, the universal object is sensible, the particular object can be felt – the particular state is intuitable. According to the essence, sensation belongs to the state, to intuition, but according to the act [sensation belongs] to the object, to feeling.
The concept – according to its essence – [belongs] to the object, to feeling – according to the act – [the concept belongs] to the state, to the intuition. As fact, the sensation is in the object – the sensible is given to the sensing subject. As product [the sensation] is in the state – the given is sensed.
This is true also with the representation. The representable receives it. It owes its *emergence* to intuition. But [representation] is in the object – modification of the object.

(The state takes – the object gives.)
<Intuition is representable.
Feeling – [is] sensible.
Sensation – can be felt.
Concept – [is] intuitable.>

Better

The intuiting subject – [is] representable.
The feeling subject – [is] sensible.
The sensing subject – can be felt.
The representing subject – [is] intuitable.

318. The active state /that arises from the universal and particular/ takes in a giving way – the suffering object /that arises from the universal and particular/ gives in a taking way. The essential state and the essential

object do both – since it arises from the universal state and the particular object – from the universal object and the particular state.

319. Drive. Propensity. Power. Sense. Matter.

320. To what extent is philosophy possible?

321. Insofar as the intuiting subject senses and can be felt, it is representable.
The feeling subject can be sensed, insofar as it represents and is intuitable.
The representing subject is intuitable, insofar as it feels and can be sensed.
The sensing subject can be felt, insofar as it intuits and is representable.

What then is intuition, feeling, representation and sensation?

Intuition is a product – that is composed of the intuiting subject and the intuitable. The intuitable is [composed of] the feeling subject and the sensible. The intuited [thing] is thus doubtless the felt [thing] and the [thing that is] sensed. Representation is composed of the representing subject and the representable, of the sensing subject and that which can be felt. That which is represented is thus the sensed [thing] and that which is felt. Feeling is composed of the feeling subject and that which can be felt. That which can be felt is [composed of] the intuiting subject and the representable. That which is felt is thus the thing which is intuited and represented. Sensation is composed of the sensing subject and the sensible, of the representing subject and the intuitable – that which is sensed is thus that which is represented and intuited.

322. Representing subject, represented thing, representation, representable, representability, etc.

323. The intuiting subject *is* representable, as the representing subject is intuitable. The intuiting subject is, however, *eo ipso* the sensing subject – the representing subject is [*eo ipso*] the feeling subject.

Not the act, but rather the product, can be made fast.
Consequently sensation would be the representable – feeling [would be] the intuitable, representation [would be] the sensible – intuition, [would be] that which can be felt.

What is representable – is also represented – when the intuiting and representing subject is active.
The intuitable is intuited when the intuiting and representing subjects are active – feeling and sensation arise together.
The sensible is sensed when the feeling and sensing subjects are suffering – that which can be felt is felt when the feeling and sensing subjects are also suffering – Representation and intuition arise together.
It is part of the concept of activity to be *prior* to suffering – to be causality – just as it is part of the concept of suffering to be *subsequent*, and to be effectivity. Each is nothing without the other.

324. Attraction of universal and particular – of the actual things set in opposition to each other – in one respect different, in one [respect] alike – [attraction of] intuition and representation – and of sensing and feeling. On the power of attraction and drive.

325. Drive is activity of a certain sort – There are only drives in the representing and intuiting subjects as such – Passion is suffering of a certain sort.

> /Pull. Inclination. Pleasure. Desire. Wish. Propensity. Will./ positive negative lack. positive, negative existence./ affects/
> /That which gives must have a given, that which takes must have a taken.

/Imagination, for the intuiting subject, is the ability to represent – the power of representation is the ability to imagine. Sense of feeling is the capacity to sense – Sense of sensation is the capacity to feel. Imagination is transcendent, /outer/ power – and immanent, /inner/ ability – Power of representation [is] immanent power, inner power – transcendent/outer/ability. Thus sense of feeling is – outer sense and inner capacity. Sense of sensation – [is] inner sense and outer capacity.

326. /Drive to completion. If the sphere of a certain power expands in a certain way, then a drive necessarily arises. The striving of a power to become realized is drive. Drive arises out of the power of attraction, if it can be called "power," since [the power of attraction] is actually a positive lack. The power of attraction is *that strengthening of foreign power through*

the sublation of its own [power]./ The more [there is] negation of the one, the more [there is] affirmation of the other.
Activity arises out of power and object. *Power* of attraction arises out of sense or receptivity, in a way, and suffering arises out of state.

/Of activity and suffering, as object and state – i.e., determined object and state, which I otherwise called particular. likewise insofar as inner ability and representability and so forth stand in relation/
/Sense of feeling and sensation – capacity – power of attraction in a way – positive, negative suffering/
/Yielding, enduring./ Need/.

327. The sphere between state and object is the sphere of reality, or actuality in the strong sense.
Through (*in*) the intuition the sensing subject and that which can be felt become representable – It has the inner ability of the power of representation. The *essential* accident, the *nature* of the intuiting subject – has the faculty of representation.
In representing, the feeling subject and the sensible thing /that which can be sensed/ become intuitable. It has the outer power of intuition – the *essence* of the representing subject has the faculty of intuition.
/The *same* (identical) *operates* at the same time, it is, in operation, one thing – that which is posited in opposition is in *essence* one – is one being. 2 belong to being – 2 also [belong to] determining – consequently 4 [belong to] *determinate being.*/

*

328. In feeling the representing subject and the intuitable/what can be intuited/ become sensible.
This has the inner capacity of the sense of sensation. The *essence* of the feeling subject has the faculty of sensation.
In the sensing subject the intuiting subject and the representable become capable of being felt.
This has the outer capacity of the sense of feeling. The *essence* of the sensing subject has the ability to feel.

329. Power is everything *positive*. Drive is posited in opposition to sense. Meanwhile I will call weakness the negative.

/Every verb expresses drive and capacity, sense and ability at once./
/*Be – ver – ge – ent – er – zer – ein*/[8]

(Selfhood. State ["Zu*stand*"], object ["Gegen*stand*"].)[9] affected power.
eit. ung. en. iß. etc./[10]
Positive – comparative – superlative. / Time. Space. Freedom – necessity./
Negation is more than lack; it is the positing of that which is posited in opposition.
/Actuality arises from contingency and necessity./

330. On the concept of standing [*des Stehens*]. Stand [*Stand*][11] – represents and is. It is not what it represents, and does not represent what it is. The state [*Zustand*] stands for [literally: "to": *Zu*] and also against [*gegen*]. Thus too the object [*Gegenstand*] [stands for and also against].

/Difference between to represent and to represent something./

Intuiting and representing lie in the concept of standing. Stand feels insofar as it is; it senses, insofar as it represents. It feels inward, in relation to itself – it senses outward in relation to [an] other – It intuits in relation to itself – it represents in relation to [an] other – this is the *Stand* in *Gegenstand* [i.e., object]. In *Zustand* [i.e., state], everything is just the opposite.

331. The causality of feeling proceeds through representation. Causality of sensation [proceeds] through intuition. The effectivity of intuiting [proceeds] through representation – the effectivity of feeling [proceeds] through sensation.

332. Power is opposed to *heaviness*. Effectiveness [is opposed to] – dependence. Science [is opposed to] opinion. Rule [is opposed to] – chance.

[8] These are all German prefixes, and most are not translatable. They have the effect of changing their root words in particular ways that bear a family resemblance across the various words using that prefix. Novalis, as is typical, is freely playing with the prefixes, hoping to make some philosophical hay from them.

[9] Again, Novalis is drawing attention to the German language, and the fact that these terms have the same root: *Stand*.

[10] All German noun endings.

[11] I am translating the German *Stand* here with the English "stand," which is one of the German meanings, to help preserve the wordplay at work. It might be thought of in the sense of "to take a stand" on something.

Evil [is opposed to] good./ Negation *teaches* us nothing/ The coarse [*Masse*] [is opposed to] refinement. The body to spirit. The state to wildness – the constant to the changeable. The thing – freedom. Life – death. The impetus – the obstacle. Impenetrability [to] space – permanence [to] time. Ideal – caricature. Love – hate. Punishment – reward. Character in general – species in general.

333. From two things posited in opposition to each other – emerges the actually *real*.

334. One can only be punished to the extent that one can be instructed, and vice versa.

> /My promise corresponds to his obligation – his promise [to] my obligation./

335. Word – deed – sign – thing – image – essence.
Toward/for [*zu*] expresses a community [*Gemeinschaft*] – Against [*gegen*] [expresses] a disjunction. Thing in common [*Gemeine Sache*] – faction.

336. /Point of view/ World is that which, as it were, has arisen from object and state. God and world are again two things posited in opposition to each other. The product is the human being. The human being is composed of body and spirit. Both are *in a certain respect*, universal – world and God, [in a certain respect] particular – God and world.

337. Philosophy can be nothing but a factual contract – just as the state arises from an original contract – that is partially tacit, partially explicit, determined on the one hand by necessity, on the other by contingency.

338. Two things posited in opposition to each other have a similar and an opposite characteristic – and both are connected.
Property is opposed to magnitude. Number (a.) is the property of the magnitude (2) – relation (1) [is] the magnitude of the property (b.).

339. Equations.

340. Verb – Substantive – adjective – particle.

341. Determining and being – determinable – and having only seem to correspond. Determination to *existence*.

342. *Beistand. Widerstand. Vorstand. Anstand. Umstand./ Hinterstand Nebenstand. Mitstand. Abstand. /Verstand, Bestand. Entstand. Gestand. Erstand. Herstand. Hinstand. Einstand. /Zweifeln./*

[Standing by [help]. Standing against [resistance]. Standing at the head [directorate]. Standing upright [Propriety]. Circumstance. Standing behind. Standing next to [bystand(er)]. Standing with. Standing apart [Distance]. /Understanding, Standing through [withstanding]. Standing forth [arising]. Standing forward [confessing]. Stand forth [come into being]. Stand here. Stand there. Stand in [Entrance]. / *Doubt* [from the Latin *dubitare*: to waver; *dubius*: moving two ways].]

343. *Ground* and *cause*.

344. An explanation suffices when it characterizes its object.

345. Ground – cause – effect.
Thing – image – essence./ Quality./
Number – magnitude – equation.

346. In what must the science that I seek consist? It must contain the universal relations of the state and the object. It must be a representation of the utmost momentary fact.

> /The essence of the concept is representable in the sign of the perception / The feeling cannot be conceived – the perception cannot be sensed / i.e., not unmediated.

347. Singular. Kind – species. /Thing is determined to the determination./

348. The actions are always the same – but their state – object and province [*Bezirk*] are different.

349. Universal – particular – contingent.

350. The perceptions are tripled fourfold – and twofold.

351. Every number is opposed to the number next to it only immediately [in an unmediated way]. On numbers – the action of 2, is very different from the positing of one and 3.

352. Division of the faculties. What is science.

353. Essence. Property. /Nature. Art./ Species.

354. Immediate – everything mediate is twofold.

355. On the determination of ground and province.

356. To set asunder. To combine.

357. Science is that – representation of the essence and properties of one whole which is established in the sign – science can engage only in the universal and the collective.

358. Concepts qualify themselves – state and object – as foundations.

359. Science must arise from the positively free (1) and the negatively bound (2), and from the negatively free (3) and the positively bound (4).

360. Alone – with – against. /Relation/

361. 1 – is freedom. 2 – [is] cause (law) – 3 – [is] dependence (consequence). 4 [is] obedience.

362. Investigation of the concepts – positive – negative.

*

363. In German, negation can best be expressed with the word *Gegen* [against]. But all affirmation is negation and vice versa – consequently

one can associate everything[12] with the *Gegen* – and the *Zu* [to], which is the expression of affirmation. Except for a few speculative words these modes are rarely indicated verbally. With respect to the enduring, to the *ground*, almost everything retains its proper name.
The opposite can easily be found if the same and the opposite characteristic are merely reversed – and what was here essence, is there made into property, and what was here property is there [made] into essence/ even in the case of that which is combined./

/Ground and sub*stance* are one – but substance is usually used for the *withstanding* thing in general/, which can be in the state, object and ground./
Concept of the ground.

/Result – fact – product – synthesis –
fruit – consequence – effect – output – product – sum – settlement – It resulted in – finding – conclusion [*Schluß*] – end – corollary [*Folgesatz*] – total – final conclusion [*Endschluß*]. Resolution [*Beschluß*]. It was found; It was shown, Something came forth. Nothing came of it. Nothing was gained. /Reward, punishment/ / Earnings / Outcome. / Exit / Work. Deciding factor. Success. Winnings. Loss. *Receipt*.

364. Purpose lies in both opposites. The medium participates in both at once. Purpose consists of intention and goal.

365. Proposition [*Satz*] – opposite [*Gegensatz*] – conclusion [*Schlußsatz*].

Addition [*Zusatz*] – contradiction [*Gegensatz*] – principle [*Grundsatz*]

366. Intuition. Representation. Sensation. Feeling. Power – Sense. Capacity. Drive. Ability. Space. Time. Way of thinking. Division of the mind. Language. Abstraction.

[12] The original text reads "allein" – "only" – instead of "everything". Mähl suggests, rightly, it seems, that this is a slip of the pen on Novalis' part, and should read "allem."

367. Abstraction consists in thinking that which in and of itself cannot be thought – what can be thought only mediately, formally – only in the opposite [*Gegensatz*].

368. Intuition appears to consist in the power of intuition, out of the ability of the intuiting subject and the capacity of that which is intuited.

> The future, the present, the previous intuition.
> The possible, the necessary, the actual [intuition].
> The simple, the compound, the fractured [intuition].
> The inner, the outer [intuition], the [intuition] in sleeping and in waking.

369. Human being – consciousness.

370. Rhythmic power./ negative negation is a property of the positive affirmation just as negative affirmation is a property of positive negation. Being is determined out of causing and vice versa.
But all nouns that don't signify their adjectival properties through a particular suffix are true personifications; they have reality, and cannot be opposed to one, but must be opposed to both their parents.

> Thus with respect to their properties they arise from essences, in respect to their essences they arise from the properties of their parents. There are always two from both sexes, or one from both sexes.
> intentional contingency. Contingent intentionality.
> Accident and intent.

371. superfluous necessity – necessary superfluity.

Abundance and pressing *need*.

Free servitude – servile freedom.

Service and power of choice

Characteristic essence – essential characteristic.

Existence and nature.
Species and kind.
Thing and mode.

372. Where must I exit, where must I go and how must I proceed?

*　　　*

*

Group IV: 373–552 (March to early summer, 1796)

373. When I ask what a thing is, I am asking about its representation and intuition – *I* am wondering only about *myself*.

[374.] All *real strife* is appearance – hence is the question of idealism and realism so stupid, so *apparent*, but for that very reason so *Johannine*.

[375.] Inapplicability of a thing, of a concept, to *itself*. Insofar as I act, I am not acted upon – the divisor is not divided, and so forth.

376. Satisfaction – dissatisfaction. /Drive. Power. Movement. Ability/ Four kinds of objects – the thought, the felt, the represented and the unrepresented. *Quantity* yields *innumerability*, unending manifoldness – quality brings unity into chaos – consequences.

377. No *positive* punishment may be meted out, only negative – even in pedagogy – *original rights* may absolutely never be annulled.

378. Schiller begins from a fixed point in his investigations and of course he can thereafter never find other relations than the proportions from which he began his determinations. His idea of morality, etc.

379. Feeling is related to thinking as being is to representing.

380. Possibility of torture. /Only the *coward* is not immortal/

381. Have the *courage* to be virtuous and you will be.[1]

382. Schiller sketches too *distinctly* to be true to the eye, like Albrecht Dürer, not like Titian – too ideally to be *natural* in the *highest* sense.

383. To set – derivation from "to spring." Marvelously significant – Character of the transition from opposing thing [*Gegengesezten*] to thing posited over against [*Entgegengesezten*] – from extreme to extreme. This is also visible in the expression – to seat oneself – Passage from movement to rest.

384. Right – is only a relation of *continuity* – *interrupted* it ceases to be.

385. It is good that our language is *clumsy* – the strong force it and it forces the weak – in the first case the appearance of power is more visible, more beautiful – in the second, inability is more noticeable – and so the realm of beauty remains purer, more noble, more unadulterated.

386. As long as there are courageous people and cowards – there will still be nobility.

/Justification of hereditary nobility, [is] relative./

387. Duties to human beings – attention – *love* – yieldingness. What they *say* doesn't matter to you.

388. Equanimity – even in the most hopeless cases. for instance, as with Sophie.[2]

389. Religion – game – opinion – diversity – love – error – enthusiasm – supernaturalness.

390. To what extent can a philosophy be universally valid and effective?

391. Take care not to lose sight of the end in the means – the pure character of humanity – modest, reasonable human conduct.

[1] The original is in French: "Ayez le *courage* d'être vertueux, et vous le serez."
[2] Sophie's condition had worsened in March of 1796, when Novalis was writing these notes.

392. *Care for old age.*

393. One always opposes the law – and this is natural.

394. Scientists – rhapsodists, or free spirits.

395. Propensity – drive. /Human beings can become anything that they reflect upon, or that they resolve [to become]./

396. Where a person places his reality, what he *fixes upon*, that is his god, his world, his everything. Relativity of morality. /Love/ Our pedantic principles. /What *pleases* – what displeases us – what attracts us – what repels us – Reality of human fantasy and will. *Freedom* of self-determination of fate, etc. I must be interested in even that which is unpleasant to me in other people.

*

397. Physiognomy. That which is constant in each face – the tone of the face.

398. Intuition – fourfold – sensible – outer and inner – in dream and in representation___

399. Positive skepticism – it is more corporeal.

400. Declamation.

401. Application of that which is set in opposition against *par tout.*

402. Official and family circumstances – French – Letters – Work for me – Fine arts – conduit [cf. #501].

403. Heldegard. Woldemar. Allwill. Gallicism – Germanism.

404. Bidet. / *Prescription.*

405. Transitions in letters. *Portrait* – Collection of traits.

406. Acquaintance – representation – concept – cognition – science.

407. Practice slowness.

408. Intuition can only be placed in opposition to the intuiting subject and the intuited thing. i.e. to its ground.

409. Everything is capable of a universal and a particular opposition.

410. Intuition is posited in opposition to sensation. Sensation is the property of intuition, intuition the property of sensation.
So also feeling and representation. But together intuition and sensation and feeling and representation are essences. Feeling and representation are properties in the state – in the object, intuition and sensation [are properties].

411. Intuition is set in opposition to ground.

> /Every thing is only first opposed to something when it is that which it is only through a determinate being of the other. Thus the child is set in opposition to the *parents* and the son [is opposed to] the daughter.

412. Science is similar to a genealogical tree.

413. Genus. Species. Kind. Individual.

414. Don't *rebuke* anything human. Everything is good only not everywhere, not always, not for everyone. The same with criticism. In judging poems, for example, dissonance is more likely to be censured in every context than strictly *artistic failures*.
Indicating as precisely as possible the domain of each poem will be criticism enough of the author's mania. Because poems can only be judged in this regard: whether they want to have a wide or narrow, a near or remote, a murky or clear, a light or dark, sublime or humble position. Thus Schiller writes for a few, Goethe for many. Nowadays there is too little thought given to instructing the reader as to how the poem must be read – under what circumstances alone it can please. Every poem has its

relations to a variety of readers and numerous circumstances – It has its own surroundings, its own world, its own god.

415. Diary – without reflections – simple relation.
After the smallpox – letter to Auguste.[3] Revised [it] that day. Delivered by Z[edtwitz?] and they are bidden to participate sometime soon. Dictation practice. Hours with my siblings. Our archive.

416. On the alternation of the pleasant and the unpleasant in the world and in daily life.

417. Nice and slow.

418. Studies. Criticism of Schiller's M[usen]-Alm[anach].

419. Only the *abiding* is worth our whole attention – the continually useful.

420. One must be able to start and stop when one wants – or one must create a *will* for oneself. The will is always reasonable – and strong. If one only wills, then one can. But one has no stable will, or none at all, if one is and behaves unreasonably – and doesn't begin and end the book when it would be clever and good.

421. The state is a person, like the individual. What human beings are to themselves, the state is to the human being. States will remain diverse as long as human beings are diverse. In essence, the state, like the human being, is always the same.

422. The rule of right will cease with barbarism.

[423.] State [*Zustand*] and object together, what are they, really. World or nature.

424. How does the relationship change in action?

[3] This reference is to his younger siblings' contraction of smallpox toward the end of March, 1796. Cf. *Novalis: Schriften*, Vol. v, p. 383.

425. The world is set in opposition to its ground. The ground is the property of the world and the world is the property of the ground. God is ground and world together.

426. Ground and world run parallel to each other and divide completely equally. They are one – consequently also in the smallest part, in everything.

427. Ground consists of law and fact. that is, the essence of ground is law and fact – its property – [is] state and object. The essence of the world is state and object – its property is law and fact.

428. Where are concepts, essence and property?

429. That in whose province these concepts first arise cannot have essence and property, world and ground.

430. The derivation of god from genus.

431. Elements of worldly wisdom.

432. The world is the mother of properties – the father of essences is the ground.

/Material and form./

433. The singer, the poet, the listener and the reader. 2 dialogue. The listener should be called *Humanus*.
The reader consists of a girl, a student and 2 older people, a professor and a landed gentleman.

434. Plan and sense and presentation of an artwork, like a novel, a comedy, and other works of this sort.
Gotter, Thümmel and Wieland seem to me to be true writerly poets – poets for reading – Klopstock is a poet for declaiming, for music.

435. Poetry is for human beings what the chorus of the Greek theater is – conduct of the beautiful rhythmic soul – the voice accompanying our

developing self – entry into the land of beauty – ubiquitous light trace of the finger of humanity – free rule – victory over raw nature in every word – its wit is the expression of free, self-reliant activity – flight – humanization. Enlightenment – rhythm – art.

436. Property means the law of an original fact – a kind of spontaneity – An appearance, revelation of essence.

/indicate – to know – show – proof – to show [*zeigen*] – witness – to signify [*zeichen*] – *inferred* [*zogen*]./

[437.] Since everything is essence, what then is property? Because all activity is for the opposed thing, existence must be in the opposed thing. Essence is only visible in its property. The visibility must thus depend on the activity of the essence – it is only perceptible insofar as it is active. Everything that is perceptible must thus be active. The property of essence, its way of being active, is thus in the opposed thing – or outside – Thus an essence is only perceived outside the opposed thing and even then only its activity and mode are perceived.

/Activity is opposed to ground – it requires a ground, a province, a product, a means and an end – a goal, a product./

That which is opposed, however, is also an essence. It is not mere essence insofar as it is property – in order to be perceptible it must be active – but this must be a different kind of activity – from the first kind – as well as a different kind of perceptibility – It must necessarily be its opposite – because the activity and the perceptibility are essence and must have an opposite in order to be able to appear.

/There are two kinds of essence, two kinds of properties – which, however, belong inseparably together, because they follow from one another/

Spontaneity [is] a receptivity – Perceptibility [is] attentiveness [perceptiveness].
Thus the essence in which the opposite reveals itself or contains its property must be receptive and attentive. Attentiveness is another kind of perceptibility – in which perceptibility reveals itself – the property of perceptibility.

Receptivity is another kind of activity – in which activity reveals itself – the property of activity.
On the other hand activity and perceptibility are again properties of receptivity and attentiveness. They are thus distinguished by their directions. Activity proceeds outward from essence – Receptivity proceeds inward – Perceptibility is outside the essence – attentiveness is inside the essence. Activity and perceptibility are opposites in the one, receptivity and attentiveness [are opposites] in the other.
An essence is like everything. From this follows that every essence is – active and perceptible in the opposites – receptive and attentive. These are the properties of essence.

438. Activity is the original property of essence, being [is] the original essence of property.

> /Activity can only be revealed through being, being only through activity/

Property is thus being through original activity and activity through being.
/Only an *exposition* of essence is possible. Essence is absolutely not cognizable – Only properties are object and state. The properties of that which is in a state [*des Zustandhabenen*] are cognized in the object – the properties of that which is an object [*des Gegenstandseyenden*] [are cognized] in the state.
One is in a state and is an object. Being expresses the original *passive* relation, in that one stands against oneself. To have expresses the passive relation of essence to property. To be expresses an *essentiality*, to have [expresses] a relation of something that *comes* upon and adds to (*received*) (*contingent*).

> /Essential and necessary are almost synonymous – but the latter expresses still more relation – it is the more specialized usage./

/Peculiar. Reverse. [Counterpart [*Widerspiel*]]./
Essence cannot be known from the properties – <it can be perceived – it can be sensed – and its activity can be felt – but still only its properties> – It [essence] is, however, nothing without its properties – consequently we don't miss anything by the fact that essence cannot be known.

> How do we find the essence? and can't we determine essence through oppositions?

Only properties can be opposed to each other. Essence can only be determined negatively. It is that which no property is – it is thus always essence that has properties – it (essence) is the ground of *everything* – the ground of activity. Its determination is positive lack of all determination.
Determination is the province of properties. Negation [is] thus the province of essence.
We don't know anything about essence except that it is the opposite of property in general. But properties can only be determined through properties and indeed this happens only through seeking out those properties that are opposed to each other – because here we find the simple activity of the essence – that reveals itself in the opposite.
The opposite is itself a mode of the original property of essence – Consequently the essence cannot be discovered through positing in opposition.
Now we will have soon discovered – that essence, as we recognize and conceive it, is also only property – and the so-called essence is only the substrate of perception and sensation – just as the so-called property is also in the opposite of essence.

439. Positing in opposition is strictly unification in that both oppose each other through a third thing – but thereby become united in One consciousness – in that here their diverse essences become One essence – their diverse properties become one property. Thereby, however, a real difference between their essence and properties is sublated and only a contingent, changing one remains.

> /E.g. in one intuition essence and property alternate as they please – because the intuitable and the intuited can both become essence or property./

The product must be sought in the third thing between opposites.

440. Concept of essence – concept of property.
The *mere* essence is not knowable – the active essence, of course, [is knowable] through its properties. Every essence must have four original properties.

> Property is in fact only the appearance of essence in opposites – i.e. essence.
> Thus every property can be merged in an essence.

441. Essence – its relationship to genus, etc. It is the universal, the lasting – the I – the active thing – but not the agitated – the opposite of active – negative activity – Property is a kind of substantive – that usually arises from verbs – and the fact of properties is the verbs themselves. On the property that expresses the verb. /Property is state./
Ground – foundation – the constant – solid – fast – the absolute ground appears to be ground in general or all ground.

/All property, all essence, all ground appear to be relative./

The changeable, contingent, becoming – can only have to do with *properties* [cf. #462].

[442.] Nature of the will. /Now only the studies./

443. Orientation in the heavens. /Constituent. Numbers. Etymology of their names./

444. The necessity that we feel of assuming an objective existence is a natural appearance of the fact of opposition.
Every thing, every concept, consists of opposites. Power and capacity – subjective power and objective capacity belong to knowledge – to determinate knowledge, or to the form of knowledge, belongs the objective ability of the subject – and the subjective sense of the object.

/Form is the having of properties./

/Thing and property correspond better. Essence has no properties, as essence – and property, as such, [has] no essence, any more than material has form and form has material. Essence is the opposite of the having of properties – material is essence – form [is] the having of properties./

Properties and essence can only have a common ground, or province – a third thing that encompasses them and whose identity is constituted by their opposition. This is the secure thing that we seek – the synthesis – the genus, etc.

Their alternating relations.

A thing is that which consists of opposed activity – of material and for and of essence and the having of properties. The thing is only possible through the positing of an opposition.
Existence, as the character of the thing, is neither the having of properties nor essence – It is both at once. It is the ground of both – what makes both possible and actual and necessary.
/Positing [*setzen*] is the verb of *Gesetz* [law]. Law is [the] *property* of activity – All doing is a positing – i.e., insofar as it is known – everything known is *posited*. Positing is the character of knowable activity. Law expresses no influence on the material of activity, but rather only [expresses influence] on its form. Activity itself could only be a law of existence of which activity would be only a particular modification – but no law can contain a doing, rather, only a *determinate* doing – because all determinate doing is positing. Determinate activity posits – Determining is, however, a better word than positing, which has only its etymology – *Gesetz* [posit: *setzen*] to recommend it. A self-determining activity is nonsense – all determinate activity presupposes a lawfulness [*Gesetzheit*], something already at hand.
Activity, like everything else, consists in opposition in one thing and requires as a consequence such a thing opposite itself – in order to be something and according to the rules of opposition this has the constituents of activity only in a reciprocal relation – Material is here what form was, and form is there what was material.
All doing is therefore a determinate doing – All being a conscious being[4] – both lawlike – everything law – the form of fact.

445. Every thing, like every ground, is relative. It is a thing insofar as its opposite is a thing – They are neither one things insofar as they are in the common province of the ground – which is then a thing. Every thing is contained in a higher thing, or a further – more extensive and intensive thing –

> /extens[ivity] and intens[ivity] must actually be a product of a single action, like affirmation and negation/

Only the whole is *real* – A thing would only be absolutely real if it was not again *a constituent*.

[4] The ordinary German word for consciousness, *Bewußtsein*, literally means "conscious being."

The whole rests more or less – like a game in which people sit on each other's knees in a circular fashion without a chair.

> /State and object are the constituents of consciousness. They both consist of material and form./

The doctrine of state and object already belongs in the theory of consciousness. But here we must seek out first the laws and facts that lie in the universal.
However, here we are classifying theory in general. This can only mean that we are investigating how in general the human spirit goes to work on theory – we observe its positing activity without regard to a determinate content – although of course [we observe it] in relation to the determinate content and even one determinate content in general.
But how then do we experience what a theory is? It must be the doctrine of the laws of a thing. The beginning must provide the definition of a thing. But definition without laws? How is that possible beforehand [*anticipando*]? How then does one even begin? Doubtless, with a separation. But still something must be given that is fixed, distinguishing – if it has something differentiating about it – consequently, through its being found among several things. It must have something in common with its context – at least its recognizable existence, but also something characteristic. The most complete knowledge of an object is when it can be determinately distinguished from everything else. Distinguishing requires, as we know, a common and a differentiating characteristic – Inasmuch as I become acquainted with a single thing, I thus become acquainted with all things – when I perform this action – I expand by consciousness, since I attach something new to it. Every cognition is thus differentiation [*Unterscheidung*] and relation / Expansion, structuration, augmentation/ in a double respect – once in an objective and once in a subjective respect – in the former there is a separation of property and a union of essence – in the latter there is a separation, as thing, and a union, as property. All four, however, in different respects. In the separation of properties, the separation of things and constituents is presupposed – the property of that which is to be distinguished is established in the union of essentialities, which precedes the separation

/quality – structure/

of properties, the plurality of things and constituents is likewise presupposed – It is only a relation to their common province – to their thingness and identity. The separation, as thing, refers to (concerns) the knowing subject and the thing known – the union, as appurtenance, refers to the identical consciousness, to the receptive consciousness.

446. All property refers to property and consequently to common essentiality.

*

447. Structure	Thing
Essence – Kind or way lat[in?]	Substance – Accident
Form, or character, property	

448. /Essent*iality* is nonsense./
Thing – structure – essence – properties.

449. A whole must consist of several [parts] – a universal [must consist] of particulars – on the other hand the universal is in several – the particular in one.

That which is in common is quantitatively different, and qualitatively identical. The particular is qualitatively different and quantitatively identical – totality contains both.

How does a thing contain its opposite?

/Theory/

/An essence refers to various properties. A property refers to various essences – the former according to quality, the latter according to quantity./

(Names.) Characteristic. Species. Independent. Appearance. Concrete. Abstract. Property is the universal of one kind. Essence is the universal of the other kind – thus also there are two different particulars.

On the concept of universal and particular.

Community – personal property. Commonality – peculiarity.

/Same – different. Together – particular. Opposite concept of the adjective particular/

Investigation of the concept of universal. /singular is the opposite concept/

450. Peculiar property – peculiar essence.
common property – common essence.

Property and essence already originally contain a universal and a particular constituent. A common being and a singular being lies in both.
These must necessarily be of different kinds.
The common constituent of property will be extent [*Umfang*] without boundaries – [the common constituent] of the peculiar [will be] boundaries without contents.
The common constituent of essence will be content without extent – [the common constituent] of the peculiar [will be] content without determinate extent.

Mere extent – bounded extent.
Mere content – determinate content.
Property without essence – mere property.

Property of essence in general – Property in general of essence in general	} determinate property

Essence without property – mere essence.

Essence with property in general – Essence in general with property in general	} determinate essence

There is a qualitative common and peculiar – and a quantitative common and peculiar.
We must attempt to investigate these concepts – but in so doing pay close attention to the third activity, the active, positing ground.
<Mere essence and property can also be considered as the *known* essence and property, in a quantitative and qualitative respect.>
The expression "like" is [considered in] a quantitative sense – "common" [is considered] in a qualitative sense.
Essence and property are concepts of quality – Now we are considering them within the province of quantity.

/Whole and parts/
/partial whole/

/What is fixed is a concept of relation – [something is] fixed only through something that is changing – as the changing is so only through a fixed thing. All change is *exchange*.
/What is constant (mere change) – qualitative – quantitative change
/Relation/
/The quantum – the qualitative – the changing quantum./
/The structure or the thing – the changing thing – the quantitative thing./
/As many facts as actual categories/

451. /Relation is the quantity term/
/The fixing [activity] of *Fingo* [I make].

Sphere	—	Relation	—	Change
/ \		/ \		/ \
Essence – property	—	Whole Part		*Cause* *Effect.*
				(state) (object)

452. I believe I have exhibited the original fact-propositions [*Thatsätze*][5] – by means of which it will now be possible for us to proceed with more assurance. They are the last products of abstraction.
Why just these and no others? That is a question that is no question – and whose ground will be developed later.

Because it is so, so is it so.

453. Genus – species – kind. State – object – /Come into the province of the thing – of relation and of change – the modifications of the mind – the properties of the soul. Spirit has sense. Matter has soul. In feeling, intuitions, etc., matter or spirit can be unity – essence at will. Both are unity – both are manifoldness in different ways.

/God and world – like matter and spirit./
(*alternating foundation.*)

[5] Here Novalis is referring obliquely to Fichte's neologism *Tathandlung* or literally "deed-act" (Breazeale translates it simply as "act"). Fichte argues that the originary act of positing is a *Tathandlung* since its occurrence is a given fact (it happens "in der Tat" – or "indeed"). Novalis wants to introduce the idea of a *Tatsatz* or literally, a "deed-proposition," a proposition that occurs as something already given.

/A thing is a thing, or a thing arises, only through crossing over into another sphere./

/The concept of counting refers only to simple being – it is a simple fixing of this simple state. 0 is only the sphere of number – the numbers themselves are the content. Without 0 no number is possible./

On the fact-propositions.

The substrate of every cognition constitutes thing, relation and change. These fact-propositions are expressions of that which always happens in cognizing, how it happens and *what* happens or arises.

454. Being expresses no absolute structure at all – but only a relation of the essence to a property in general – a capacity for being determined. It is an absolute relation. Nothing in the world *is merely* anything; Being does not express identity. One knows nothing of a thing if one knows only that it *is* – in actual understanding. Being in the ordinary sense expresses the properties and relations and the change of an object. Being stands in relation to properties. Thus it *is* no Thing further for us than the totality [*Inbegriff*] of the properties known by us. A thing can have more or less being – *Only the All is absolute*. We ourselves only *are* insofar as we know ourselves. The identity judgments are parallelisms – They teach nothing new – and nothing is in them except the pure form of judgment, without matter – It is an attribution without attribution – activity without product.

455. We thus say nothing at all about a thing when we say: it is. Being expresses only, as was said, that which is already merely at hand – the known in a universal form. I am – means I find myself in a universal relation, or *I change* – It is part of change in general without an opposite – an exposing to all possible use, to original thoughts[.] Refrain – repetition – expression of mere activity without object and content – first *play* –

456. Being expresses a permanence of positing, of change, of activity, of the productive action – and it is a mere concept of *presence*. In the temporal world being is a rhythmical relation. Being literally expresses the active and passive character of the exchange between the *positing* and the *positable*, [between] *sphere* and *content*.

457. Fixing one's attention on the expression: I am or he is – should produce a concept of a prototype [*Inbegriff*] – the intuition of a prototype – It should fix the mind on an individual thing. Reason thereby fixes a manifold in a unity – [reason] signifies a certain combination with this concept – *to a possible end.*

458. Person for *thing.*

459. On the verb "to have."

460. All philosophy is only explanation of that which is there – the putting together of that which belongs together – separating of that which is different – exhibition of the pure thing, of true relation, of actual change.

461. If someone were to ask me why the sun comes up every morning, and I answered him, because the earth turns on its axis in a certain period of time – then I must presuppose familiar perceptions of space on his part. I show him the application of a *familiar thing* to an unfamiliar one – I combine a subjective state of his with an objective one – I add something to the store of his knowledge. All wisdom thus consists in the application of a familiar thing to an unfamiliar one – insertion of a *suitable* thing to *what it suits.*

> We know only insofar as we have, and vice versa.
>
> /Activity in a sphere is a spheric activity or an active sphere. All change in the determined [is] doubly determined / Affirmation and negation./ We only know what is, and there is only what we know – because it is the same – one power, etc./

Neither of them is the first or the second.

*

462. We can find the capacity of cognizing being in the individual – where there is a cognition – there is also a being. We cannot develop anything about the cessation of being and cognition based on changes in this individual. As genus we do not cease to be, but only as individual. Cognition

is a universal state that is not bound to a single case. When we speak of us, we are speaking of the genus and the individual. Our I is genus and individual – universal and particular. The contingent or individual form of our I does not cease to be only for the individual form – death only puts an end to *egoism*. The individual form remains only for the whole, insofar as it became a universal. We speak of the I – as one, and it is in fact two, that are thoroughly different – but absolute correlates. The contingent must disappear, the good must remain. The contingent was contingent, the essential remains essential.

What you really love remains with you.

One does not know what one wants if one wants to fix on the contingent – about *love*.

/*One wants* the contingent *contingently*./

The universal of every moment remains, because it is in the whole. In every moment, in every appearance, the whole is operating. Humanity, the eternal, is ubiquitous – because it knows neither time nor space – we are, we live, we believe [*denken*] in God, because this is the personified genus.
It is not a universal in our sense, a particular. Can you say it is here, or there?
It is all, it is *over all* [*überall*: everywhere]; In whom we live, breathe and have our being.
All reverence endures forever – all truth – everything personal.

463. Where there is a being there must also be a knowing.

464. /Feeling and perceiving relate to being; representation and sensation [relate] to knowing – but only in the

Individual./

Every individual consists of heterogeneous constituents.

/All inquiry can only touch the individual – and the universal that we display is part of a collective universal, or it is the expressions of the genus, of the whole in the individual/.

All of the theory must be given completely – philosophy can do nothing but order. Imagination supplies the materials to judgment for lingering in unknown lands, but in order to deliver actual materials, not figments, [imagination] must be *rational* – which it can be in countless different degrees – it has to do with its *pure* self-activity. The purer the imagination, the truer it will be.

465. What kind of theory am I looking for? I am looking for that in us which takes itself to be ordering – to be bringing the changes in us under laws in order to construct an intuitive and conceptual whole out of it, according to which I can order my inner appearance, and clarify for myself *one* schema.
A schema contains the spheres of a content that is determined with respect to its *nature* but not actually given – and the alternating engagement of these spheres with each other in order to yield a *universally* determined product. The genera must also be known already. The schema only simplifies the treatment of an *individual case*, because it teaches me to apply the *universal* laws of the genus of these cases, and thus saves me the trouble of repeatedly seeking out the laws for this case.

466. All learning is a joining to – a becoming acquainted with – an enlargement – a quantitive action.
We learn nothing new from simple quality, quantity and relation. We are born with simple quality, quantity and relation – i.e., with compartments without contents. However, they are absolute correlates – They want to be filled – They are nothing without content – They have a drive to be, consequently to have content, because they exist only insofar as they have content, actually.
Our mind is schematic throughout. More precisely examined, all our concepts are generic concepts.

/Relation is being affected by a sphere./

The individual is only genus in certain relations, isolated through an objective and subjective action. The genus is that in it which is universally determining, otherwise we would not know which genus predominates – the genus is what sets the tone. This must be what is peculiar to the genus – the law of its existence – this can only be absolutely one, because otherwise it would be property [*Eigenschaft*] – the genus would be determined

through another genus – because all plurality is the product of several spheres.
But is there a genus that would be such a strict genus?
When we speak of genus, we understand by that: A common fundamental character – but we do not find genera always contained again in more comprehensive ones – every genus becomes kind – the genus that seems to be the highest to us is thing – but is this really a genus. Representation is still higher than thing. But all genus is representation.
In order to find the laws of genus at all, we must come to know representation better.
If everything consists of genera that simply limit and contain each other alternately, then knowledge of representation must lead us in the right direction and thoroughly introduce us to the essence and the properties of genera.

/Property expresses nothing but the relations of a sphere to another. Property has no essence, essence has no properties – sphere has essence, sphere has properties./

/Sphere and genus are one./

In what does representation consist? All genus arises in it – consequently it cannot itself be genus or kind – that would be a transcendent extension of an immanent law – a form outside its sphere – a genus outside genus – A sphere first arises here, thus it must be something other than sphere. If it were the highest genus, however – the genus of genera, or the actually absolute genus, since the others are only kinds, then at least its original basis must lie in something other than in something contained in it or subsumed under its laws. It would be the most universal of the universal, its law would thus be active everywhere – It would combine the whole into one – It would contain the schematic law of everything – Everything would be an individual case in its realm. But an individual case could not indeed be possible in the highest genus? Then how is it to be distinguished? It is in fact only one, and one cannot be two. We still really know absolutely nothing about the origin of genus – what sort of unity it arises from.
In the end, indeed, every genus necessarily presupposes a more comprehensive thing – a space – and if that is so, then a highest genus is just a nonentity. The universal presupposes the individual, the individual presupposes the universal – the concept of genus, kind and the individual

has only a regulative, classificatory use – no reality in itself, because otherwise it would be unending. We must not pursue the idea, otherwise we will end in the spaces of nonsense. Every regulative idea applies to the eternal – but it contains no independent relation to an actual thing – An eternity, a ray of sun, can be incorporated within it – It remains always the same – because it is entirely beyond the sphere of the actual – of that which is actually the case. It is a law of representation – a schematic concept.

467. Genus is the sphere of a mental action – interaction of the determining and the co-determining on the determinable to produce a determined [thing].
Occurrence of this action as cause is origin of the concept of essence in actuality – [occurrence of this action] as effect [is] origin of the concept of property. Genus is both together.
This action can occur in countless modifications – as action and as product.

468. The common sphere of opposed concepts is the sphere of their common product – if things want to affect each other – i.e., reciprocally influence each other, they must have a common sphere – in this [sphere] the properties are also determined.

/Essence is what is excluded by form and vice versa./

469. Can I seek a schema for myself, since I am the schematizer?

470. The Categories contain the original properties of genus in general and are always available – only not as object – but as subject – form and matter of the object and context of everything.

Quantitative – relative – qualitative and modal.
/Quantity is the form of content.
Quality [is] the matter of content.
Relation – the form of interaction.
Modality – the matter of interaction./

The possible is the product of the efficacy of a determining thing – The actual is the product of both determining things. The necessary is a double product depending on how the constraints of the universal and the particular differ. Actual – necessitated *possibly actual* (modus) – Possibly necessitated actual, *possible* (modus) – The former is an absolute presupposition – where a common effect exists, a particular activity must have taken place – The latter is a relative presupposition, a mere relation – a mere efficacy of the thinking determining subject – a particular efficacy is possible without a common consequence or cause.

/There must be an effecting and a counter-effecting in the common efficacy – two positive opposites/

We are a product of the genus and the individual – we are often affected only by the former, often only by the latter – usually by both. We are their middle sphere – their common relation – their *realizable*. With respect to procedure what they have in common is the actions of the Categories.

What then is the individual?

The I is that which is determinable between the genus and the individual.

471. Formal – and material laws of thought.

/Thought is the *other half* of being for us / just as being is the other half of thinking/

The subject is presupposed in all consciousness – it is the absolute active state of consciousness. However, it is not prior to consciousness, but rather with consciousness – nevertheless [it is] the common outer sphere – the universal scene – space. /It is thus no more an absolute subject than it is an absolute space./

/action – act – /fact/ –/

472. Reason is the simplifier –

/Simple./

It has a feeling of quantity – a feeling of quality, relation and modality. Each affects us through its opposite – consequently through ourselves – when we are the universal opposite – the affected must also be the affecting thing. A thing thus affects in virtue of its original properties – Its properties of this sort are, however, only the common products of the

thing in itself and of the subject – since, however, each is active only in the opposite – so the subject is active insofar as it is a thing – the thing is active insofar as it is subject. Every state, every fact-act [*Tathandlung*] presupposes another – It is the same as with genus – all quest for the first [action] is nonsense – it is a *regulative idea*.
We cannot measure the content of reason by its form, or its form by its content – both are unending – and philosophy can never be
primal history, but rather
must be, and remain, the law of unmediated existence – because it is nothing more. It may not pursue its ideas, but only represent them.

/Sphere has its content from form, its form from content. It can thus be determined – i.e., one can speak of its content and of its form – [sphere] is a *pure* determinable./

We find throughout an *available* and an *emergent* – the available must, however, be twofold. /In actuality there is no becoming thing, no past thing, but only a present – that is, an available thing.

473. Imagination – understanding – both [are] in the sphere of reason.

474. /If these were the *spheres* of reason, and the Categories the form of reason, then all that would be left for us to seek out would be their content, if it is not already contained in the Categories./

The Categories contain the relation of both spheres and their relation to reason.

475. Form is sphere – It lies between the universal content and the particular. *Both emerge* through it; because they are only relative concepts.

476. The act of representing is a free action. It consists of the universal representing subject and of the particular representing subject and its *form* –.
All efficacy, self-activity, is free. Reason is also free. The characteristic of *humanity* is *reason* – It wants a content, regardless of what kind – It is the determiner of content in general, i.e., of all content. Reason is universal sphere. In it everything advances – consequently also in its forms.

What do we mean by the representing subject? The scene of representation, or its cause – but cause is only a regulative concept, an idea of reason – it would thus be foolish to attribute real efficacy to it. We are thus looking for a non-thing. Representation is a determined thing in our sphere. From all of this we can easily gather that also even our so-called "I" can be represented – because representation is free – and can contain everything that is given. Thinking does not belong to genus – Such and such a thought is mere property of the individual.
The I is absolutely united in 2 absolutely divided parts – but as such it is representable and therefore we can represent reason for ourselves, in a certain way, because all opposition can be thought. Because *everything* is an opposite, *everything* can be thought.

477. We think of the representation too much as a representing subject, as active, i.e., in motion, causal – because this is only an *idea*. We can indeed represent the representation "I" – because since there everything is representation, a representation can indeed become material of another representation.

/This must of course still be cast in another language./

/Character of the individual/

478. The person[s] of the verb – I, you, he, etc. are the substrate of essentiality in the judgment – to which something should and can be attributed. The predicate is either contained in the verb, a simple, or a compound.
I is an expression of the singular, which <has representations> judges. /Difference between representing, being a representation, having a representation./ The word "to represent" does not qualify as a generic word for the product of thought. "To judge" is better. To represent is not an active verb, but is neutral – To represent is not an action – not a relational [concept], but rather only a concept of quality. "It represents" expresses a meaning – either a reproduction of form – or an arbitrary [act of] being posited for an other thing.

/Nature of the verb./

The I is only, as with everything, in its sphere, I or the somewhat I [*das Etwas Ich*].

Everything operates its essence for itself – cause, influence, relation – are only ideas – There is nothing real behind them – they are ideal *actions*.

479. Representation – genus – *concepts in general* are nothing real – they have only an ideal use. Hence also I, etc. is a regulative idea.

The whole of philosophy is only a science of reason – only of regulative use – exclusively ideal – without the slightest reality in the actual sense.

480. Reason itself is only an ordering idea.

/but what then is the use, the practical influence, of philosophy?/

481. Knowing – its use by Luther. /Instinct, *drive*, bees, etc. Art/

What is reality? and which reality does the doctrine of reason have – Overall, to what [does] knowing belong.

/Metaphysics of morals – e.g., about greeting/

482. Willing – better – worse – property – character.

483. Naive and sentimental[6] – objective – subjective.
The parents are more naive – so also the ancients.

484. I am too much on the surface – not a still, inner life – kernel – of working from an inner, middle point outward – but rather on the surface – zigzagging – horizontally – unstable and without character – play – accident – no lawlike effect – trace of independence – expression of *one* essence.

485. Crooked line – victory of free nature over the rule.

486. Concept of language – grammar.

487. 0 is the positive non-determination. Infinity – the negative determination in general. X or the name – also negative determination in general.

[6] A reference to Schiller's essay of 1795–1796: "On Naive and Sentimental Poetry."

488. Inner hearing – like inner vision.

489. One must exercise all his powers and develop them regularly – imagination – like reason – judgment, etc. I am now developing reason, and it also deserves to be first – since it teaches us to find the way.

Religion – Jesus, etc.

490. Science is only one half. Faith is the other.

491. We should simply become acquainted with the matter of spirit and the spirit of matter.

492. Reason and fantasy is religion –
reason and understanding is science.

493. What is faith?

494. Everything – cosmos.

495. Is language indispensable to thought.

496. Theory will never be able to determine whether virtue or vice is preferable – It can only order – exhibit forms of thought.

497. Acting in accordance with principles is not valuable for the sake of the principles, but for the structure of the soul which presupposes it. Whoever can act on principles must be a valuable man [*Mann*] – but his principles do not make him valuable, only that which he makes of them – concepts of his actual conduct – forms of thought of his being.

498. Practical reason is pure imagination.

499. Concepts, words *influence the opposite* – whence the power of words and their value.

500. Where there are many words there must also be many transactions – like the circulation of money.

501. Now I can do nothing better than to finish the studies and work leisurely on French. 2–3 hours every day must bear fruit eventually. Also, before finishing the Studies I cannot think properly about other sciences or even take on occupations. My spirit will gain much from the study of the French language, since I will become more informed, more *skillful*, and richer in phrases. The more *peacefully* and *freely* I will work, the more secure and uniform my style must become.
Studies – French – Fine arts – Letters – Officialia – official readings.

502. I – has, perhaps, like all ideas of reason merely regulative, classificatory use – Nothing at all in relation to reality.

What is reality?

/Space and time in the common sphere (modality) arise from quality and quantity according to the laws of change/

503. Faith is sensation of knowledge – representation [is] knowledge of sensation. Thoughts – thinking – is what is predominant in knowledge – as feeling [is predominant] in faith.

Idea, Concept	–	Feeling, Sensation
Thought		Feeling

504. Why must everything I do now be so *painful* – nothing peaceful – at leisure – calm –

505. One can also fulfill one's vocation without philosophy, if one lives in accordance with what the wisest and best did and taught, and makes experience and common sense[7] his guide. With both plus industry one can rally oneself to all life's tasks and not be without resources. The pure feeling of the nature of the thing – this is what is called healthy human understanding – and this is indispensable even to the scholar, the scientific architect. Practice can make it easier to use – and genuine life force unconstrained by opinions, etc., keeps it pure. /Its development is slow – its existence sudden./

[7] *Gesunden Menschenverstand*: literally, "healthy human understanding."

One will never lose the way if one attends to the universal in us and around us. By universal we mean here the universal of reason – thence the necessary respect for *universal morality*, the voice of the people, etc. – the enduring in us – the consequence insofar as it is not a *particular* (not rational) one – (the *final* consequence).

506. The science /idea of *the* whole or of *a* whole. /difference between "the" and "a(n)."// and a science. /The I – One I/

507. Reason and individual in harmonic activity – is life force. Theory of *life force*.

508. To what extent do we never reach the ideal? Insofar as it would annihilate itself. In order to have the effect of an ideal, it may not stand in the sphere of ordinary *reality*. The nobility of the I consists in free elevation above itself – consequently the I can in a certain respect never be elevated absolutely – because then its efficacy, its enjoyment, i.e., its triumph – in short the I itself would cease to exist. Vice is an eternally escalating torment (negation) (feeling of powerlessness) – dependence upon the involuntary – Virtue [is] an eternally escalating enjoyment – affirmation – feeling *of power* – independence from the contingent. Just as the vicious, because of its *identity* can never lack opportunities to be virtuous – so virtue never lacks opportunity – the quantity of duration has no influence on worth – were viciousness to gain victory to the thousandth degree below 0, it would be *worth* the same as the virtuous battling to triumph to the thousandth degree above 0. A moment can run through the space or time that divides them – because here there are no relations of quantity – They are two absolutely separated spheres that we, however, represent to ourselves quantitatively – and every triumph and every defeat is imagined as a step forward or a step back. Habit is a relief for the good and an impediment for the evil – and herein lies the difference of longer and shorter – the punishment of the persistently evil person – the reward of the persistently virtuous one.

509. Judgment presupposes a law and a given case.

510. Man must control his nature and secure right and mastery for the *individual* in himself – mastery of the will is proper to him – and the

submission of sensation. Woman must obey nature – constrain her individuality – her sensation must determine her will. In the former sensation is the servant, in the latter, the will [is the servant] – She must have a subordinated will, he must have a subordinated sensation. (He simplifies the universal, she universalizes the singular.) He and she both serve reason – He is the ideal of content – She is the soul of form. Both have the universal and particular of a different kind – His individuality and her universality both have a singular root – and so also his universality and her individuality.

511. Preservation of individuality – preservation of the genus – these are their natural purposes in procreation. The first, the feminine, the other, the masculine.
The satisfaction of this drive on his side, or his enjoyment, takes the form of the triumph of his drive, his power over the opposite, the attractive. Her enjoyment consists in the nursing of her longing, her needs, through a *feeling* of power, not a sensation of power./ She wills, but her sensation resists and can only be suspended momentarily by an alien power.
He senses – but does not will – and his will can only be momentarily suspended through an alien yieldingness.

512. In every analysis of a concept it is still only a concept that we take apart, and yet a concept arises out of two opposed genera. A concept, like all progeny, is not an aggregate of its parents, but an independent being, like one of its parents.

On *Neutra*

513. The peculiar sphere of genus is the species, or the individual. It exists only through the latter.

514. The original of that which is conceived is lacking in the concept.

515. The totality of reason makes up, as it were, the body of the determined concept – Its remaining determined universalities. All properties of an object are *ideally* really at hand a priori – this determined existence, however, does not depend on the subject. The matter of the properties is at hand in reason. Their form in nature. The matter of the essence is thus in nature, the form of it is contained in reason.

516. Sphere – form – matter – these are the three fundamental concepts from which everything is formed, or better, of which everything consists. These are constantly together – related inseparably.
In what way are the Categories always together?

517. "Sphere" can perhaps be translated by "concept."

518. Science consists of form, matter and sphere. Form consists of the form of being and the form of thought – Matter [consists] of the matter of being and the matter of thought. Sphere is the human being. The being of science is only a knowable being and a knowable thought – theoretical being, theoretical thought – Being in the no-longer-being – Thought in the no-longer-thought, or – Being, as concept, thought, as image – both held fast in the third, in the *imagining subject* – in the imagination – whose identical matter is the two forms of being and thought, whose identical form is the two matters of being and of thought.

519. The man obeys himself as object – the woman as subject. The man must transform his sensations into concepts, the woman her concepts into sensations.
The concept does not deceive him, sensation does not deceive her.

520. Merriment and good mood.

521. *Art* – science – handicraft – play – nature – genius.
Knowing how. ability. knowing that. to know. to make. /to cause *a thing*[8]/ conceive. understand. insight. grasp.

522. The concept is as much a thing as intuition. But no thing is in itself knowable – therefore –

523. The faculty of knowledge is also not knowable as a thing in itself.

524. Being does not correspond to property. Substance and accident are clearer expressions of the actual meaning.

[8] *Verursachen*: The German word actually contains the root *Sache* – "thing."

525. On love.

526. Definition – contains the *objective concept* of the thing.

527. In order to determine an intuition, etc., the subject must be anticipated – or the subjective structure of the thing gives us the order. We determine concepts through their objective structure – we premise its universal being, i.e., its independent being, and order it thereafter.

528. In the concept, the subject is the sphere of accidents. In the *thing*, the object is the sphere of contingencies.

529. Probably all *universal* concepts are limited in this way – namely, like object and subject, by the application of their faculty of determination.

530. On inner sense.

531. There is a *free* (causal) *content* and a *free* (causal) *form* – and a *free* (causal) *sphere* – and also a bound, dependent form – sphere and matter.

532. Closer investigation of the Categories.

533. As cause – effect – as effect – cause. /The caused, as independent – the causal as independent – the caused as dependent (dependent on an alien cause), the cause as dependent (dependent on an alien cause).

534. On *left* and *right*.

535. One must already essentially have the concept in mind – that one is supposed to be learning.

536. Uncertainty is the source of all error. Sphere of absolute certainty is God in the proper sense – or the common sphere of object and subject. Sphere of relative *certainty*, or of knowledge, our I.

> /This relative certainty – is relative to its accidents – absolute with respect to its substance. as absolute it is caused, as relative it is causal./

537. If a thing is determined in the whole, then it is also determined in the individual.

538. In *all* and *everything* there are 2 absolute and relative opposite spheres. Through them all determinations are given. Both together constitute one sphere – They determine themselves through reciprocal self-determination.

539. Matter – form – and sphere of science. Sphere is subject – matter and form are object. The former is thus subjectivity of the object – the latter is objectivity of the subject.

/Subject and object exchange in the sphere of consciousness/

540. Science contains the propositions according to which the subject can obtain representations from the object.

541. (Representation) Intuition and concept together make idea. An ideal quale, quantum and relatum make up the whole of a science.

542. The science of science is a very subaltern science – because it is a very determined one.

543. Thought – feeling, etc. are states. /Memory and imagination/

/Object – state./

544. Which objects are actually scientific? or what in a science is actually science?
Proper, firm determination of the concept of science – difference between it and description – knowledge – insight – experience.

545. One must not seek *one's own* legitimation in the world.

546. On *religion*.

547. Purpose – Determination of determination.

548. Consciousness – necessary medium of change.

549. The greater the extension of the concept, the smaller its content. /The genus is in the kind, and the kind is completely contained in the individual – precisely the opposite of the universal of nature./

550. Existence – inherence [*Insistenz*] or subsistence.

551. Can a real name be given to the absolute opposite in general?

552. *Objective* – *subjective* reason. /Modality – relations to the cause./ a priori – relation – *relatio* – quantity and relation – form – quality and modality – matter. /Concept of disjunction. /Discursive unity./ Extensive, intensive quantity.

*   *

*

Group v: 553–568 (summer, 1796)

REMARKS ON THE *WISSENSCHAFTSLEHRE*

553.1. Difference between fact and fact-act, page 4.
p. 5,[1] a is a – seems to me to be nothing but a repetition of the bringing forth of the a to being. It can express a strengthening. No connotations are involved, and it qualifies therefore as a logical copula. Often such an identity judgment expresses a sharpened distinction – a sharp attention to the peculiar character of that which is in danger of being confused with something else. The sphere a is determined through the sphere a. a is the name of an unknown sphere. The first a is a characteristic posited, the second a is an essential posited – the former is presupposed, the latter is posited. The concept a is set in opposition to the a that is available.
Their common sphere, their scene, is the I – the subject. The first a is already available in the I – the other also – They are only connected.

> /These reflections on this simple proposition must deliver to us the foundations of all philosophy/

a is a emerges from predication of the *simple*; simply on account of quantity, quality, relation, modality or their composites.

*

[1] Reference is to Fichte's *Grundlage der gesammten Wissenschaftslehre, als Handschrift für seine Zuhörer* (Leipzig: Chr. E. Gabler, 1794).

554. All explanation must begin with a fact. But from which fact must all explanation proceed? It must be a fact that lies at the basis of all other facts and needs no further explanation, but rather itself first makes possible all explanation. The explanation thus proceeds from the fact of all facts, or from the single original fact. It must be inexplicable, that is, its complete concept must be given with it. It is its concept – its concept is it. It is explained insofar as it is, and is insofar as it is explained. The law of every appearance must be contained within it – It gives the unity of all knowledge – Everything must be deduced from it. It gives the certainty of all certainty – absolute certainty. The point is simply that everything leads back to it. Its relationships to the unending body of the known are the unity for which our theoretical reason strives.

555. [The] Law of the concept and [the] law of the object must be identical – only separable in reflection -/Concept and intuition are identical when referred to the I, separate when one reflects upon both without referring them to the I./ If I reflect specifically upon the I, then there is no Not-I – if I reflect without reflecting specifically upon the I, then there is a Not-I. *Free reflection* is about the Not-I – *determinate* reflection is about the I. In both cases the I is free and unfree, only in different ways. It is free in that it reflects upon itself as unfree, as a Not-I. It is free in that it reflects upon itself as free, as an I. In the former it is free as intelligence, in the latter as pure I. In the former it separates its reflecting activity from its being – it goes outside itself – in the latter it unites both [reflecting activity and its being] – it goes into itself. It must do the first in order to be able to do the other. The last is the end, the first is the means – the end occasions the means. The means effects the end. /All knowledge should produce morality – the moral drive, the drive toward freedom occasion knowledge./ To be free is the tendency of the I – the capacity to be free is the productive imagination. – *Harmony* is the condition of its activity – *of* [*its*] *oscillating*, between opposites. Being one with yourself is thus the fundamental condition of the highest end – to Be, or to be free. All being, being in general, is nothing but being free – *oscillating* between extremes that necessarily are to be united and necessarily are to be separated. All reality radiates from this light-point of oscillation – everything is contained in it – object and subject have their being through it, not it through them. I-ness or productive power of

imagination, the *oscillating* – determine, produce the extremes between which oscillation occurs – This is a deception, but only in the realm of ordinary understanding. Otherwise it is something thoroughly real, because the oscillating, its cause, is the source, the mother of all reality, [is] reality itself.

On the nature of this oscillation.

556. Morality must be the core of our existence, if it is to be for us what it wants to be. Its end, its origin, must be the *ideal of being*. An unending *realization of being* would be the vocation of the I. Its striving would be toward ever more being. From 'I am' the path of evil descends, the path of good ascends. The highest philosophy is ethics. Therefore all philosophy begins with 'I am.' The highest proposition of knowledge must be an expression of the fact that grounds all knowledge as means, that refers to the end of the I that is to be achieved or aimed at through *knowledge*/ in the broadest sense as existence in the world of sense,/ namely, total freedom. The I appears to be contradictory if the nature of its efficacy, the productive imagination, is not recognized, in that the achievement of its end seems to be thwarted, as it were, by the means chosen – but precisely in this way it acts in harmony with itself, to be consistent I want to say, it must [act] thus, because of its nature – namely because it is nothing but an *oscillating*, etc. and thus precisely only creates, and can create, what it seeks to create – It cannot create anything at all without proceeding in this way – because all creation is about being and being is oscillation, etc.

/What is must appear to contradict itself, insofar as one, as it were, resolves it into its constituent parts, which one must as it were be forced to do because of the nature of reflection.
/Being, Being I, being free and oscillating are synonyms – one expression refers to the others – it is simply a matter of a single fact – It is only the predicates of the single concept I – Concept and fact are, however, identical here. I is inconceivable, because it is already its concept in that it is – its only possible concept is given with its being.

By "fact" one usually thinks of action, something that is proceeding or has happened in time. But the fact that is under discussion here must be

thought of as completely spiritual, not singular, not temporal – almost like a moment that encompasses the eternal universe, conceives it in itself – in which we live, move and have our being – an unending fact that transpires completely in every moment – [an] *identical eternally acting* genius – *being I*. Relations of consciousness to this
mysterious being of things.

/Transition from this concept to the actual world – /application of it./

557. Categories – context of the practical and theoretical I.

*

NOTEWORTHY PASSAGES AND REMARKS UPON READING THE *WISSENSCHAFTSLEHRE*

558. I and not-I are *abstracta*. They don't behave, like estates in opposition to each other, but rather I and not-I are at work in every empirical action indifferently. The canon, the schema of every action, but of course also the matter of [the action], is exhibited in the *Wissenschaftslehre*.

559. All reality that we can speak of must be a *thinkable* one. Consequently the principle of all reality, the guaranty of it, the ground of thinking, is – *Sum* [i.e., I am]. Philosophy is limited strictly to the determinate modification – *of consciousness*. [Philosophy] is modest – it remains within its borders. It grasps what it contains, or what falls under it. Freedom of reflection leads to a freedom of the acting I.

560. Philosophizing is an activity of intelligence. At what level does philosophy stand?

561. The *human being* is as much Not-I as I.

562. I is only thinkable through a not-I. An I is of course only an I insofar as it is a not-I – for the rest, it could be what it wants – only it would not be an I.

563. The ground of the law of nature that the action without reaction of every force continues eternally – where does [this principle] lie in the I – it can explain much about the I.

564. When one speaks philosophically of that which is to come, for example, of the annihilation of the not-I, then one guards against the illusion that there would come a point in time where this would take place – In the first place it is in and of itself a contradiction that something could take place in time that supersedes all time, like all transplanting of the non-sensible, thinkable, and subjective into the sensible world of appearances. In every moment that we freely act there is such a triumph of the infinite I over the finite one; for this moment the Not-I is really annihilated – only not in terms of sensible existence.
As it should and shall be, so is it – the thing remains forever, only the form changes ceaselessly. Time can never cease – we cannot *think away* time – because time is indeed the condition of the thinking being – time ceases only with the cessation of thought. Thought outside time is an absurdity.

565. For the living being the world becomes more and more unending – therefore there can never come an end to the connecting of the manifold, a state of inactivity for the thinking I – Golden ages might appear – but they do not bring the end of things – the goal of the human being is not the golden age – the human being should exist eternally and be a beautifully ordered individual and endure – this is the tendency of human nature.

*

566. Philosophizing must be a unique kind of thinking. What do I do when I philosophize? I reflect upon a ground. The ground of philosophizing is thus a striving after the thought of a ground. Ground is not, however, a cause in the literal sense – but rather a constitution – connection with the whole. All philosophizing must therefore end in an absolute ground. Now if this were not given, if this concept contained an impossibility – then the drive to philosophize would be an unending activity – and without end because there would be an eternal urge for an absolute ground that can be satisfied only relatively – and that would therefore never cease. Unending free activity in us arises through the free renunciation of the

absolute – the only possible absolute that can be given us and that we only find through our inability to attain and know an absolute. This absolute that is given to us can only be known negatively, insofar as we act and find that what we seek cannot be attained through action.
This could be called an absolute postulate. All searching for *a single principle* would be like the attempt to square the circle. /Perpetual motion. Philosophers' stone./ (Negative knowledge./ (Reason would be the capacity to posit and retain such an absolute object./ (Understanding extended through imagination/ striving for freedom would thus be that striving to philosophize, the drive toward knowledge of the ground. Philosophy, the result of philosophizing, arises accordingly through *interruption* of the drive toward knowledge of the ground – through standing still at the point where one is. Abstraction from the absolute ground and validation of the actual absolute ground of freedom through connection (enlargement) of that which is to be explained / to a whole. The more manifold the members of the whole, the more vivid will be the sensation of absolute freedom – the more connected, the more whole it is, the more effective, intuitable, *clarified*, is the absolute ground of all grounding, i.e., freedom, in it. The *manifoldness* bears witness to the energy, vividness of practical freedom – the *connection* [bears witness] to the activity of theoretical freedom. The first comprises *actions* – the other [comprises] treatments. By this I understand the acts of actual reflection that have to do with mere acts of thought. (Reflection does not include all thought, but only thought that is treated, contemplated) The I signifies that negatively known absolute – what is left over after all abstraction – what can only be known through action and what only realizes itself through eternal lack. /Thus eternity is realized temporally in spite of the fact that time contradicts eternity./ The I becomes effective and determinate in itself only in its *opposite*. /Insofar as I ask "What is that?" I demand the *externalizing* of the thing in itself – I want to know – *what is* it? Of course I already know that it *is* this or that thing, but what sort of a thing? This is what I want to know – and here I step into the sphere of the subjective.

/I never find intuition because I must seek it through reflection and vice versa./

567. What acts in the first place for me – from where do I borrow my concepts? – necessarily I – necessarily from myself. I am for myself the

ground of all thought, the absolute ground, whose I is only known to me through actions – the ground of all grounds for me, the principle of my philosophy is my I. I can make this I the ground of all my philosophizing only in a negative way – by trying to cognize / to act as much as possible and to connect these as exactly as possible; The latter through reflection/. The more unmediated and directly I can derive something from the I, the better cognized and grounded it is for me./

/To ground is to philosophize. To *think up* [*something*] [*erdenken*] is to poeticize. To think over [*bedenken*] and to consider [*betrachten*] is the same thing. Sensing/pure thinking is a mere concept – a generic concept. But genus is nothing apart from the individual [cf. #53]. thus one always thinks in a particular way: one grounds, one invents, etc./

/I cannot become acquainted with the individual through the genus, rather through the individual I become acquainted with the genus, but of course one must always have the idea of the genus in mind when considering the individual./

(Fichtean philosophy is a call to self-activity – I cannot thoroughly explain something to someone unless I refer him to himself, unless I bid him to perform the same action that clarified it for me. I can teach someone to philosophize when I teach him to do it as *I* do it – when he does what I do, he is what I am, is there, where I am.)
/All art begins with invention or imitation/
/Now if the actions that I take are *natural ones*, all other actions are unnatural and do not attain the goal that they have and must have in mind – human beings contradict themselves. They do not contradict themselves when they act in accordance with their nature. For this reason evil people, for example, remain in eternal contradiction with themselves./ Different material first brings about differentiation with respect to that for which a ground is sought. Thus the ancients also called the doctrine of nature, etc. philosophy – we have limited it to the thinking of a ground of *representations* and sensations, in short to the alterations of the subject./

/On the expression – soul – /soul of the whole//

568. It is generally recognized that soul and body are distinct. Everyone who recognizes this distinction thereby establishes an association between the two because of their mutual interaction. Both have a double role in this reciprocal action – either they affect each other in themselves directly or a third something acts through one of them upon the other. That is, at the same time the body serves to communicate outer objects to the soul via the senses, and insofar as it is itself an outer object, it acts on itself as such, through [the effect of] the senses upon the soul. Naturally the soul operates in the same way in return and from this it is shown that this path, the senses, are a common, undivided property of the body and the soul. Just as there are outer objects to which [set of things] the body belongs, so as well there are inner objects to which the soul belongs. These operate on the body and outer objects in general, via the senses, as already mentioned, and in this way maintain the return countereffect. Now the difficulty is to explain the *senses*.

/generic concept of the senses/

Sensing always involves a body and a soul. Their union is mediated by the senses. The senses are simply not self-acting – they receive and give what they get – they are the medium of reciprocal interaction.

> /The soul either does *not distinguish* actual existence in the momentary appearance, the actual state, from necessary existence in the idea, the posited, ideal state, /state of free being, without [a] lively power of distinguishing/ or [the soul] distinguishes both. Now in the latter case it finds the actual state in harmony with itself or in contradiction with itself – the first is the feeling of pleasure, of liking, the other is the feeling of displeasure, of disliking. Both are departures from the natural state and therefore only momentary in the broader sense. In the first, feeling is the form of the natural state, of the artistic state, the agreeable and pleasure-inducing. In the other the compulsion suffered by the natural necessity of the contingent is what is disagreeable and painful.

The ground of the senses, sense, must be negative matter and negative spirit – both the same – consequently absolute matter and absolute

spirit – which are one. Hence probably the element of imagination – of the I – of the one and only absolute anticipated – that is to be found through the negation of everything absolute.
Now we must not think of this finding as material or spiritual – It is neither one, because in a certain way it is both. It is a product of the imagination, which we *believe in*, without being able ever to know it according to its nature or ours. It is also in and of itself nothing readily available, but rather that which, as object of a necessary idea, lies at the basis of the particular senses and explains them – and makes them amenable to theoretical treatment.

/The highest principle must be absolutely nothing given, but rather must be freely made, something *composed*, *devised*, in order to ground a universal metaphysical system that begins with and proceeds toward freedom. / All philosophizing aims at emancipation./

We search for this substrate isolated in the particular senses – that is, in connection with an outer or inner object. Light, sound, etc. are modifications, individual instances of the genus of sense.

/Distinguish organ and sense/

/From this we see incidentally that the I is fundamentally nothing – everything must be *given* to it – But something can only be given to it and the given only becomes something through the I. The I is not an encyclopedia, but rather a universal principle. This also illuminates the matter of deductions a priori. The I cannot deduce from itself what is not given to it – but with something's being given comes also the I's warrant and power to deduce it. What is given to the I belongs to it for eternity – because the I is nothing but the principle of appropriation. Everything that steps into its sphere belongs to it – because the essence of its being consists in this conversion to its own use. Appropriation is the original activity of its nature/ [Cf. #468.]

/Inner, outer organ – kinds of inner and outer objects that presuppose particular organs and thereby make visible, comprehensible, a new modification of sense./

/Two ways to look at things – from above downward or from below upward – through this switch what was at first negative becomes positive, and vice versa. Both ways must be used at once./
/Sense and consciousness. The latter is nothing but: actuality of the one or the other world mediated by sense.

*   *

*

Group VI: 569–667 (summer to fall, 1796)

569. *De Officio judicis.*

570. Intelligence and sensory being – what is simple in the one is manifold in the other and vice versa – The same with freedom and compulsion – universality and particularity – quality – quantity – relation – modality – suffering and acting – affirmation [*Position*] – negation.

571. On the productive imagination. In the mere concept of determination lies the concept of reciprocal determination, of opposition, of substantiality. It also contains within it the reason why the highest determination always determines itself as well. The determination of the unending is always determination. Being – being determined. a|———|b thus the division of the ground.[1]

572. Adam and Eve. What is brought about through a revolution must be sublated through a revolution. /Bite of the apple/

573. If a concept is [of an] accident, its constituent parts stand in an altered order than where [it is of] substance. Its constituents are, however, likewise substance and accident – consequently if the whole concept is accident, its subsistence preexists in it and is substance. /Right and proper./

[1] Novalis seems to be indicating a line from point a to point b, perhaps suggesting, as does Kant in the Deduction of the Categories in the *Critique of Pure Reason*, that "we cannot think a line without *drawing* it in thought," that is, without ordering representions spatially in inner sense (*Critique of Pure Reason* B 154ff.).

574. On reconciliation – its necessity – faith and the sphere of the Christian religion.

575. Categories – original properties of a noumenon.

576. In man reason sets the tone, in woman, feeling /both positive/. The morality of the woman is grounded in feeling – as the morality of the man is grounded in reason.

577. On the various kind of entertainments of both sexes.

> /The man may desire the *sensuous* in *rational* form, the woman may desire the *rational* in *sensuous* form./

The *peripheral being* of the man is the *primary being* of the woman.

578. The greatest possession is the imagination.

579. Men most naturally know how to entertain women well, and women most naturally know how to entertain men well.

580. Positive activity opposes negative passion, not positive [passion].

581. Distinction of the indistinguishable.

582. [Distinguishing] Right from passing judgment – to judge – to distinguish and to relate.[2] [The former] Refers to a determinate exclusion of a determinate object. All right is grounded in property. The universal I possesses its accidents *ipso jure* [by law] – and indeed [possesses them] by virtue of its identity *ex jure identitatis*. The necessity of its existence grounds this right – which, however, is not yet a right in this sphere – because there is nothing here that the I could exclude.

It is so because it must be so.
It must be so because it is so.

[2] Novalis is here playing with the German, underlining the "unter" in *unterscheiden* to hint at a certain kind of "separation" – one that is "under." The original phrase is "*unter*scheiden und beziehen."

Right first arises in the sphere of individuals. [It] has an absolute ground in the sphere of the absolute genus. The individual who has a right is its real ground – that which is excluded is its ideal ground. I have a right to that from which I exclude everything else. All right aims for permission. Matter and form of the substance of right – its accident is the object to which I have a right. The latter [object] must be so structured that it can have a particular, exclusive relation to an individual. The matter of the substance of right is determined through the individual who has a right – the form [of the substance of right is determined] through the individual who is excluded. In both determinations the structure cooperates with the accidents.

> /*That* and *one*. /The genus consists of species – this is best expressed in Latin by the word *genus*, which means genus and species. /generic, special and individual concept./ *The* [generic] human being has, as such no rights – but he has rights against *a* [particular] person, against the quantitative person. Only substance has rights, never the accidents; because only the substance can, in general, *have* [something]. /Real, personal rights, or better – generic, special, and individual rights./

583. Double nerves – of the outer and inner sense – they can both only be cured by each other – destruction of the whole machine through dissipation is of course also damaging to the nerves – But in this case they suffer only mediately – in the former case [where the whole machine is not destroyed?] [they suffer] directly and in this case I simply mean the reciprocal cure.

> /Inner sensibility opposes outer sensibility when a desire gives way to representation./

[584.] The Kantian Categories are merely for accidental substance.

585. The right of the genus derogates the rights of individuals and so forth.

586. Factual. Natural.

587. The idea of a whole must *thoroughly* govern and modify an aesthetic work. Even in the most capricious books. [Christoph Martin] Wieland, [Jean Paul Friedrich] Richter and most comics are often lacking in this regard.[3] Their works contain so outrageously *much* that is superficial and boring, and actually just hors d'œuvres. Rarely is the plan and the *grand* arrangement aesthetic. They have only aesthetic or comic moods, not aesthetic comic sense or *spirit* /Unity of diversity/

[588.] There must be nothing arbitrary, lawless in a particular mode of action of the human spirit – Everywhere art and science. All science is something positive – or better, it must be grounded on something given. It is complete knowledge of an *object* – art – the perfect application of knowledge.

589. Other more expressive number terms.

590. On the nature of the *word*. Every word has its specific meaning, its connotations, its false and thoroughly arbitrary meanings. Etymology differs – genetically – pragmatically –/how it should be used/

*

591. Concept – judgment and conclusion differ according to quantity or according to form in general.

592. Closer examination of the Categories.

593. Consciousness insofar as it is an accident of an object – as accident of a subject – as substance of a subject – as substance of an object.

594. The subject can have objective accidents, it can have objective substance. It determines itself in the former as substance – in the latter as accident. The object behaves the same way.

[3] Wieland (1733–1813) was an extremely popular writer of the German "Rokoko" and an influential editor (*Der Teutsche Merkur*) and translator. Jean Paul (1763–1825), as he was known, was a controversial writer of the German "Klassik," disliked by Goethe and Schiller among others, but highly praised by later German writers such as Adalbert Stifter and Stefan George who saw his work as proto-impressionist.

/Subject and object are only ideal differences, like left and right./

595. Subject does not arise out of object, and vice versa. Theory of the subject.

596. Rights of animality – rights of humanity – rights of the I.

[597.] The Categories.

Modality contains the determinations of mere undetermined *existence.* /in the world of sense/ Quality contains the determinations of existence in the world of thought.
Relation – [contains] the determinations of both through the I, with respect to their matter.
Quantity – [contains] the determinations of both through the I, with respect to their form.

598. Every single predicable expresses a manifold relation.

599. Quantity.

Unity – modal quantity.
Plurality – modal-qualitative quantity.
Totality – modal-qualitative relative quantity.

Relation.

1 – modal relation.
2 – modal-qualitative relation.
3 – modal-quantitative qualitative relation.

Quality.

Reality – modal quality.
Negation – modal-relative quality.
Limitation – modal-relative quantitative quality.

Modality –

1. qualitative modality.
2. qualitative-relative modality.
3. qualitative-relative quantitative modality.

600. Principles of algebra applied to metaphysics.

General application of the already discovered *certain* laws of nature.

601. Contradiction and opposition.

1. Real contradiction and ideal opposition.
2. Real opposition and ideal contradiction.

602. It is part of the nature of determination that it excludes two spheres – the sphere that gives it form (Gestalt), the sphere that gives it matter (content – essence).

603. Not – only refers to the sphere of excluded determination in general.

604. Nothing can be determined immediately, directly; that is, [nothing] can influence any object [immediately, directly].
God could create the world only according to an idea, consequently only through mediated creation. All efficacy is mediate. No thing can affect another unmediated, operate thing upon thing, but rather only mediately through appearance, activity or suffering, in a communal sphere – this is the universal sensorium – it is the sphere of freedom, and the sphere of compulsion.

605. In order to become acquainted with a thing I must observe it as an *appearance*. Here it is in the communal field – Here it is mine – here I can influence it – It is an object – Here I can determine its state – Its relations to me, to itself, to the sensorium, to others.

606. *Opposing* evil to virtue does evil too much honor.

*

607. Border settlements.

608. On the law of nature:

Nature makes no leaps.

609. That which contradicts itself does not oppose itself, and that which opposes itself does not contradict itself – because both change in opposed spheres.

/Man and woman/

610. Subject / Substance/
Subjective. Accidents
/ \
objective substance of the subject — objective accidents of the subject.

The same with the object.

611. What actually is substance? What I before called sphere.

612. Metaphysical words are, as it were, only letters – like the formulae in algebra. They are only schematized substances.

613. How then does one see corporeally? The same as in consciousness – through productive imagination. Consciousness is *eye*, *ear*, and *feeling* for the inner and outer sense – unified through itself – because it consists, and must consist, of nothing but oppositions.

614. Formation of single sentences – a kind of gleaning. One remark clearly *carried out*. /Periods/

615. The *art* of living happily.

616. Saxon constitution.

617. No universal *system* of political economy, etc., is possible.

618. There is One essential component of virtue – all virtue is *one*. Different virtues arise out of virtue in several kinds of relations.

619. It is crude and spiritless to communicate only for the sake of the content – the content, the material, must not tyrannize us. We must

communicate ourselves *purposively* – artfully – sensibly – Our presentation must not be unworthy of us – it must be appropriate to its public, to its purpose – It must take advantage of the time and the place.

620. Only moral and character improvements are real improvements – all others without exception are only modes, only alteration, only insignificant improvements.

621. On the evil in the world? On punishment.

[622.] On the character of words. Sensation words – concept words – phrases – figures – *repetitions* – concise – precise – effortless – ponderous – tedious – disagreeable – uneven – confused – wearisome – melodious – symmetrical – harmonious – more fantasy – more sensitivity – more understanding – more reason – lively – dry – locality of the style – color of the style. – Relation of the expression to the thought – in how many ways can a thought be expressed – component parts of the thought.

623. Dreams of the future – is a thousand-year Reich possible – will all vices one day be expunged? When the education of reason will be perfected [cf. #648, 651].

624. Acquiescence to misfortune and physical suffering. One must arrest all *sensitivities*.

625. Do human beings owe nothing to the *nobility*? Are they mature enough to do without the nobility?

*

626. People change themselves in the face of extremes, and are only *that which* they can be in their environment and *against* objects and human opponents – thence variability of character and relative character in general.

627. Fortune and misfortune – both negative and positive.

628. The latin poet.

629. The point cannot be thought as moved. /Determinate sphere of determination./ Principles of definition. /Naming/

630. On the ordering of thoughts. According to what is a thought ordered? How is a description begun? One advances either according to the time – or one proceeds from the universal to the particular. A sensible object is described analytically – a spiritual [object is described] synthetically – in the former case one begins with the most universal – in the latter with the most particular. We are looking for the ordering with which a concept *should* be grasped. The ordering of the *necessary* I. In a whole, everything must hang together in an orderly fashion. What connects thoughts? /It is the same as with everything – grounded either in the *subject*, or in the object./

631. Does my mistake, the reason I cannot get any further, perhaps lie in the fact that I cannot grasp and retain a whole?

632. A book can have very different sorts of interest. The author, the reader, a purpose, an incident, its mere individual existence can be the axis around which it turns.

633. We awaken activity when we give it stimulating material. /The I must posit itself as presenting./ What is essential to presentation is what is inessential to the object/There is a particular power of presenting – that merely presents for the sake of presenting – presenting in order to present is *free* presenting. This is only to suggest that it is not the object as such but rather *the I*, as ground of activity, that should determine activity. The artwork thereby acquires a free, independent, ideal character – an imposing spirit – because it is the *visible* product of an I – But the I posits itself determinately in this manner, because it posits itself as an unending I – because it must posit itself as a perpetually presenting I – it thus posits itself as free, as a determinate presenting I. /The object may only be the kernel, the type, the fixed point – the formative power first creatively develops the beautiful whole in and through it. Put differently – the object should determine us, as product of the I, and not as mere object./ Difference between oral and written presentation./ Necessity of rule-governed temporal divisions./ Change of spheres is necessary in

a completed presentation. The sensible must be presented as spiritual, and the spiritual as sensible./ Speech, like song, demands a completely different text than writing. Speech stands between music and writing. Science of declamation a priori./ Concerning what is to be distinguished and what is to be connected in the composition./ How does one find the whole in the parts and the parts in the whole?/ The inessential must be treated only as the medium, as that which connects – hence only this integrating and forward-leading characteristic must be marked out./ Not one superficial word is permitted.

/We stand now only at the beginning of the art of the writer/

Wherever there are several units, they must give up some of their claims, their freedom – So that a *community* then exists. Generic similarity of *the whole* in general – for example of a state or a composition.

634. Voice [*Stimme*] – tune/mood [*Stimmung*] – to tune/put in a certain mood [*stimmen*] – determine [*bestimmen*] – agree with [*einstimmen*]. "Voice" expresses a self-constituting thing. "Mood" arises out of two things acting and two things acted upon.

635. What are the requirements of a rational state? Political science – political knowledge[4] – statesmanship [political art]. /In science everything must be grounded and connected in and through itself – in knowledge we find only individual characteristics of a whole, without *inner* connection. Methodology and applied science constitute the art [of politics]./

636. Every independent material whole must consist of two branches that are distinguishable only in reflection, that together are one and something – thus [it is with] science, knowledge and art.

637. Presentation is an externalization of an inner state, of inner changes – appearance [is an externalization of] the inner object. /The outer object changes in and through the I with the concept, and the intuition is produced. The inner object changes in and through the I with *a body appropriate to it* and the sign arises. In the former the object is body – in

[4] The term Novalis uses in what follows is *Kenntnis*, which is not wisdom so much as a kind of knowledge by acquaintance.

the latter the object is spirit. Common consciousness mistakes what has arisen, the intuition, and the sign, for the body because it does not know how to abstract – it is not *self-active*, but only of necessity *acted upon* – it is only *half*, not *whole*.

638. Military science – military knowledge – art of warfare.

639. Art is: the cultivation of our causal influence – *a certain sort of wanting* – according to an idea – affecting and wanting are one here. Art is cultivated only by the frequent practice of our influence, whereby it becomes more determined and powerful.

*

Development of Concepts

640. Love – natural law – criminal law – sociability – *art* – state – constitution – religion – marriage – sickness – political economy

---

641. The expression criminal law is dim and obscure. It must be grounded in natural law.
Relations of the subject, as object, seem to me to contain the concept of right.
Objective determinations of the subject would thus be what we had to investigate, or the objective accidents of the subject. The subject with objective substance is opposed to the subject with objective accidents. Right is generated from these. *It flows from the latter and it is determined through the former.* The latter has the right but only through the former is it in the right. (From the latter it has matter, from the former the form of existence – from the latter [it has] the form of subsistence, from the former the matter of subsistence – from the latter [it has] objective structure, from the former its subjective structure – the sphere gives it the whole.

From the second [i.e., the subject with objective substance], modality and relation.
From the first [i.e., the subject with objective accidents], quality and quantity.

1. Modality –

The matter of modality from the second – actuality.
The form of modality – from the first – possibility.
The sphericality of modality from both – necessity.

2. Relation –

The matter of relation – from the second – inherence and effect [cf. #644].
The form of relation – from the first – cause and subsistence [cf. #644].
The determinate field of influence – from both – alternating mastery and subordination – or community.

3. Quality –

The matter of quality from the first – reality.
The form of quality – from the second – negation.
The determinate field of influence – from the whole – limitation.

4. Quantity –

The matter of quantity from the first – unity.
The form of quantity from the second – plurality.
The determinate field of influence – from both – totality.

642. Different meanings of the word "right" and its relatives.

643. Which objects can be objects of right? The I cannot be limited or excluded. It thus only has rights insofar as it is limited, that is, excluded. How is that possible?
So the I, as such, can have no rights? But then the quantitative, etc., I can have rights. The I as appearance has rights.
The I as appearance is determined through Categories. These are the rubrics under which I must undertake the determination of the I.

644. We are here considering the I as substance – hence all determinations are accidents.

/Determination is an *identical* relative concept, a self-opposing object, a state with one voice./
/A contradictory state is unitary as an object/

What is object in the sphere of a state is substance in the sphere of accidents.

Categories – are real relationships that are a priori because they have an ideal ground. They are necessary possible ways of thinking actual thoughts, or, they necessitate the possibility of the actual, they alternate the substance and accidents of cause and effect, they *generalize* the unity of the manifold, they limit the reality of negation.

/being there – being together – being apart – being structured

645. The inner and the outer oppose each other. "I" is the concept of the inner – consequently the I is always with the inner.

646. The concept of an identical whole includes that the laws of the whole, the necessary conditions of the whole, are also the laws and necessary conditions of *the parts* – The grandest object is handled by the very same formulae as is the *slightest*. In the whole everything must be whole – In the I everything must be I and so forth. /All determination is a being determined-in-itself – an emergent thing in itself – or a *being* in itself. /It can be only up to the I whether it wants to immortalize its individuality or not./ The I is always one with itself and is always opposed to itself – it means one and the same thing./ All unification must occur from *one side*. An activity out of two opposed points can never become one / Self-consciousness is only apparently tied to a particular individual. The actual ground [of self-consciousness] lies in the sensorium and in *both determining things* outside it./ The devil and God are the extremes out of which humanity arises. The devil is the destructive, God is the creative *power*/ Drive is *outside* us *in a way*. Reason does not drive and is not driven – which is *one and the same* thing./ The highest perfection of the thinking intelligence is to be free, *to be taken up* as free, even with respect to what is *alien*, *given*; that is, to let a free thing, an alien free thing, be – for instance a *truth* that has been read. To let what is received be an independent influence. / we *are* only insofar as we want to be or let ourselves be / what holds for one holds for all / State is the determined thing from which

emanates at once both an affecting and an affected thing / Concept and object must be demonstrated at the same time./ Right arises from the *universal* essence of reason or from the concept of humanity / on the Categories./

[647.] Quantity of time – quantity of space – quantity of understanding – of reason. On religion. Anything can be elevated to a chosen point, if it is aimed at from all sides and everything is reduced to it. What constitutes God can be constituted from a nutshell. Every *fixation* on an object is as *correct*, but also as *unjust*, as a 'one true religion' – human beings draw more from it [the fixation] than their humanity permits – disregarding the fact that they can make of it anything they want. Reality of temporal appearances – influence of space and time on our concepts and ideas./ Philosophy must be all-encompassing./ Fichte's propositions must be more reducible to universal propositions./ The more freely reason, understanding and imagination, etc. play stylistically, the more their free movements are already visible on the surface, the more fully voiced and hence more harmonized is the style, then the more spirited [the style] is./ Objects must not do violence to us – They must not hem us in, not rule [*bestimmen*] beyond the *borders*./ An object is an object, even if it is God –/ Efficacy is only possible through connection – but all connection occurs via a medium – like, for instance, the way I move the fingers of my hand./ What is individuality outside time?/ Why the determined thing exerts so much power – the determinate in the world of sense and the world of spirit – We must seek to create an inner world that is an actual pendant to the outer world – that, insofar as it is in direct opposition to [the outer world] at every point, constantly increases our freedom. Because our freedom necessarily proceeds from determination – the more we rid ourselves of our determinations, the freer we become. All determinations proceed outward from us – we create a world out of ourselves – and thereby become more and more free, since freedom is only thinkable in opposition to a world – The more we determine, the more we lay out what is in us – the freer – more substantial – we become – we set aside, as it were, more and more that which is inessential and approach the thoroughly pure, simple essence of our I. Our [creative] power gets as much free play as it has world *under it*. But since our *nature*, or the fullness of our being, is unending, we can never reach this goal *in time* – But since we are also in a sphere outside time, we must reach it there in every moment, or better, if we want, in this sphere we are able to be pure simple substance. /Here is morality and peace of mind, because an endless striving after what hovers ever out of reach before us seems unbearable./

[648.] All determination occurs by the substance of the object uniting with the accidents [*Accidens*] of the subject and vice versa – or better, because substance always lies between the opposites and all opposites are one – but each of the opposites is necessarily constituted out of two components of which one is shared, although it is not a quantitatively shared component, but rather a quantitative separate one – thus this shared component is sought – and in this way both are combined./ The world of sense and the world of spirit are only opposed to each other during the process of change. If the object/ as I want to portray the content of the world of sense here/ is manifold, then the subject is simple, the former constant, the latter changeable – the former substance the latter inherence, and vice versa. / Substance is *merely an idea* – it is the *whole* that directly reflects what is directly intuited – Inherence [*Accidens*] is only its alternate concept – it indicates its state, the sum of relations that the whole has as *whole*. Inherence can at bottom only be used in the plural./ To what extent *must* a person live in *obedience*. /to God and men?/ /character of language – universal language – whence the variety of languages – prophesy of the future – thousand-year Reich. New religion./ An authentic philosophical system must systematize freedom and unendingness, or, to express it more strikingly, it must systematize systemlessness. Only such a system can avoid the errors of system and be accused of neither *injustice* nor anarchy.

649. The Categories are synthetic concepts of accidents a priori./ Reason corresponds to time, understanding to space./ Why are there 12? / Solo act: 3 unities; of the aesthetic whole – change – transitions – related sensations by analogy to music – how [do] they readily replace each other? Combinations – aesthetic purposes./ Only two realms / Morality struggles with physical freedom – mastery – Mere choice [*Willkür*] [struggles] with God – Independence from outer and inner contingencies – The sphere of morality of the I supersedes all thesis and antithesis – It is beyond the laws, the sphere of influence of theoretical determination./ On freedom – Singular determinations are necessary – but reason must direct the change – a person must only be determined insofar as, because he is in the realm of determination, he must be determined – that

is, he must be determined – but not in this or that way, etc. All material limits freedom – all action extends it./ Man must be without any sensation / Philanthropy toward humanity./ Does the unexpected in an occurrence lie *without* or *within* us?/ Novelty – habit – to take pleasure in the everyday / Every Category, like every pure concept, has one unique and one shared characteristic – hence one always runs in circles when examining such a concept./ In [matters of] *style*, either the object in general or the the particular object rules; either the state or the idea, either the symbol or the word, the gestalt, genesis or use / Character / of the word./ Difference between the right to my own person and to a thing./ I can treat a person as a thing, when it does not cancel all [my] right to it through its perfected morality, for instance, the right to a female on a deserted island./ permission? / Gradations of activities for the preservation of the animal spirits./ Life sentence / The universal system of philosophy must be, like time, a thread with which one can run through endless determinations – It must be a system of the most manifold unity, of endless expansion, a compass of freedom – neither formal nor material system – /We must seek the dichotomy everywhere./ On fantasy systems that are endlessly possible – However, there still remain material systems, hence only aesthetic compositions – but these do not have to be pure philosophy – [Philosophy] contains only laws of orientation and absolutely no content or its form in the ordinary sense – It is neither formal nor material./ Every synthetic concept contains 2 special opposed concepts as concepts of inherence, as concepts between which it alternates, or better, [as concepts] which change through it./ Until now concepts of God were quite correct concepts of human beings – *qua* intelligence./ *Pure sensation*, whence comes that which is the most certain touchstone of truth, etc.? Our sensation excludes and includes – but does not determine – In its totality it is the unconscious intuition of the world of spirit – we sense an objective whole – and with every determination of the faculty of knowledge we sense a certain right or wrong, without being able, without special activity of the imagination, etc., to state it. This relationship gives much excellent material to the faculty of judgment./

650. That which can be found outside time can only be active, or visible, in time./ Why universal philosophy cannot be a *positive system* – It can contain nothing but the form of the complete activity of spirit in *a*

determination./ In order to form something one must have an object before one – either one designs it out of oneself or finds it outwardly./

[651.] Only the most perfect person can design the most perfect philosophy. Human beings stand in thorough reciprocal interaction with themselves – and in inward connection – Every error, every virtue must have a universal sphere of influence, a total influence – A person cannot have a genuine virtue here and not have it there./ The Categories are only synthetic concepts a priori. So should there not be synthetic ideas a priori and synthetic intuitions and sensations? Our states are only agglomerations. Are states in the proper sense of the word only conceivable by a very ideal imagination? Our states are states – and they are not. How does this occur? A proposition is true when we intuit it with the power of truth, when we elevate it to an idea./ Sphere of indifference – always the same. Sphere of difference – alteration./ Synthetic sphere – change./ The endless idea of our freedom also involves an endless series of our appearances in a world of sense – We will not be bound to the single appearance in our earthly body on this planet./ There are 3 spheres everywhere. They are determined only with respect to themselves – Their efficacy is as diverse as the parts of infinity. But they are always the same – The material and the form of their *appearances* may be as diverse as it likes. They are completely indifferent with respect to their respective determinations. They are what they are, do what they do, endure what they endure, simply for their own sake. In order to be realized they must be applied singly – i.e., in single appearances – however, they are and remain eternally virginal – eternally themselves – undivided and free./ It is so with all ideas. Their *appearance* appears only to transform them./ It is so with *humanity* / It is *the same* in the whole and the individual./ Ideas elevate themselves – they don't lower themselves: / Principle of perfection in humanity – Humanity would not be humanity – if a thousand-year Reich were not necessarily coming. The principle is visible in every detail of everyday life – *in everything*. The true always survives – The good prevails – The human being rises again – Art forms itself – Science arises – and only the contingent, the individual, disappears – It is the battle of the transitory with the enduring – finally Hercules does learn to kill the ever-growing Hydra – finally victory must become the order of the day – result of the most calculated, exact art – Art must triumph over the crude multitude[5] – Practice makes perfect./ *Art of wisdom* and *science* of wisdom./ Sphere of reality (of property) – shared material of opposition./ Every part of the opposed substances – is constituted *again* out of *both* / Totality is only the completeness of the relations./ How do parts arise in substance – and become independent? / We must thoroughly reflect upon the synthetic connection of the opposites – thus also upon the connection between the world of sense and of spirit. In the products of each world what is unique [to that world] is only that which predominates. Idea belongs as much to the world of sense as feeling belongs to the world of spirit./ I maintain that analysis and synthesis are actually opposed actions – what is their synthetic character – or their shared sphere? / All pains must have a maximum – in short, all unpleasant states must have their determination – their limits – their order – they must stand under the same laws as states of pleasure. The greatest pain can only be a moment – thetic – antithetic pain. Pleasure and pain alternate: / Human beings often tend to grasp at what is obviously harmful, to damage themselves willfully out of spite. It is still an expression of freedom./ Must something be opposed to all faculties and powers of the mind? What is that? / In which sphere is everything that is whole a part? and in which [sphere] is every part a whole? / There are only two original elements and a one sphere of appearance for them./ Love – as a synthetic power / It all depends on whether we assimilate something to the inner sphere of our free activity – and what hinders that [assimilation], so that we suffer and become dependent upon it. Even the greatest misfortune must be assimilated in this sphere if it is to actually affect us – otherwise it remains alien and outside us –/

[652.] Property in our proper sense is only a positive concept, that is, one that would come to an end under conditions of barbarism. Positive law must have positive foundations a priori. Property is the only thing that has the possibility of expressing its freedom in the world of sense./ What is analytic in the world of spirit is synthetic in the world of sense and vice versa./ In this way analysis and synthesis are interchangeable concepts – Each takes the place of the other and alternates into the opposite sphere – namely that of which analysis and synthesis are predicated./

[5] "Die rohe Masse." This phrase is ambiguous between "raw matter" or "substance" and "crude mob." Novalis is quite capable of saying either, and I have tried to preserve the ambiguity here.

Strength can be replaced by *balance* – and every human being should remain in balance – because this is actually the state of freedom./ What does it mean, that virtue should be loved for its own sake? / Real thought must be an opposing of 2 material, opposed spheres. Thetic – antithetic opposition – Only opposed things can be opposed – a determinable must correspond to every act, that is, to all [acts of] determining. Activity is a synthetic concept – that grounds a change between subject and object – It is the medium, the vehicle of all change – change and activity alternately condition one another. Thus activity creates nothing new, but rather only combines the existing thing with a correlative efficacy. Activity is the third material sphere – through which all formation is made possible and actual.

/Sphere misdirects us to false concepts – better mere matter./

Thetic – antithetic and synthetic matter
This is the grounding of cause and effect. But how are substance and inherence grounded? Only together are they a whole – a something – Everything must be in either one or the other – None of these materials is dispensable – taken together in their totality they are the cosmos. This is of course a fantasy intuition – Already its own product. Since they are inseparable they must put everything back together – what can be determined to be cause and effect – substance and accident – necessary negation, necessary affirmation.

/In the category of disjunction something becomes negatively determined through affirmation and through negation becomes affirmatively determined./ In the category of causality, causality is determined through dependence and vice versa, that is, something causal is determined to be dependent, and something dependent is determined as causal./ In the category of substantiality something is determined to be substance through its accidents, and as an accident through its substance./

653. Our inner world must thoroughly correspond to the outer world, down to the smallest detail – because they are set up in opposition to each other in the whole. What is opposed to itself in the one case is reversed in the other – nothing but *antithetical* determinations.

654. Something can occur for me only through action – because something comes into my sphere – something occurs between me and my self. Only through my activity is a Being possible for me. I push my boundaries forward as it were – I gain something. This something must be a non-active thing – something static.

655. For this reason pain must be bearable – because we posit it for ourselves – and we thus cease to suffer as we thereby become active.

656. Cause and effect is better expressed in the first category of relation – the determining thing – the determinable or the determinative – the accentuated – and that which fills out – the connecting thing.

657. How do obscure sensations and intuitions determine us so powerfully? Because as objects, they stimulate our efficacious power.

658. Is an organon of pure schematic possible, or is a pure schematic itself the original organon?

Or does only the combination of pure schematic as theoretical form with pure metaphysics as practical material deliver the actual organon, which Fichte presents us in his *Wissenschaftslehre* – and which is one and indivisible?

659. /Free and necessary I – There is no suffering at all in the I. The I is both action and product at once. Wanting and representing are reciprocal determinations – the I is nothing more than wanting and representing. What is distinguished by the outer world is the practical I. Only the practical I can be perceived – because this is also the actual fundamental I. The I actually does not have faculties – it exists only insofar as it posits itself and posits itself only insofar as it exists – /To be a complete I is an *art* – One can do and one is what one *wants*. One is more or less an I according as one wants./

On the synthetic sphere between being and positing.

660. Accidents can inhere in absolutely only one object. But substance includes both accidents combined – but how is this combination possible? – Every object as object, that is in the action through which it is and

becomes an object – has a voiced and a silent side, a resisting and a free part, a side that is turned toward and a side that is turned away – it is voiced and silent, resistant and free at once – what was divided ideally between both accidents now rests only on that which has been claimed, and the opposite rests on the other. Consequently only one accident is intuitable at a time. /Matter and form are always independently grounded by each other – Their encounter is conditioned not by themselves but by a third thing, the object – and this is in turn conditioned by the action of the I./

661. The object simply cannot be investigated in any other way – except insofar as it is an object, that is, insofar as it is part of the act in which it is an object:

662. Object of the necessary and of the free I.

Everything must be voluntary, i.e., objective, that is to be freely determined by human beings – or better, by which they are freely to determine themselves. The more independent of reason something is, the more capable – of being a determining ground – Herein lies the mystery of the magic of everything positive – everything that cannot be clarified – of all formulae – of idolatrous images – of superstition, etc. With this the necessary I comes into play – effective representation switches directly with its products – Hence the more closely it approaches its product – the more certainly effective representations switch places with it. /This is why the past and present have such an incredible effect on us, because the more independent an object is of our efficacy – the more freely our efficacy plays – thus also the special *everydayness* of the present. Here the mind is compelled to a determinate efficacy and the *necessary* I is too much *sensed*, on the other hand there the necessary I is, as it were, more separated and so the representing I senses its freedom more./ Sensation of freedom is sensation of pleasure – /Being determined without being determined, like the object. So, in the I: the most inner feeling of the immutable./ In that the I feels its suffering and its activity it is more than an object – subject and object at once. How can it be both at once – in that it reflects upon itself – In reflection, arising from both, is an incessant interchange – or an endless interchange – because one is driven from one to the other – thus the I is now object, now subject – according as one looks, and must look, now here, now there. Reflection and object are accidents – the I is the One that they constitute – and since reflection only consists in opposition, it incessantly opposes.

663. Fantasy, understanding, memory, etc. are ways of acting that can be modified in the most diverse ways. For example, there is a fantastic understanding – an understanding[6] fantasy – in short they are the necessary accidents of a rational being – that only become something in combination – however, where now the one, now the other predominates – They are the I's ways of acting in determinate interchanging spheres.

664. On periods – objectivity and subjectivity of style. Unity – circles – effortlessness – character – mood of the period. /Effortless, unconstrained overview of the period/ /Fixed character for which everything flows effortlessly, calmly and leisurely, flows in the agreeable order of self-limiting freedom/

665. To every real thing there belongs a duality – the one has the matter of the essential and the form of the contingent, and the other has the matter of the contingent and the form of the essential.

666. Every science arises out of the appearance of the I in a determinate sphere – out of the *manner of treating* a certain material. A material must treat of itself in order to be treated – /mere suffering, merely being active, are abstract states./ Everything suffers only insofar as it is active and vice versa. There are as many ways of suffering as there are ways of acting.

667. On humanity. Its pure complete development must first be in the art of the individual – and only then pass over to the great masses of people and then the species. To what extent is the species an individual?

*   *

*

[6] Also: "reasonable."

Index

Cambridge texts in the history of philosophy

Titles published in the series thus far

Aristotle *Nicomachean Ethics* (edited by Roger Crisp)
Arnauld and Nicole *Logic or the Art of Thinking* (edited by Jill Vance Buroker)
Bacon *The New Organon* (edited by Lisa Jardine and Michael Silverthorne)
Boyle *A Free Enquiry into the Vulgarly Received Notion of Nature* (edited by Edward B. Davis and Michael Hunter)
Bruno *Cause, Principle and Unity* and *Essays on Magic* (edited by Richard Blackwell and Robert de Lucca with an introduction by Alfonso Ingegno)
Cavendish *Observations upon Experimental Philosophy* (edited by Eileen O'Neill)
Cicero *On Moral Ends* (edited by Julia Annas, translated by Raphael Woolf)
Clarke *A Demonstration of the Being and Attributes of God and Other Writings* (edited by Ezio Vailati)
Classic and Romantic German Aesthetics (edited by J. M. Bernstein)
Condillac *Essay on the Origin of Human Knowledge* (edited by Hans Aarsleff)
Conway *The Principles of the Most Ancient and Modern Philosophy* (edited by Allison P. Coudert and Taylor Corse)
Cudworth *A Treatise Concerning Eternal and Immutable Morality* with *A Treatise of Freewill* (edited by Sarah Hutton)
Descartes *Meditations on First Philosophy*, with selections from the *Objections and Replies* (edited by John Cottingham)
Descartes *The World and Other Writings* (edited by Stephen Gaukroger)
Fichte *Foundations of Natural Right* (edited by Frederick Neuhouser, translated by Michael Baur)
Hobbes and Bramhall on Liberty and Necessity (edited by Vere Chappell)
Humboldt *On Language* (edited by Michael Losonsky, translated by Peter Heath)
Kant *Critique of Practical Reason* (edited by Mary Gregor with an introduction by Andrews Reath)
Kant *Groundwork of the Metaphysics of Morals* (edited by Mary Gregor with an introduction by Christine M. Korsgaard)
Kant *The Metaphysics of Morals* (edited by Mary Gregor with an introduction by Roger Sullivan)
Kant *Prolegomena to any Future Metaphysics* (edited by Gary Hatfield)
Kant *Religion within the Boundaries of Mere Reason and Other Writings* (edited by Allen Wood and George di Giovanni with an introduction by Robert Merrihew Adams)
La Mettrie *Machine Man and Other Writings* (edited by Ann Thomson)
Leibniz *New Essays on Human Understanding* (edited by Peter Remnant and Jonathan Bennett)
Malebranche *Dialogues on Metaphysics and on Religion* (edited by Nicholas Jolley and David Scott)
Malebranche *The Search after Truth* (edited by Thomas M. Lennon and Paul J. Olscamp)

Melanchthon *Orations on Philosophy and Education* (edited by Sachiko Kusukawa, translated by Christine Salazar)
Mendelssohn *Philosophical Writings* (edited by Daniel O. Dahlstrom)
Nietzsche *Beyond Good and Evil* (edited by Rolf-Peter Horstmann and Judith Norman)
Nietzsche *The Birth of Tragedy and Other Writings* (edited by Raymond Geuss and Ronald Speirs)
Nietzsche *Daybreak* (edited by Maudemarie Clark and Brian Leiter, translated by R. J. Hollingdale)
Nietzsche *The Gay Science* (edited by Bernard Williams, translated by Josefine Nauckhoff)
Nietzsche *Human, All Too Human* (translated by R. J. Hollingdale with an introduction by Richard Schacht)
Nietzsche *Untimely Meditations* (edited by Daniel Breazeale, translated by R. J. Hollingdale)
Nietzsche *Writings from the Late Notebooks* (edited by Rüdiger Bittner, translated by Kate Sturge)
Novalis *Fichte Studies* (edited by Jane Kneller)
Schleiermacher *Hermeneutics and Criticism* (edited by Andrew Bowie)
Schleiermacher *Lectures on Philosophical Ethics* (edited by Robert Louden, translated by Louise Adey Huish)
Schleiermacher *On Religion: Speeches to its Cultured Despisers* (edited by Richard Crouter)
Schopenhauer *Prize Essay on the Freedom of the Will* (edited by Günter Zöller)
Sextus Empiricus *Outlines of Scepticism* (edited by Julia Annas and Jonathan Barnes)
Shaftesbury *Characteristics of Men, Manners, Opinions, Times* (edited by Lawrence Klein)
Adam Smith *The Theory of Moral Sentiments* (edited by Knud Haakonssen)
Voltaire *Treatise on Tolerance and Other Writings* (edited by Simon Harvey)